POLLUTION CONTROL
THE LAW IN SCOTLAND

Charles Smith, WS
Partner, Brodies, WS

Neil A Collar
Associate, Brodies, WS

Mark R Poustie
Lecturer in Law, University of Strathclyde

T&T CLARK
EDINBURGH
1997

T&T CLARK LTD
59 GEORGE STREET
EDINBURGH EH2 2LQ
SCOTLAND

First edition (*Scots Law and the Environment:
Liability for Contaminated Land*), 1992

Second edition, 1997

ISBN 0 567 00525 9

British Library Cataloguing-in-Publication Data
A catalogue record for this book is available from the British Library

Typeset by Fakenham Photosetting Ltd, Fakenham, Norfolk
Printed and bound by MPG Books, Bodmin

To Our Parents

Preface

This book has its origins in *Scots Law and the Environment: Liability for Contaminated Land*, written by the Environmental Law Group at Brodies and published by T & T Clark in 1992. In 1995, at the time of the passing of the Environment Act of that year, discussions took place with T & T Clark about the possibility of a second edition.

As a result of these discussions, it was felt appropriate that the text should be considerably expanded and should cover not only liability for contaminated land but also all the main aspects of environmental law in Scotland, both common law and statutory. More detail has been added on those aspects of the law which were covered in the first edition and a considerable amount of updating has been undertaken to take account of the legislation which is now in force.

Many more case and statutory references have been introduced with a view to making the text useful for practitioners and students. The opportunity has been taken to organise the text by reference to specific areas of common law and regulatory liability. Much of the material is entirely new, including Chapter 1, which now serves as a general introduction to environmental law in Scotland, describing the sources of environmental law, the Scottish and other regulators, the common features of regulatory régimes and regulatory powers of entry, Chapter 4 on environmental information, Chapter 5 on the interface between planning and environmental law, Chapter 6 on contaminated land, Chapter 8 on water, Chapter 9 on integrated pollution control and air pollution control, Chapter 10 on statutory nuisance and noise, and Chapter 11 on radioactive substances. The appendices, some of them containing a substantial amount of detail, attempt to provide assistance in tabular form on such matters as Criminal Liability for Environmental Matters, Liability for Clean-Up Costs for Environmental Matters, and Civil Liability for Environmental Matters.

The guiding principle has been to produce a book which is capable of use by those who have a reasonably good grounding in the subject and also of being read by any person who comes fresh to the subject of environmental law. The book is therefore intended to serve as a source of reference and as an introduction to the key areas of environmental law in Scotland.

Environmental law, as ever, continues to be in a state of flux, although perhaps less so than at the time of publication of the first edition. Every attempt has been made to draw the reader's attention to future legislative or other proposals which may affect the areas described. Instead of being inserted in separate chapters, these proposals have been described within the chapter which most closely relates to their subject-matter.

Except as otherwise indicated, the law is stated as at 31st March 1997. A special mention must be made, however, of the provisions of Chapter 6, paragraphs 6.4 to 6.6, which describe the new contaminated land régime contained in Part IIA of the Environmental Protection Act 1990, as inserted by the Environment Act 1995. The text is based on the consultation draft of the implementing guidance and regulations issued in September 1996. At the date of going to press, the new provisions have still not been brought into force and it is possible, if not probable, that amendments will be made to the drafts of the guidance and implementing regulations prior to commencement. T & T Clark have kindly agreed to publish a supplement to this book as and when the new régime is brought into force.

A Scottish Parliament is to be set up by the year 2000 as part of the Labour Government's devolution proposals for Scotland and Wales. The government's White Paper, Scotland's Parliament (Scottish Office, Cm 3658, July 1997), indicates that land use planning, pollution control functions in relation to air, land and water pollution and 'the functions of the Scottish Environment Protection Agency' are to be devolved matters within the competence of the Scottish Parliament, but that nuclear safety issues are to be reserved to the UK Parliament. The White Paper does not expressly mention radioactive substances functions and hence it is not yet clear whether they will fall within the Scottish Parliament's competence, especially in the light of the reservation of nuclear safety issues, presumably under the Nuclear Installations Act 1965, to the UK Parliament. The proposals are that the Scottish Parliament will be able to amend or repeal existing UK Acts of Parliament within its areas of competence and will also be able to pass new legislation in relation to such devolved matters. The Scottish Parliament will also be able to scrutinise the activities of or legislate in respect of public bodies listed in the White Paper, which include SEPA. The devolution proposals do not affect the sovereignty of the UK Parliament, which means that Westminster will be able to repeal or amend the devolution legislation.

Given the constraints of EC environmental legislation, it is unlikely that a Scottish Parliament would be able to alter the substantive framework of environmental legislation in Scotland. It is more likely (simply by way of example of the true scope for use of the devolved powers) that the membership of SEPA's board could be changed when the current members' terms expire; that guidance to SEPA could be altered; and that more distinctively Scottish policies – in relation to air quality, for example – could be developed. The provisions of the Environment Act 1995 in relation to SEPA could also be amended – for example, to give SEPA a principal statutory aim which it currently lacks and to strengthen the general duties which SEPA has, for example, in relation to conservation by virtue of s.32(1).

Other legislative proposals of note which may impact on environmental law include the proposed incorporation of the European Convention on Human Rights into UK domestic law (Chapter 2, paragraph 2.13) and the proposed passing of a Freedom of Information Act. The latter may have an impact on the current provisions relating to access to environmental information (see Chapter 4). Since the government had not published White Papers on these proposals at the time of writing it is not possible to comment on them further.

There are many people who must be thanked in connection with the preparation of this book. In particular, a debt of gratitude is owed to the publishers, T & T Clark, for their patience and forbearance as a number of deadlines for submission of text were missed or only partially met. A number of people within Brodies' Environmental Law Group have assisted in the preparation of the text and, in particular, thanks are due to Douglas Taylor, who provided invaluable assistance in co-ordinating the text and preparing the appendices, to Jim Colquhoun, the firm's librarian, who hunted down concrete details in response to more or less obscurely worded requests for information, and to William Holligan and Calum Wilson who assisted with a number of queries on civil and criminal litigation. A great debt is owed by me personally to various secretaries who have coped with my handwriting and computer illiteracy, in particular Lesley Montgomery and Catriona Mitchell.

Finally, I would like to express my most sincere thanks to my co-authors, Neil Collar of Brodies and Mark Poustie of the University of Strathclyde. Without their contributions, advice, assistance and attendance at editorial meetings, this book would not have been written.

Charles Smith
Brodies, WS
15 Atholl Crescent
Edinburgh EH3 8HA
September 1997

Contents

TABLE OF CASES

TABLES OF STATUTES

STATUTORY INSTRUMENTS

INTERNATIONAL LEGISLATION

Abbreviations

AC	Appeal Cases
All ER	All England Law Reports
APC	Air Pollution Control
B App	Bell's Appeals (Law Reports)
BATNEEC	Best Available Techniques Not Entailing Excessive Cost
BPEO	Best Practicable Environmental Option
C-	European Court of Justice Case Numbers
CA	Court of Appeal
CBI	Confederation of British Industry
CFCs	Chlorofluorocarbons
Cm	Command Paper
CMLR	Common Market Law Reports
COM	Commission (Directive)
COPA	Control of Pollution Act 1974
CRI	Chemical Releases Inventory
Crim LR	Criminal Law Review
D	Dunlop (Session Cases)
EA	Environment Act 1995
EC	European Communities
ECJ	European Court of Justice
ECHR	European Convention on Human Rights
ECR	European Court Reports
EEA	European Environment Agency
EEC	European Economic Community
EGCS	Estates Gazette Case Summaries
ELM	Environmental Law and Management
ENDS Report	Environmental Data Services Report
ENTRUST	Environment Trust Scheme Regulatory Body Ltd
Env LB	Environmental Law Bulletin
Env LR	Environmental Law Reports
EPA	Environmental Protection Act 1990
EU	European Union
F	Fraser (Session Cases)
FRPB	Forth River Purification Board
GWD	Greens Weekly Digest
HC	House of Commons
HL	House of Lords
HLR	Housing Law Reports
HMIP	Her Majesty's Inspectorate of Pollution
HMIPI	Her Majesty's Industrial Pollution Inspectorate

HSE	Health and Safety Executive
IPC	Integrated Pollution Control
IPPC	Integrated Pollution Prevention and Control
IRLR	Industrial Relations Law Reports
JPL	Journal of Planning and Environment Law
KB	King's Bench (Law Reports)
LAAPC	Local Authority Air Pollution Control
LAPC	Local Air Pollution Control
LMELR	Land Management and Environmental Law Reports
LGR	Local Government Reports
LR	Law Reports
M	McPherson (Session Cases)
NII	Nuclear Installations Inspectorate
NPPG	National Planning Policy Guidelines
NRA	National Rivers Authority
N & SNA	Noise and Statutory Nuisance Act 1993
OJ	Official Journal (of the European Communities)
PAN	Planning Advice Note
PCBs	Polychlorinated Biphenyls
PLR	Planning Law Reports
QBD	Queen's Bench Division (Law Reports)
R	Rettie (Session Cases)
RPA	River Purification Authority
RSA	Radioactive Substances Act 1993
SC	Session Cases
SCCR	Scottish Criminal Case Reports
SCLR	Scottish Civil Law Reports
SEPA	Scottish Environment Protection Agency
SLT	Scots Law Times
SNH	Scottish Natural Heritage
SPEL	Scottish Planning & Environmental Law
THORP	Thermal Oxide Reprocessing Plant
WCA	Waste Collection Authority
WDA	Waste Disposal Authority
WLR	Weekly Law Reports
WRA	Waste Regulation Authority

Chapter 1

THE LEGAL FRAMEWORK (1):
SOURCES; THE REGULATORS; THE REGULATORY
RÉGIMES; REGULATORS' POWERS OF ENTRY

1.1 INTRODUCTION
The purpose of this chapter is to set out the broad framework within which environmental law and regulation presently operate in Scotland. It examines four topics, an understanding of which it is hoped will assist in making sense of later chapters, by providing a common thread. Consideration is therefore given to the following:

— the sources of environmental law in Scotland;

— the Scottish environmental regulators;

— common features of the regulatory régimes;

— powers of entry available to regulators.

1.2 SOURCES OF ENVIRONMENTAL LAW
1.2.1 Introduction
The development of environmental law as a separate and distinct discipline can probably be traced back to the mid-1980s, just at the time when the government was considering bringing forward the legislation which eventually became the Environmental Protection Act 1990(EPA). It coincided with a period of considerable public concern about environmental matters and indeed with the enactment of a large amount of European environmental legislation. However, it should not be thought that environmental protection was absent before that time. The common law of nuisance was used in the nineteenth century to protect property owners' interests, mainly from the effects of water pollution, which was then widespread and serious, so much so that many rivers were little more than open sewers. As late as the 1850s, the curtains of the Houses of Parliament were coated with lime in an attempt to neutralise the stench of the River Thames. Legislation in respect of the protection of public health from polluting activities and in respect of water pollution can be traced to the middle years of the nineteenth century when it was realised that damage to the environment and harm to human health could not go on unchecked. In Scotland, and until very recently, statutory nuisances were regulated by the Public Health (Scotland) Act 1897. During the twentieth century, efforts to contain water pollution were reinforced and the creation after the Second World

1

War of the river purification boards played a major part in improving water quality in many Scottish rivers. Permits were required in respect of specified polluting activities from as early as 1906 in terms of the Alkali etc Works Regulation Act of that year which, again, has only just been fully repealed in England and Wales, and which is likely shortly to be repealed in Scotland as well. Air quality was addressed by means of the Clean Air Acts in the 1950s, following particularly serious smogs in London. The enactment of the Control of Pollution Act 1974 (COPA) represented a major step forward in the development of a permit-based system in respect of the disposal of waste and discharges to water. This statute, much amended, still regulates water pollution in Scotland.

All these various threads, each with their own history, have tended to come together in the last ten years to form an identifiable body of legislation and of case-law which has evolved into a separate discipline. This can be seen in its purest form in the ground-breaking concept of integrated pollution control (IPC), as introduced by Part I of EPA. The aim of IPC is to have a single permit regulating discharges and omissions to air, water and land from processes considered to be the most likely to give rise to pollution. The 1990 Act also strengthened the regulation of waste disposal, restated the law of statutory nuisance, legislated for genetically modified organisms, introduced street litter control notices and sought to address the proliferation of abandoned shopping trolleys. With this Act, environmental law came of age.

There are four principal sources of environmental law in Scotland:

(1) the common law;

(2) UK legislation;

(3) European legislation; and

(4) international law.

1.2.2 The common law

The common law may be distinguished from statute law in the sense that the common law is developed by the courts in decided cases, rather than by Parliament passing legislation. In the field of environmental protection, it occupies a considerably less significant position than statutory law, but it is nevertheless important in providing a means whereby, subject to satisfying the appropriate liability tests and the test of title and interest to sue, one person may seek damages from another in respect of contamination or other pollution. The principal areas of the common law which are of relevance in the context of environmental protection are the law of nuisance and the law of negligence, both of which are discussed in some detail in Chapter 2. There are, however, limitations on the effectiveness of common law remedies as a means of environmental protection, and these are further explored in Chapter 3.

1.2.3 Legislation

Much of the framework for environmental protection in Scotland is to be found in statutes. The most important of these are COPA, EPA and the Environment Act 1995 (EA), although there are many others. The majority of statutory provisions operate by means of the use of a 'command and control' system of regulation. This has the effect of criminalising certain conduct, save insofar as it is carried out in accordance with a licence, permit, authorisation or consent. In turn, these licences are made subject to conditions, the purpose of which is to aim to protect the environment from the polluting activity being carried on, and breach of these conditions is generally also a criminal offence. Thus, in the field of waste regulation, it is a criminal offence to keep, treat, dispose of or deposit waste without an appropriate licence or without an exemption from the requirement to have a licence. The licence, once granted, may be seen as a permission to pollute, while the conditions in that licence aim to limit the environmental consequences of that polluting activity.

The complexity of environmental legislation is generally such that the statutes themselves operate as a framework, with the more detailed regulation being left to the making of delegated legislation in the form of statutory instruments. Again, this may be seen in the context of waste regulation where not only is Part II of EPA relevant, but so also are the Waste Management Licensing Regulations 1994 (SI 1994/1056). Additionally, what may be described as 'soft law' mechanisms are also used. These take various forms. In the context of waste, section 34 of EPA imposes a duty of care as respects waste, but much of the detail on the content of that duty of care is to be found in a code of practice which, although it does not have legislative effect, is a document to which the courts are directed to have regard when considering any prosecution in respect of a breach of the duty of care. In the context of IPC (Part I of EPA), guidance has been issued on the meaning of BATNEEC ('best available techniques not entailing excessive cost'), by both the Department of the Environment and the Scottish Office, but this is purely interpretative and thus it is not necessary to have regard to it. At the other end of the scale are certain parts of the guidance proposed to be issued in terms of the new contaminated land régime contained in Part IIA of EPA. This 'guidance' states that enforcing authorities must act 'in accordance with' its provisions which will effectively make it legislation by another name.

The various relevant legislative systems are considered, under their appropriate pollution control heading, in later chapters. In recent years there has been a limited move away from 'command and control' legislation to market-based environmental protection mechanisms. The more significant of these are examined in Chapter 2.

1.2.4 European legislation

Strictly speaking, this is not a separate category of legislation as by virtue of the European Communities Act 1972 European law is expressly stated to form part of the law of the UK and therefore of the law of Scotland. However, it is considered separately here because of its considerable influence upon environmental legislation in the UK. This influence is not always apparent, because in many cases European legislation is implemented either by UK statutes or alternatively by statutory instruments. Taking an example from waste regulation, the definition of waste which is applicable in terms of UK legislation is now taken straight from the European Framework Directive on waste and is therefore identical throughout all the countries of the European Union. Similarly, the Special Waste Regulations 1996 (SI 1996/972), which control particularly dangerous wastes, implement the EC Hazardous Waste Directive (91/689/EEC) and also make use of the EU hazardous waste list. There are numerous other examples of this approach.

Historically, the 1957 Treaty of Rome made no mention of environmental protection. However, in October 1972 the EC agreed to adopt the first of its Environmental Action Programmes. This ran from 1973–1976 and set out the objectives and principles of a European Community-wide environmental policy which was to be implemented primarily by means of legislation at European level. The present Environmental Action Programme is the Fifth ('Towards Sustainability'). This programme runs from 1993–2000 and differs markedly from its predecessors in its emphasis on a new approach to environmental protection involving a range of policy instruments rather than the traditional legislative 'command and control' approach. It also stresses the need for integration of environmental protection into all economic activities and the need for shared responsibility between member states, industry and the public.

The lack of specific environmental provision in the Treaty of Rome was remedied by the Single European Act 1987 which introduced a new Environment Title into the Treaty, contained in articles 130R–T. The objectives set out in article 130R(1) of the Treaty were very wide in scope, namely

— to preserve, protect and improve the quality of the environment;

— to contribute towards protecting human health;

— to ensure the prudent and rational utilisation of natural resources.

Additionally, article 130R(2) stated that

'Action by the Community relating to the environment shall be based on the principles that preventive action should be taken, that environmental damage should as a priority be rectified at source and that the polluter should pay. Environmental protection requirements shall be a component of the Community's other policies.'

This legislative underpinning of the Community's activities on environmental matters was extremely important as it provided for the first time a clear legal base for environmental policy at European level. In making explicit the principle that environmental protection requirements were to be a component of the Community's other policies, article 130R(2) also enshrined the concept that environmental requirements must not only be imposed for their own sake but must also be integrated into the other policies adopted at European level.

Finally, the Treaty on European Union of 1993 (the Maastricht Treaty) introduced, in terms of a replacement article 2 of the Treaty of Rome, the promotion of 'sustainable and non-inflationary growth respecting the environment'. It also introduced into article 130R(2) of

4

the Treaty the use of the precautionary principle as the basis for environmental policy, this principle having very recently been adopted at international level at the Rio summit (see paragraph 1.2.5).

The result of this, and other changes introduced by the Maastricht Treaty, produces the following text for articles 130R(1) and (2) of the Treaty of Rome.

'1. Community policy on the environment shall contribute to pursuit of the following objectives:

— preserving, protecting and improving the quality of the environment;

— protecting human health;

— prudent and rational utilization of natural resources;

— promoting measures at international level to deal with regional or worldwide environmental problems.

2. Community policy on the environment shall aim at a high level of protection taking into account the diversity of situations in the various regions of the Community. It shall be based on the precautionary principle and on the principles that preventive action should be taken, that environmental damage should as a priority be rectified at source and that the polluter should pay. Environmental protection requirements must be integrated into the definition and implementation of other Community policies.

'In this context, harmonization measures answering these requirements shall include, where appropriate, a safeguard clause allowing Member States to take provisional measures, for non-economic environmental reasons, subject to a Community inspection procedure.'

Although consideration of the means whereby EC legislation is adopted is outwith the scope of this book, it should be noted that voting by qualified majority, rather than by unanimity of member states, has become the norm in respect of most environmental measures, that the power of the European Parliament to amend draft legislation proposed by the European Commission has been significantly strengthened and that, in certain cases, the Parliament has a power of veto over legislation.

In essence, the provisions of European law applying in the UK are derived from four distinct sources:

— provisions of the 1957 Treaty of Rome (as amended by the Single European Act and the Maastricht Treaty), which are directly applicable in the UK as a member state. Not all the provisions of the Treaty of Rome have this status, but those worded adequately specifically to constitute binding legal obligations will do so;

— regulations made by the Commission under authority of the Treaty. These regulations are directly applicable in the UK without the requirement that they be the subject of national legislation bringing them into force;

— directives, which are also issued by the Commission under authority of the Treaty. These generally require to be the subject of specific national measures bringing them into force in the country concerned although there may be circumstances in which directives are also applicable in the member state without specific enabling legislation having been brought into force. This point is considered in more detail in Chapter 2; and

— decisions, issued by the Commission under the authority of the Treaty, which are binding only upon those to whom they are addressed without the need for further implementing legislation.

Of the foregoing, it is directives which are the most important legislative mechanism in the environmental context. A very large amount of environmental legislation has been adopted by the Commission, so much so that it has become increasingly difficult for the Commission to police its implementation, primarily because of staffing and funding constraints. There has therefore been a tendency for the topics of environmental directives to be more carefully chosen in recent years and to be the subject of fuller prior consultation with those affected and member states, with the result that, although the number of such directives may have decreased, the quality has improved. The declared aim of the Commission is that Community environmental legislation should be drafted so as to attain maximum clarity, transparency and certainty, which it is hoped will make implementation simpler and quicker.

As to implementation, the Commission issued a communication on 22nd October 1996 (COM (96) 500. final) which suggests addressing the problems by means of (1) establishing guidelines with a view to improving compliance inspection in member states, (2) setting minimum criteria for the handling of complaints and investigation procedures in member states, and (3) considering the need for guidelines with a view to increasing the use of national courts as a forum for litigation on Community environmental legislation, with particular reference to providing access to the courts for environmental groups. These proposals are at a relatively early stage and are couched in terms of making recommendations rather than proposing legislation. Nevertheless, the issue of implementation is considered fundamental by the present European Environment Commissioner, not only because of the implications for protection of the environment, but also because poor implementation calls into question the credibility of the Community and its institutions.

The European Court of Justice (ECJ) has the task of interpreting the legislative acts of the Commission which are brought before it. Its decisions are therefore an important source of interpretation of European law and cannot be ignored by member states or indeed by the courts of member states. In fact, because European law is part of the law of Scotland and because of article 5 of the Treaty of Rome (which provides that member states are under a duty to take all necessary steps to meet their obligations under European law), member states (and the courts in member states) must give effect to European law even in circumstances where it conflicts with national law. This is the doctrine of supremacy of European law (see paragraph 2.12.2).

1.2.5 International law

Consideration of international environmental law falls outwith the scope of this book, but it should not be overlooked as a means of environmental regulation at a higher level. For example, the phasing out of CFCs in refrigerants is the direct result of the Vienna Convention and the Montreal Protocol thereto. Similarly, the statutory régime in relation to nuclear contamination which applies in the UK by virtue of the Nuclear Installations Act 1965 is the direct result of the Paris Convention of 1960 on third-party liability for nuclear occurrences. Not only, therefore, do international treaties impose obligations on signatory states, but they also inform legislative thinking at national level. Since the UN summit at Stockholm in 1972, when environmental law came on to the international agenda, over 100 international treaties with an environmental content have been entered into. Although it is true that many of these do not impose particularly strong obligations on signatories, there has been a tendency for some of these treaties to be strengthened in terms of the obligations which they impose by means of later protocols. The Rio summit in 1992 gave a major impetus to sustainable development in policy terms, as also to the precautionary principle. Each of these concepts informs more recent environmental legislation to some degree.

1.3 THE SCOTTISH ENVIRONMENTAL REGULATORS

1.3.1 Secretary of State for Scotland/Scottish Office

The Secretary of State is involved in the environmental arena in three important respects. First, he has significant reserve powers under many environmental statutes. For one example, see the Scottish Environment Protection Agency's (SEPA's) pollution control functions, discussed at paragraph 1.3.2.3.

Secondly, he is in many cases responsible for producing guidance (often in collaboration with the Department of the Environment and the Welsh Office) on various environmental law issues (eg, the Duty of Care for Waste Code of Practice). Scottish Office policy documents are often very similar to the relevant English document (eg, guidance to SEPA).

Thirdly, the Secretary of State also deals with appeals in respect of the granting, suspension, modification and revocation of environmental permits and consents.

The Scottish Office is developing an Internet site at http://www.open. gov.uk/scotoff/scofhom.htm

1.3.2 The Scottish Environment Protection Agency (SEPA)

The principal environmental regulator in Scotland is SEPA, which is responsible for the following pollution control functions.

Function	Statute and former regulator
Air pollution control	Alkali etc Works Regulation Act 1906; Health and Safety at Work etc Act 1974 (Her Majesty's Industrial Pollution Inspectorate (HMIPI))

Waste regulation	COPA; Control of Pollution (Amendment) Act 1989; EPA, Part II (former district and islands councils)
Local air pollution control	EPA, Part I, Part B processes (former district and islands councils)
Integrated pollution control	EPA, Part I, Part A processes (HMIPI and River Purification Authorities (RPAs))
Radioactive substances control	Radioactive Substances Act 1993 (RSA) (HMIPI)
Water pollution control	COPA; Rivers (Prevention of Pollution) (Scotland) Acts 1951 and 1965 (RPAs)
Producer responsibility for packaging waste (registration and compliance)	EA, sections 93–95 and the Producer Responsibility Obligations (Packaging Waste) Regulations 1997
Remediation etc of contaminated land ('special sites' only)	EPA, Part IIA, as inserted by EA (not yet in force)

1.3.2.1 SEPA: policy background

The government's case for SEPA is set out in the Consultation Paper, Improving Scotland's Environment: The Way Forward, 1992. This argued that with the establishment of IPC, the time was ripe to integrate the administration of pollution control in Scotland. This was required (1) to overcome the potential for overlap between existing agencies – for example, HMIPI and RPAs in relation to IPC; (2) to overcome the potential for a conflict of interest where the regulator was responsible for regulating itself – for example, in the case of district and islands councils who as waste regulation authorities were responsible for regulating their own disposal and treatment facilities; and (3) to bring together the necessary expertise and resources to deal with pollution control. The government saw the one-stop shop approach as having considerable advantages for industry and the integrated approach to pollution control as having considerable advantages for the environment. Accordingly it recommended the establishment of SEPA as an independent body operating at arm's length from government with full powers, bringing together the functions of HMIPI, RPAs and certain functions of local authorities, namely air pollution control (APC) under Part I of EPA and waste regulation.

1.3.2.2 SEPA: status and organisation

SEPA is a non-departmental public body accountable to Parliament through the Secretary of State for Scotland. It came into existence on 12th October 1995 and became operational on 1st April 1996. It consists of a main board and three regional boards. The main board has twelve members comprising a Chairman, a Chief Executive and ten other members from a variety of backgrounds including agriculture, fisheries, industry, local authorities, nature conservation and the former RPAs.

SEPA's headquarters are in Stirling. It has a devolved structure with three regional boards (North, based in Dingwall; East, based in Riccarton near Edinburgh; and West, based in East Kilbride) which are to exercise delegated executive functions of the main board. There are also seventeen local offices around the country in addition to the Stirling HQ and the regional HQs. Broadly speaking, policy matters are dealt with in Stirling, while the activities related to regulation are carried out from the regional HQs and the local offices. SEPA has a staff complement of about 600 people, of whom about eighty are based in the Stirling HQ.

Concern regarding SEPA's accountability has been expressed given that all its main board members have been appointed by the Secretary of State in contrast, for example, to the position of the former RPAs, half of whose members were appointed by local authorities within the board area and half by the Secretary of State. However, lack of connection with local areas may be an advantage as SEPA may thereby be more independent in its approach to environmental protection.

1.3.2.3 SEPA: aims, objectives, duties

SEPA has no principal statutory aim in contrast to the Environment Agency (the equivalent body in England and Wales) which by section 4 of EA is required to discharge its functions so as to make a contribution to sustainable development. SEPA's aims and objectives are supplied in guidance from the Secretary of State and section 31 of EA specifies that this guidance must indicate what contribution SEPA should make to sustainable development. In performing its functions SEPA must have regard to such guidance.

The fact that SEPA must have regard to the section 31 guidance means that its actions could be challenged in the courts only where it completely ignored the guidance or considered the wrong guidance. If it had regard to the guidance and decided in the circumstances to depart from it that could only be challenged where such a decision was manifestly unreasonable.

Despite the government's professed aim that SEPA should be an independent, arm's length body, it is clear that the Secretary of State can exercise very considerable influence over the policy direction which SEPA takes by means of the section 31 guidance. For example, SEPA cannot itself develop a definition of sustainable development but must have regard to the Secretary of State's guidance on this issue.

The guidance in terms of section 31 was issued by the Secretary of State in November 1996. It states that the principal aim of SEPA is

> 'to provide an efficient and integrated environmental protection system for Scotland, which will both improve the environment and contribute to the Government's goal of sustainable development'.

This principal aim is expressly stated to be subject to the provisions of EA and in particular to section 39 of that Act, dealing with costs and benefits (see below).

The principal objectives of SEPA are stated to be the following, namely, to

> 'adopt, across all its functions, an integrated approach to environmental protection and enhancement, which considers impacts of substances and activities on all environmental media and on natural resources;
>
> 'work with all relevant sectors of society, including regulated organisations, to develop approaches which deliver environmental requirements and goals without imposing excessive costs (in relation to benefits gained) on regulated organisations and society as a whole;
>
> 'adopt clear and effective procedures for serving its customers, including developing single points of contact through which regulated organisations can deal with SEPA;
>
> 'operate to high professional standards, based on sound science, information and analysis of the environment and of processes which affect it;
>
> 'organise its activities in ways which reflect good environmental and management practice and provide value for money for those who pay its charges and taxpayers as a whole;
>
> 'provide clear and readily available advice and information on its work; and
>
> 'develop a close and responsive relationship with the public, local authorities and other representatives of local communities, and regulated organisations'.

The emphasis, therefore, is on an integrated approach to environmental protection, the establishment of close relationships with sectors of society and the public, efficiency and responsiveness and the avoidance of the imposition of excessive costs.

On sustainable development itself, the following matters are emphasised:

— a holistic approach to the protection and management of the environment;

— the taking of a long-term perspective;

— conserving and enhancing biodiversity;

— the encouragement of improved technologies and management techniques;

— the discharge of regulatory functions in partnership with regulated organisations;

— the development of close and responsive relationships with the public and local authorities;

— the provision of high-quality information and advice.

In summary, there is a considerable emphasis on the adoption of a partnership approach, wherever that is possible, with business, the public, local authorities and other representatives of local communities, as also other bodies with sustainable development functions (such as Scottish Natural Heritage (SNH)). This is made expressly clear in paragraph 19 of the background information to the Secretary of State's guidance.

Enforcement policy is a very important aspect of SEPA's activities. This is currently still under discussion within SEPA, but it is likely that the policy, once it emerges, will be based upon a hierarchy of procedures ranging from discussions, through meetings, warning letters and enforcement notices, to reports for prosecution. The declared intent is to produce a policy which is fair, reasonable and open.

SEPA will also operate within a complex web of duties. It has duties – for example, in terms of section 34 of EA – to promote the cleanliness of waters; to conserve water resources as far as is reasonably practicable; and, in considering any proposals, to have regard to the desirability of protecting the natural heritage. However, most of these duties are not absolute but must be discharged 'in so far as is reasonably practicable' or are merely 'to have regard to the desirability' of doing something. This means that SEPA has some degree of discretion in discharging these duties. Essentially its officers will be performing balancing acts whenever they consider proposals, such as an application for an IPC authorisation, or whether to take enforcement action. The discharge of many of these duties has required SEPA to enter into memoranda of understanding with appropriate bodies – for example, SNH, the Scottish water authorities, the Health and Safety Executive, harbour authorities and the police.

One duty which came in for much criticism is the duty in section 39 of EA to take account of costs and benefits in the performance of its functions. Environmentalists believed that this would result in watered down environmental protection while the CBI welcomed the provision. In fact the duty is of fairly limited application in that (1) it does not apply where SEPA must discharge a duty; (2) it does not apply where it would be unreasonable for it to do so; and (3) it is only a duty to take account of costs and benefits, not a duty to apply and follow rigidly a cost-benefit analysis. In any case, existing provisions already require regulators to consider costs and benefits as, for example, in the application of BATNEEC under the IPC régime in terms of Part I of EPA.

1.3.2.4 SEPA: functions

As the government originally envisaged, SEPA has taken over the functions of HMIPI (IPC, radioactive substances regulation); RPAs (IPC, water pollution control); and certain local authority functions (APC under Part I of EPA and waste regulation). SEPA took over all these functions as from 1st April 1996 ('the transfer date').

SEPA also has a number of new functions in relation to the development of a national waste strategy, an air quality strategy and a role in relation to certain contaminated land which is designated as a 'special site'. It will also have a new duty to provide advice on flood risk to planning authorities and a consultative role in relation to prescribed drainage works.

However, it is not as integrated a body in this regard as it might have been. Flood defence powers and indeed a duty to inspect watercourses for potential to cause flooding and to take steps to prevent or mitigate such flooding are vested in local authorities (see the Flood Prevention (Scotland) Act 1961, as to be amended by the Flood Prevention and

11

Land Drainage (Scotland) Act 1997) which leaves a division of responsibility in relation to flooding which is absent south of the border. Furthermore, SEPA does not have an extensive catchment management role in that it has minimal powers to protect water resources, unlike the Agency south of the border. Additional selective controls over water abstraction are, however, likely to be introduced in the near future. In relation to nuclear issues, there remains a fragmented approach with the Nuclear Installations Inspectorate (NII) (part of the Health and Safety Executive) retaining responsibility for the licensing of nuclear installations and SEPA taking over HMIPI's responsibilities for authorising the disposal of radioactive materials. Other functions, such as the licensing of the dumping of waste at sea, remain with the Secretary of State. SEPA has no direct conservation functions: SNH is the lead conservation agency in Scotland. As a result of this, the extent to which SEPA can be said to be a truly integrated body is doubtful.

Furthermore, it should be noted that the establishment of SEPA does not mean that a business will require only one environmental licence for a particular process (unless it happens to be an IPC process). If a business was previously regulated by a local authority in relation to its emissions to air and by a river purification board in relation to discharges to water, it will still have two licences from SEPA, ie, an air pollution authorisation and a discharge consent.

1.3.2.5 SEPA: likely benefits and problems

Clearly the adoption of an integrated approach to pollution control and a one-stop shop will bring benefits for both business and the environment. The quality of authorisations etc may well improve significantly. Furthermore, the adoption of uniform procedures and policies nationally on issues such as enforcement should bring benefits.

However, there remain doubts about the extent to which SEPA is actually a truly integrated body. More fundamentally, however, there are valid concerns that SEPA is not really independent at all, but very much a creature of the Secretary of State since he may give SEPA directions (EA, section 40) and influence its actions through guidance. SEPA's independence is further undermined by the fact that the Treasury holds the purse strings for most (about 75 per cent) of its budget.

SEPA has an Internet site at http://www.sepa.org.uk/ where press releases may be accessed.

1.3.3 Councils established by virtue of the Local Government etc (Scotland) Act 1994

A major reorganisation of local government in Scotland took place on 1st April 1996, as a result of which the previous two-tier structure of regional and district councils was replaced by a single-tier approach involving the creation of thirty-two councils covering the whole of Scotland. At the same time, the creation of SEPA resulted in the transfer of the functions of local authority air pollution control and waste regulation from district councils to that organisation. Additionally, the functions of regional councils in respect of the provision of water and sewerage collection and treatment were transferred to the three new

Scottish water authorities. Nevertheless, local councils remain responsible for a number of functions of some importance in the context of environmental protection.

Function	Statute
General planning control	Town and Country Planning (Scotland) Act 1997
Hazardous substances control (planning)	Planning (Hazardous Substances) (Scotland) Act 1997
Statutory nuisance	EPA, Part III
Waste collection	EPA, Part II
Waste disposal	EPA, Part II
Air pollution control (smoke)	Clean Air Act 1993
Flood prevention and defence	Flood Prevention (Scotland) Act 1961, as amended by the Flood Prevention and Land Drainage (Scotland) Act 1997 (not yet in force);
Air quality management	EA, Part IV (not yet in force)
Identification and remediation of contaminated land (excluding remediation of sites which are not 'special sites')	EPA, Part IIA, as inserted by EA (not yet in force)

1.3.4 Water authorities established by virtue of the Local Government etc (Scotland) Act 1994

At the same time as the creation of SEPA and the new local councils (1st April 1996) three new water authorities were created in Scotland, namely the North of Scotland Water Authority, the East of Scotland Water Authority and the West of Scotland Water Authority. Albeit that they are primarily concerned with the provision of water, they have significant pollution control functions in that they are responsible not only for water quality but also for the collection and treatment of waste water and sewerage. In contrast to the position in England, where these functions are discharged by means of privatised utilities, the Scottish water authorities are public sector bodies.

Function	Statute and former regulator
Water pollution control	Water (Scotland) Act 1980; Sewerage (Scotland) Act 1968 (former regional and islands councils)

1.3.5 Health and Safety Executive (HSE)

The primary function of HSE is the enforcement of the Health and

Safety at Work etc Act 1974 and statutory instruments made there-under. This legislation comprises a comprehensive and large body of rules for ensuring the health, safety and welfare of persons at work, consideration of which is beyond the scope of this book. However, insofar as its functions relate to the storage, handling and carriage of dangerous materials and hazardous substances, it has a role which complements that of environmental protection.

Function	*Statute*
Nuclear installations regulation	Nuclear Installations Act 1965
Health and safety at work	Health and Safety at Work etc Act 1974

1.3.6 Department of the Environment, Transport and the Regions (DETR)

Although the DETR is not a Scottish environmental regulator, it is nevertheless a useful point of contact in relation to legislation and policy which applies to all of Great Britain. As a London-based department, it tends to take the lead in such matters (for example, in the national air quality strategy and in the development of the guidance on the new contaminated land powers contained in Part IIA of EPA) and is often able to provide more up-to-date information than the Scottish Office. The DETR has an Internet site at http://www.open.gov.uk/doe/doehome.html where access is available to its press releases, up-to-date air quality monitoring and drinking water quality information, etc.

1.3.7 The European Commission

The European Commission initiates EC legislation on all matters, including the environment. However, it also has a role which may be described as regulatory, in the sense that it is the guardian of the European treaties. In that capacity, it must ensure the correct and proper implementation of EC legislation and take proceedings against member states if that legislation is not properly enacted by those member states. The topic of enforcement proceedings by the Commission is considered at paragraph 2.12.3.

1.3.8 The European Environment Agency

The European Environment Agency (EEA) was established in 1990, in terms of Regulation 1210/90/EEC. Although it is not a regulator, it does have an important role in respect of obtaining, collating and then disseminating data, research and other information about the environment. For example, it receives data from member states on all aspects of regulatory control, such as information on waste arisings and methods of disposal. Its information and knowledge will assist the Commission in formulating proposals for new environmental legislation and in reviewing existing legislation. It is based in Copenhagen and presently has a staff of about seventy people.

1.4 COMMON FEATURES OF THE REGULATORY RÉGIMES

This section considers certain common features of the environmental regulatory régimes imposed by statute and applicable in Scotland. These features are of most relevance in respect of IPC and local air pollution control (LAPC) in terms of Part I of EPA, waste management licensing in terms of Part II of EPA, water pollution control in terms of Part II of COPA, radioactive substances control in terms of RSA and the licensing of nuclear installations in terms of the Nuclear Installations Act 1965, although certain other régimes share some of these common features – for example, the new contaminated land powers in Part IIA of EPA and statutory nuisance in terms of Part III of EPA. The essential features are

— the criminalisation of certain conduct except insofar as permitted by a licence, permit, authorisation or consent, usually with potentially heavy fine penalties attached and the possibility of imprisonment;

— the imposition of such criminal liability upon 'any person' who carries out an unconsented activity;

— the imposition of criminal liability on directors and other officers of bodies corporate and on members of bodies corporate in circumstances where they have consented to or connived at the commission of a criminal offence by that body corporate or where the offence is attributable to their neglect;

— the involvement of a regulatory body to police the regulatory system, ie, to grant or refuse consents, to impose appropriate conditions in consents, to vary or revoke consents, and to enforce compliance;

— a system and procedure for applying for, considering and granting the necessary licences, permits, authorisations or consents, with appropriate appeal mechanisms;

— a system and procedure for the variation of conditions attached to licences, authorisations, permits or consents;

— a system and procedure for the suspension and/or revocation of licences, authorisations, permits or consents;

— the ability on the part of the regulatory authority to review the relevant licence, authorisation, permit or consent on a regular basis in order to keep abreast with changing environmental technologies and changing priorities;

— a system and procedure requiring the effects of acts or omissions carried out in breach of a licence, or without a licence, to be remedied, either at the hand of the regulator with cost recovery from the liable person, or at the hand of the liable person (generally known as statutory clean-up powers);

— in some cases, the imposition of statutory civil liability in respect of the consequences of criminal conduct (ie, acts carried out without a licence or in breach of a licence condition);

— the provision of public registers containing details of licences, authorisations, permits and consents, variations thereto, suspension and
revocation notices and the like;

— the availability of powers of entry and of obtaining information on
the part of the regulatory authorities for the purpose of implementing their duties under the relevant regulatory system.

All the above produce regulatory systems in respect of specific areas
of control which are necessarily complicated and sometimes difficult to
understand. Nevertheless, once the basic framework is appreciated, the
nuts and bolts of each regulatory system can be more readily understood. The reason that the regulatory systems are there in the first place
is because of the perception (almost certainly correct) that the market
would not regulate itself so as to provide the requisite degree of environmental protection, principally because of the cost element involved. The
tightening of environmental legislation in recent years has almost invari-
ably come about because the market place has not sufficiently (or at all)
taken account of the environmental consequences of its operation.

An important aspect of the regulatory régimes is the powers of entry
which are made available to regulators in order to facilitate the exercise
of their various pollution control functions. These powers are now
mostly to be found in EA and merit separate consideration, first,
because they are truly a common feature and, secondly, to avoid repeti-
tion in subsequent chapters.

1.5 POWERS OF ENTRY/OBTAINING INFORMATION
1.5.1 Introduction
This section considers powers of entry available to SEPA and local authorities in Scotland. Prior to the enactment of EA, the powers of entry of
regulatory authorities were contained in a number of different statutes,
enacted at different times, and relating to different pollution control
functions. This inevitably resulted in a number of discrepancies between
the powers of entry available, as between regulated sectors and regulatory authorities. The opportunity was therefore taken in EA to create a
single set of provisions dealing with powers of entry which covers most,
although not all, environmental statutes. These powers are contained in
sections 108–110 of and Schedule 18 to EA.

1.5.2 Scope of powers
Section 108(1) of EA provides that a person who appears suitable to an
enforcing authority may be authorised in writing by that authority to
exercise the powers specified in section 108(4) for the purpose

— of determining whether any provision of the 'pollution control enactments' in the case of that authority is being, or has been, complied with;

— of exercising or performing one or more of the 'pollution control
functions' of that authority; or

— of determining whether and, if so, how such a function should be
exercised or performed.

Section 108(15) explains that 'pollution control enactments', in relation to an enforcing authority, means the enactments and instruments relating to the pollution control functions of that authority. The same subsection defines 'pollution control functions' as well. In relation to SEPA, these are the functions conferred or imposed on it by or under

— the Alkali etc Works Regulation Act 1906;

— Part III of the Rivers (Prevention of Pollution) (Scotland) Act 1951;

— the Rivers (Prevention of Pollution) (Scotland) Act 1965;

— Part I of the Health and Safety at Work etc Act 1974;

— Parts I, IA and II of COPA (waste, water pollution);

— the Control of Pollution (Amendment) Act 1989;

— Parts I, II and IIA of EPA (IPC, LAPC, waste, and contaminated land);

— section 19 of the Clean Air Act 1993 (smoke control areas);

— RSA;

— regulations made by virtue of section 2(2) of the European Communities Act 1972, to the extent that the regulations relate to pollution (broadly, European environmental directives and the like).

In relation to local authorities in Scotland, the 'pollution control functions' in relation to which the powers of entry may be exercised are

— functions conferred under Part IIA of EPA (contaminated land);

— functions conferred by or under regulations made by virtue of Part IV of EA (air quality);

— functions conferred by or under regulations made by virtue of section 2(2) of the European Communities Act 1972, to the extent that the regulations relate to pollution (broadly, European environmental directives and the like).

The powers of entry are exercisable in relation to 'premises', which is defined in section 108(15) of EA as meaning any land, vehicle, vessel or mobile plant.

It should be noted that the general power of entry does not extend to cover the functions of local authorities in respect of statutory nuisance (EPA, Part III), noise under COPA, and air pollution under the Clean Air Act 1993 (with the exception of smoke control areas).

Additionally, section 108(2) permits the powers of entry to be exercised by SEPA for the purpose of enabling SEPA to carry out assessments or reports as may be required in terms of section 33(3) of EA. Section 33(3) provides that, if required by the Secretary of State to do so, SEPA shall

— carry out assessments of the effect or likely effect on the environment of existing or potential levels of pollution of the environment and report its findings to the Secretary of State; or

— prepare and send to the Secretary of State a report identifying the options which SEPA considers to be available for preventing or minimising or remedying or mitigating the effects of pollution of the environment (whether generally or specifically), and the costs and benefits of the options identified by SEPA.

However, the power contained in section 108(2) may only be exercised in relation to a matter covered by section 33(3) of EA where the Secretary of State, having required the assessment to be carried out or the report to be prepared, has also notified SEPA that the assessment or report appears to him to relate to an incident or possible incident involving or having the potential to involve serious pollution of the environment, or serious harm to human health, or danger to life or health.

1.5.3 Content of power of entry

It must be remembered that before the powers of entry may be exercised at all, the relevant enforcing authority must confer a written authorisation on a suitable person, that the authorisation must specify the powers which are permitted to be exercised, and that the exercise of the powers must be for one of the purposes referred to in section 108(1) of EA or alternatively for the purpose set out in section 108(2) as limited by section 108(3).

The powers cover not only entry to premises, but also the taking of measurements, photographs, recordings and samples, the removal of articles or substances, and the obtaining of information and records. These powers are specified in section 108(4) and include the following:

— to enter at any reasonable time (or, in an emergency, at any time and, if need be, by force) any premises;

— on entering any premises, to take

— any other person duly authorised by the enforcing authority and, if the authorised person has reasonable cause to apprehend any serious obstruction in the execution of his duty, a constable; and

— any equipment or materials required for any purpose for which the power of entry is being exercised;

— to make such examination and investigation as may in any circumstances be necessary;

— to direct that premises or any part of them, or anything in them, shall be left undisturbed (whether generally or in particular respects) for so long as is reasonably necessary for the purpose of an examination or investigation;

— to take such measurements and photographs and make such recordings as are considered necessary for the purpose of any examination or investigation;

— to take samples, or cause samples to be taken, of any articles or substances found in or on any premises and of the air, water or land in, on or in the vicinity of, the premises;

— in the case of any article or substance found in or on any premises, being an article or substance which appears to the authorised person to have caused or to be likely to cause pollution of the environment or harm to human health, to cause it to be dismantled or subjected to any process or test (but not so as to damage or destroy it, unless that is necessary);

— in the case of any article or substance as referred to in the immediately preceding paragraph, to take possession of it and detain it for so long as is necessary for all or any of the following purposes

   — to examine it, or cause it to be examined, and to do, or cause to be done, to it anything which the authorised person has power to do in terms of the immediately preceding paragraph;

   — to ensure that it is not tampered with before examination of it is completed;

   — to ensure that it is available for use as evidence in any proceedings for an offence under the pollution control enactments in the case of the enforcing authority under whose authorisation the authorised person acts or in any other proceedings relating to a variation notice, enforcement notice or prohibition notice under those enactments;

— to require any person whom the authorised person has reasonable cause to believe to be able to give any information relevant to any examination or investigation to answer (in the absence of persons other than a person nominated by that person to be present and any persons whom the authorised person may allow to be present) such questions as the authorised person thinks fit to ask and to sign a declaration of the truth of his answers;

— to require the production of, or where the information is recorded in computerised form, the furnishing of extracts from, any records

   — required to be kept under the pollution control enactments for the enforcing authority under whose authorisation the authorised person acts; or

   — which it is necessary for the authorised person to see for the purposes of an examination or investigation;

and to inspect and take copies of, or of any entry in, the records;

— to require any person to afford the authorised person such facilities and assistance with respect to any matters or things within that person's control or in relation to which that person has responsibilities as are necessary to enable the authorised person to exercise any of the powers conferred upon him by section 108.

There is also provision in section 108(4) for additional powers to be conferred by regulations made by the Secretary of State – no such regulations have been made to date.

Section 108(5) makes clear that the powers include the power to carry out experimental borings or other works on the premises and to install, keep or maintain monitoring and other apparatus there.

Section 108(6) provides that, except in an emergency, in any case where it is proposed to enter any premises used for residential purposes, or to take heavy equipment on to any premises which are to be entered, at least seven days' notice of the proposed entry must be given to the person who appears to the authorised person to be in occupation of the premises, and such entry must be taken either with the consent of the person in occupation of those premises or under the authority of a warrant granted by virtue of Schedule 18 to EA.

Similarly, except in the case of emergency, section 108(7) provides that where an authorised person proposes to enter any premises and entry has been refused and the authorised person apprehends on reasonable grounds that the use of force may be necessary to effect entry, or the authorised person apprehends on reasonable grounds that entry is likely to be refused and that the use of force may be necessary to effect entry, then any entry may only be effected under the authority of a warrant granted in terms of Schedule 18.

For obvious reasons, the powers are somewhat more draconian in the case of 'emergency' and that concept is defined in section 108(15) as being a case in which it appears to the authorised person in question

— that there is an immediate risk of serious pollution of the environment or serious harm to human health; or

— that circumstances exist which are likely to endanger life or health;

and that immediate entry to those premises is necessary to verify the existence of that risk or those circumstances or to ascertain the cause of that risk or those circumstances or to effect a remedy.

For the purposes of dealing with situations where entry is refused or it is apprehended on reasonable grounds that entry is likely to be refused and, in either case, the use of force may be necessary to effect the entry, the enforcing authority must apply to a sheriff or a justice of the peace under Schedule 18 to EA for a warrant. This is not, however, required in cases of emergency.

It is worth noting that where any person provides information pursuant to the exercise of the section 108 power of entry, no answer given by that person in pursuance of the requirement to provide information is to be admissible in evidence against that person in criminal proceedings (section 108(12)), although the failure to provide the information is itself an offence (see paragraph 1.5.4). Additionally, section 108(13) provides that nothing in section 108 is to be taken to compel the production by any person of a document of which he would on the grounds of legal professional privilege be entitled to withhold production on an order for the production of documents in an action in the Court of Session – in other words, documents protected by legal professional privilege need not be disclosed and it is not an offence to fail to disclose them.

Section 109 confers power on an authorised person to deal with articles or substances found by the authorised person on premises which he has reasonable cause to believe to be a cause of imminent danger of serious pollution of the environment or serious harm to human health. In these circumstances, the authorised person may seize the article or substance and cause it to be rendered harmless. If he should do so, he must prepare and sign a written report giving particulars of the circumstances in which the article or substance was seized and rendered harmless and give a signed copy of that report to a responsible person at the premises where the article or substance was found by him and, unless that person is also the owner of the article or substance in question, serve a signed copy of the report on the owner. This power, therefore, enables immediate action to be taken in respect of particularly dangerous articles or substances.

It should be noted that although sections 108 and 109 of EA are the most obvious means whereby a pollution control authority may obtain entry to premises and information, they are not the only available means. By way of example, section 71 of EPA states that the Secretary of State, or a waste regulation authority, may require any person to furnish such information specified in a notice in writing as the Secretary of State or the authority reasonably consider that he or it needs for the purpose of the discharge of their respective functions under Part II of EPA (waste regulation). Once again, failure to comply with such a requirement is a criminal offence carrying with it an appropriate fine penalty or, on conviction on indictment, a fine or imprisonment for a term not exceeding two years. The important point, however, to note about section 71 of EPA is that there is no provision to the effect that any answer given by a person in pursuance of such a notice is not to be admissible in evidence against that person in later criminal proceedings. For a case in which this section was used in circumstances where one might have expected the predecessor of section 108 in Part II of EPA (section 69, which did contain protection against self-incrimination) to be used, and where the use of section 71 was upheld, see *R* v *Hertfordshire County Council and Others* [1997] Env LR 114. It is not clear that this decision is altogether logical, but it demonstrates that the English courts, at least, are prepared to put environmental protection above the rights of persons who might otherwise incriminate themselves to remain silent.

1.5.4 Sanctions

Section 110 provides that it is a criminal offence for any person intentionally to obstruct an authorised person in the exercise or performance of his powers or duties. It is also an offence for a person, without reasonable excuse,

— to fail to comply with any requirement imposed under section 108;

— to fail or refuse to provide facilities or assistance or any information or to permit any inspection reasonably required by an authorised person in the execution of his powers or duties under or by virtue of section 108; or

— to prevent any other person from appearing before an authorised person, or answering any question to which an authorised person may require an answer, pursuant to the powers contained in section 108(4).

The offence of intentional obstruction carries with it a maximum penalty on summary conviction of a fine not exceeding level 5 on the standard scale, except in circumstances where the authorised person is obstructed in the execution of the powers conferred under section 109, where the penalty on summary conviction is a fine not exceeding the statutory maximum with a penalty on conviction on indictment of a fine or to imprisonment for a term not exceeding two years, or to both. In the case of the other offences referred to, the maximum penalty on summary conviction is a fine not exceeding level 5 on the standard scale.

1.5.5 Conclusion

The powers of entry contained in sections 108 and 109 of EA are broadly expressed and wide ranging. It is worth noting that there is no provision requiring any premises inspected, examined or tested to be restored to their original condition after inspection nor for compensation to be paid for any damage sustained by reason of exercise of these powers. On the other hand, the costs of such an entry or inspection will fall to be met by the relevant enforcing authority. For obvious reasons, defences to any failure to comply with the requests of an authorised person under the entry powers are very limited.

Although specific mention of these powers is not made elsewhere in this book, or only in passing, the availability of EA powers of entry should be borne in mind in respect of all aspects of pollution control which are covered elsewhere, with the exception of statutory nuisance in terms of Part III of EPA and, obviously, common law remedies, these powers of entry being entirely statutory and related to statutory matters.

Chapter 2

THE LEGAL FRAMEWORK (2): CIVIL LIABILITY; JUDICIAL REVIEW; CRIMINAL LIABILITY; EC LAW; MARKET MECHANISMS

2.1 INTRODUCTION

This chapter contains an examination of the general legal framework within which environmental law exists. The application of civil liability, judicial review, criminal liability, EC law and market mechanisms in the context of environmental protection are considered.

2.2 CIVIL LIABILITY
2.2.1 Introduction

Civil law must first be distinguished from criminal law. Criminal law exists to punish conduct which society has determined merits such punishment. Civil law exists primarily to uphold obligations which may be incurred voluntarily – for example, contracts – or involuntarily – for example, the obligation not to cause unintentional harm to another person. Civil law is therefore largely concerned with upholding standards of conduct by ensuring that individuals or businesses fulfil their obligations. In this section we are principally concerned with obligations which arise involuntarily. The most relevant in terms of environmental law are the areas of law known as nuisance and delict. Civil liability may also be imposed by statute and we consider areas in which Parliament has legislated for civil liability. For an example of the possible application of contract law in an environmental law context, see paragraph 8.4.8.3.

It is up to a person to pursue a civil law action involving a claim based on nuisance or delict. There is no positive duty on any person to do so although Parliament has imposed such duties on local authorities in relation to statutory nuisances (see paragraph 2.6.1 and Chapter 10) and the new contaminated land régime (see paragraph 2.6.4 and Chapter 6). This means that one of the principal drawbacks to its usefulness as a tool for controlling pollution is that many people may not wish to take action even if they are entitled to do so. Other drawbacks include legal limitations on who may sue and the potential costs and risks involved in litigating. It should be noted that a person who commences a civil action in Scotland is known as the pursuer and the person being sued is known as the defender. The equivalent terms in England and Wales are plaintiff and defendant.

Before we examine the law of nuisance, delict and statutory civil liability in some detail, it should be noted that a civil action may be raised

23

in either the sheriff court or the Outer House of the Court of Session, which are accordingly known as courts of first instance. In cases of statutory civil liability, the statute sometimes prescribes which court an action should be brought in. There is no limit on the sum which can be sued for in either court. However, the more complex the litigation – and most environmental litigation is complex - the more likely it is to be raised in the Court of Session. This is borne out by the fact that most recent environmental civil liability actions have been commenced in the Outer House (eg, *Logan* v *Wang* 1991 SLT 580; *Drummond* v *Lord Advocate* 1996 GWD 33-1987; *Barr & Stroud Ltd* v *West of Scotland Water Authority* 1996 GWD 36-2126) although some interdict cases have been heard in the sheriff court (eg, *Clyde River Purification Board* v *Balfour Beatty Ltd*, Dumbarton Sheriff Court, 1991, unreported; and *Stonehaven and District Angling Association* v *Stonehaven Recreation Ground Trustees and Stonehaven Tennis Club* (1997) 60 SPEL 36).

Appeal may be made from the sheriff court either to the Sheriff Principal or directly to the Inner House of the Court of Session. If a person appeals to the Sheriff Principal and is not satisfied with the outcome, he can then appeal from the Sheriff Principal to the Inner House of the Court of Session. From the Inner House of the Court of Session it is possible to appeal to the House of Lords. If an action is commenced in the Outer House, an appeal must be taken first to the Inner House and only thereafter to the House of Lords. If questions of EC law are at issue, a reference to the European Court of Justice (ECJ) in Luxembourg may be made (see paragraph 2.12.4).

The onus of proof in a civil action lies with the pursuer and the evidence led must prove the case 'on the balance of probabilities'.

2.2.2 Nuisance: definition

The common law of nuisance is extremely broad in its application and protects the right of an owner or occupier to 'comfortable enjoyment' of his property. A nuisance arises where one person so uses his property as to cause serious disturbance, substantial inconvenience or material damage to a neighbour or his property (*Watt* v *Jamieson* 1954 SC 56). Such interference with 'comfortable enjoyment' may clearly be caused by various types of pollution.

The disturbance, inconvenience or damage will be actionable when it is more than is reasonably tolerable taking into account all the circumstances and effects of the offensive conduct. Tolerability is judged from the standpoint of the victim and not of the author of the alleged nuisance. The victim is only expected to take ordinary measures to protect himself from nuisance.

The relevant circumstances to which the courts will have regard in determining whether the conduct complained of is more than reasonably tolerable include:

— the type of harm;

— the extent of harm;

— the interest harmed;

— the locality;

— the sensitivity to harm; and

— the difficulty or otherwise of preventing harm.

Although the social utility of the activity from which the harm arises can never serve to deny a person a remedy in nuisance (*Webster* v *Lord Advocate* 1984 SLT 13) it is considered in deciding whether the balance of convenience favours granting an interim interdict. For example, in *Barr & Stroud Ltd* v *West of Scotland Water Authority*, although accepting that there was a triable issue in relation to the existence of a nuisance, the court refused to grant an interim interdict preventing the defenders from operating the source of the alleged nuisance, Shieldhall Sewage Works in Glasgow, which the pursuers contended was interfering with their business, since this would cause untreated sewage to flow into the rivers Clyde and Cart and the public would be the first to suffer (see also paragraph 2.2.6).

2.2.3 Requirements of a successful nuisance action

The basis for liability is *culpa* or fault. The English law rule in *Rylands* v *Fletcher* (1868) LR 3 HL 330 that liability for the escape of dangerous things – for example, landfill gas or leachate – is strict does not apply in Scotland (*RHM Bakeries (Scotland) Ltd* v *Strathclyde Regional Council* 1985 SLT 214). Nevertheless, in Scotland, the escape of a dangerous thing, such as a pollutant into water, gives rise to a very strong presumption of fault. However, it should be noted that the requirement to show *culpa* or fault applies only where the pursuer is seeking damages for some form of loss. The remedy of interdict may nevertheless be available without having to prove fault by the party causing the alleged nuisance.

The usual categories of *culpa* are malice, intent, recklessness and negligence (*Kennedy* v *Glenbelle Ltd* 1996 SLT 1186). However, in that case the Inner House held that a nuisance action might also be based on a situation where the defender had indulged in conduct which gave rise to a special risk of abnormal damage from which fault might be implied if damage resulted from that conduct. Such conduct would appear to be an example of recklessness. Liability in nuisance does not arise merely by reason of ownership as in England and Wales and therefore some degree of personal responsibility is required.

The pursuer must also prove that the activity complained of actually is causing or has caused the harm in question and this may be problematic. Establishing causation may require expert witnesses and may not be easy if there is conflicting evidence about the possible causes of the harm. For example, in *Shotts Iron Co* v *Inglis* (1882) 9 R (HL) 78 it was established by expert evidence that acidic vapours from the appellants' operations were causing damage to the respondent's trees, in the face of conflicting evidence that the trees were planted too close together in poor soil. However, in *Graham & Graham* v *Rechem International* [1996] Env LR 158 the plaintiffs failed to establish that emissions from the defendants' incinerator had caused harm to their dairy herd since the most plausible explanation was a condition known as fat cow syndrome brought on by the plaintiffs' own inappropriate animal husbandry.

The type of damage suffered by the pursuer must also be reasonably foreseeable (*Cambridge Water Co* v *Eastern Counties Leather plc* [1994] 1 All ER 53). Although this was an English case, it seems certain that a similar requirement would apply in Scotland. It may be the case that, as in *Cambridge Water Co*, where pollution has, or is alleged to have, occurred before the evolution of modern scientific techniques, the level of awareness at the time may not have been such that it could fairly be alleged that the polluter could reasonably have foreseen the consequences of his actings. However, in *Graham & Graham* v *Rechem International* it was held that where it is known that the operation of a plant can and does result in the emission of substances known to be toxic into the environment, such harm or damage as may be proved to have been caused by such toxic substances when emitted is foreseeable harm.

2.2.4 Persons who may raise a nuisance action

Since nuisance is a remedy connected with the 'comfortable enjoyment' of property, title to sue depends largely on an interest in land. This has been confirmed by the English House of Lords decision in *Hunter and Others* v *Canary Wharf Ltd and London Docklands Development Corporation* [1997] 2 All ER 426. This has restricted those with title to sue to those persons with an interest in property, ie, owners and tenants, overturning the more liberal approach adopted by the Court of Appeal which had accepted that other occupiers, such as those occupying a property under licence and children, also had title to sue. It is likely that this approach will be followed in Scotland. Those with an interest in property include tenants of fishings who have title to sue in respect of nuisances which interfere with their rights (*Stonehaven and District Angling Association* v *Stonehaven Recreation Ground Trustees and Stonehaven Tennis Club*).

It would also appear that members of the public may have title to sue where a nuisance interferes with a public right. Such an action is known as an *actio popularis* (eg, *Potter* v *Hamilton* (1870) 8 M 1064). So, for example, since members of the public have title to assert the existence of a public right of way (*Torrie* v *Duke of Atholl* (1849) 12 D 328; affd (1852) 1 Macq 61) they may well enjoy title to take action in relation to a nuisance which materially affects their use or enjoyment of a public right of way. Since planning authorities have a statutory duty to keep public rights of way within their areas open and free from obstruction (Countryside (Scotland) Act 1967, section 46) this could also involve them in taking action against pollution which was causing a nuisance on a right of way. Furthermore, it is clear that the public have a right to use the foreshore (*Fergusson* v *Pollok* (1901) 3 F 1140), for example, for recreational purposes and may enforce that right along with the Lord Advocate since the right is vested in the Crown (*Officers of State* v *Smith* (1846) 8 D 711; (1849) B App 487). It would seem to follow therefore that members of the public could take action against nuisance interfering with the public right to use the foreshore. Finally, it seems clear that members of the public could take action against pollution which amounted to a material interference with a public right of navigation (*Crown Estate Commissioners* v *Fairlie Yacht Slip Ltd* 1979 SC 156).

However, it has been held that material interference is something more than inconvenience or a nuisance (*Walford* v *David* 1989 SLT 876).

2.2.5 Persons who may be liable for nuisance

The person who causes the nuisance may obviously be sued. This may often be the occupier of land who is not necessarily the owner. However, it seems clear that owners and licensers may also be liable even if they did not cause the nuisance. For example, in *Gourock Ropework Co Ltd* v *Greenock Corporation* 1966 SLT 125, a case involving the blockage of a water course by contractors working on the owner's land which caused damage to neighbouring property, it was held that the liability of the owner depended on whether the owner ought to have foreseen the damage. If the owner had knowledge or means of knowledge that a nuisance was likely to be committed he would be liable. Where contractors are carrying out operations which are not inherently dangerous nor likely to require precautions to be taken to prevent damage to others, the landowners will not be liable (*Noble's Trustees* v *Economic Forestry (Scotland) Ltd* 1988 SLT 662). In *Webster* v *Lord Advocate* the Secretary of State licensed the erection of the Edinburgh Military Tattoo grandstand and obliged the contractors not to cause a nuisance. However, he took no steps to enforce this contractual provision and declarator was granted against him. It would therefore appear that landlords may be liable for nuisances caused by their tenants where they have anti-nuisance clauses in their leases but fail to monitor or enforce such clauses.

2.2.6 Defences

Various defences may be open to the defender. These would obviously include arguments that the alleged nuisance was not actually a nuisance and/or that someone other than the defender had caused the nuisance. However, in addition or in the alternative it might be open to the defender to argue that the nuisance was actually authorised by statute or that the pursuer had lost the right to complain about the nuisance.

It is possible for Parliament expressly to absolve a person from liability for creating a nuisance – for example, as a consequence of a large-scale construction project (*Allen* v *Gulf Oil Refining Ltd* [1981] AC 1001). However, the availability of this defence would depend on the terms of the statute. The possession of a licence from a regulatory body is not the equivalent of statutory authority. Thus, possession of planning permission is not necessarily a defence to a nuisance action (*Wheeler* v *JJ Saunders Ltd* [1995] Env LR 286; *Hunter and Others* v *Canary Wharf Ltd and London Docklands Development Corporation*). By implication it is clear that possession of an environmental licence from SEPA or another environmental regulator would not provide a complete defence. Where the licence's conditions were being breached, the licence would provide no defence. However, it would also appear following *Wheeler* that even where the licence conditions were being complied with, they would not necessarily amount to a defence if they were permitting a nuisance to continue or exist. This would also appear to be the implication of *R* v *Carrick District Council*, ex parte *Shelley and Another* [1996] Env LR 273, albeit in the context of a statutory nuisance, in which the court clearly considered that the existence of a discharge consent issued by the National Rivers Authority (NRA) did not affect the duty of a local authority to serve an abatement notice where it was established that a statutory nuisance existed.

It is not possible to acquire a right to pollute by the operation of the doctrine of prescription since the act would continue to be unlawful (usually in terms of both criminal and civil law). It appears, however, that individuals may lose their rights to take action against a nuisance by acquiescing in a nuisance for the relevant prescriptive period, which is twenty years (the Prescription and Limitation (Scotland) Act 1973, section 8). However, they would still be able to complain about an increase in the level of pollution (*McGavin* v *McIntyre and Others* (1890) 17 R 818; *Kennaway* v *Thompson* [1981] QB 88; *Webster* v *Lord Advocate*).

It is not possible to argue that the social utility of the activity complained of acts as a defence. So, for example, in *Webster* v *Lord Advocate* the social utility of the Edinburgh Military Tattoo and associated annual grandstand construction works did not deprive a pursuer of a remedy in relation to noise nuisance caused by the construction works. However, the form of remedy granted was nevertheless affected by the social utility of the Tattoo. Although an interdict was granted preventing the construction of the Tattoo grandstand, its operation was suspended for six months to enable the contractors to devise a quieter method of erecting the scaffolding. The social utility of the activity complained of may also be considered if an interim interdict is sought. In *Barr & Stroud Ltd* v *West of Scotland Water Authority* the court would not grant an interim interdict preventing the operation of a sewage works which was allegedly causing an odour nuisance interfering with a neighbouring business since the social utility of continuing to operate the sewage works and hence not having raw sewage overflowing into two rivers outweighed the business interest affected.

Finally, it is not a defence to argue that the pursuer came to the nuisance. Remedies are available to a person whether he came to the nuisance or the nuisance came to him (*Webster* v *Lord Advocate*).

2.2.7 Remedies
2.2.7.1 Interdict
An interdict is a remedy which would prevent the conduct or activity complained of from continuing or from being repeated or even from commencing.

To obtain an interdict it is necessary to establish that the conduct complained of would constitute or constitutes a nuisance and that it is either likely to occur or occur again or is continuing.

It is also possible to obtain an interim interdict which is an order preserving the rights of parties pending final determination of the issues. If an interim interdict is being sought, the person seeking the order will require to demonstrate to the court's satisfaction that there is a prima facie case and that the balance of convenience favours granting an interdict. This may involve weighing up the effect of the alleged nuisance on the pursuer against the social utility of permitting the alleged nuisance to continue, pending determination of whether it is a nuisance (*Barr & Stroud Ltd* v *West of Scotland Water Authority*). A financial undertaking for the respondent's costs known as a caution may be required from a petitioner for interim interdict. Should caution not be forthcoming the interim interdict may be refused.

If an interdict is obtained wrongfully, ie, in circumstances which did not entitle the party seeking the order to the interdict, that party may be liable in damages. This may often be the case with an interim interdict where the issues have not yet been fully determined. This may serve as a major deterrent to such actions. In England and Wales the position is similar with the courts requiring a cross-undertaking in damages before an interlocutory injunction (the English equivalent of an interim interdict) may be obtained (*R* v *HM Inspectorate of Pollution and Another*, ex parte *Greenpeace Ltd* [1994] 4 All ER 321).

Although interdict is essentially a negative remedy, it has been used in creative ways by judges. For example, in *Shotts Iron Co* v *Inglis* an interdict was granted preventing the appellants from carrying out the operations in the manner which had hitherto caused the air pollution complained of or in any other manner which would cause such pollution. This is an example of what might be described as a technology-forcing interdict. Another such example is *Webster* v *Lord Advocate*, which is discussed in paragraph 2.2.6.

Actions for interdict may be raised in the appropriate sheriff court or the Court of Session in Edinburgh. If an interdict is obtained in the sheriff court it will only apply to the territorial extent of the particular sheriffdom. However, if the order is obtained in the Court of Session it may apply to the whole of Scotland if that is required.

2.2.7.2 Damages

As noted above damages are available when actual loss, injury or harm occurs. In Scotland *culpa* must be proved if damages are claimed. Although damages for pure economic loss (eg, the loss of the value of a house) may not be recovered it is unlikely that economic loss cannot be associated with loss of amenity or enjoyment of property (see, eg, *Bone* v *Seale* [1975] 1 All ER 787).

2.3 DELICT
2.3.1 Introduction

The principal private law action for damages for personal injury or property damage is based on the law of delict. Under the law of delict, liability is again based upon *culpa* or fault but in this case want of due care for unintentional harm, ie, negligence, rather than on the basis of what is more than reasonably tolerable as in the case of nuisance (see paragraph 2.2.2). The principles of liability in such actions are broadly the same in Scotland as in England and Wales.

There is considerable confusion over the boundaries between liability under nuisance and negligence. As discussed above at paragraph 2.2.2, nuisance is a remedy related to enjoyment of property. If a person's enjoyment of his property is materially affected then he is entitled to a remedy. This can extend to nuisances which cause not only inconvenience but also those which cause actual physical damage. In the case of physical damage to property there is a clear overlap with negligence. However, there is no overlap in the case of personal injury. If personal injury is suffered, the appropriate action is in negligence. To get around this confusion as a matter of practice it is usual to plead both grounds of action in a case. This is known as 'the blunderbuss approach' (eg, *Cambridge Water Co* v *Eastern Counties Leather plc*; *Graham & Graham* v *Rechem International*). Another relevant issue is that where conduct is continuing, the appropriate action would normally be based on nuisance, whereas if it is a one-off accident, the appropriate action would normally be based on negligence although a one-off incident which causes damage may be a nuisance under normal nuisance principles (*Crown River Cruises* v *Kimbolton Fireworks* [1996] 8 ELM 119; and, in England and Wales, under the rule in *Rylands* v *Fletcher* (see paragraph 2.2.3)). It has, however, been held that a one-off rave held in an isolated location did not exceed what was reasonably tolerable (*Cumnock and Doon Valley District Council* v *Dance Energy Associates Ltd* 1992 GWD 25-1441).

2.3.2 Requirements of successful negligence action

For a negligence action to succeed, the pursuer must essentially show

— that the defender owed the pursuer a duty of care;

— that the defender failed in the performance of that duty, falling below the requisite standard of care by reason of negligence; and

— that the damage, loss or injury allegedly suffered by the pursuer was caused by the act complained of.

The test for establishing whether a person owes another a duty of care is whether the defender can reasonably foresee that his conduct will cause harm to the pursuer. In assessing what is reasonably foreseeable it is necessary to look at the harm which occurred and not at what actually happened (*Hughes* v *Lord Advocate* 1963 SC (HL) 31). Importantly for civil liability in an environmental context, where something is not a known hazard at the time, harm resulting from it cannot be reasonably foreseen (*Cambridge Water Co* v *Eastern Counties Leather plc*). However, where something is a known hazard resulting loss or injury will be reasonably foreseeable (*Graham & Graham* v *Rechem International*). For example, in *Margereson* v *J W Roberts Ltd*; *Hancock* v *J W Roberts Ltd* [1996] Env LR 304 the Court of Appeal held that evidence from as early as 1900 linked asbestos with lung damage and that it was not necessary for the defendants to have foreseen the exact type of injury or damage suffered by the plaintiffs; it was enough that the defendants had reasonably foreseen some type of pulmonary injury, not necessarily mesothelioma.

The principles applicable in terms of causation were discussed at paragraph 2.2.3. However, it should be noted that in *Graham & Graham* v *Rechem International*. it was held that it was only necessary to demonstrate that the causal mechanism was a material contribution to the injury complained of rather than the dominant cause.

2.3.3 Title to sue
The ability to sue depends upon being owed a duty of care by the defender.

2.3.4 Parties who can be sued
Liability may obviously attach to the person who caused the harm. However, under principles of vicarious liability, another person may be liable for the harm caused. For example, an employer is liable for the actings of his employees which are within the scope of their employment.

2.3.5 Remedies
The principal remedy for loss or injury suffered by reason of unintentional harm caused by want of due care or negligence is damages to provide compensation for pain, injury, suffering and loss of earnings. Recovery for pure economic loss, such as the loss of the value of a house, is not generally available (*Merlin and Others* v *British Nuclear Fuels Ltd* [1990] 2 QB 557; [1990] 3 All ER 711). However, it has been held that economic losses resulting from radioactive contamination of a property which amounted to physical damage and rendered the property unsaleable until it had been decontaminated are recoverable even though the contamination did not pose an actual risk to human or animal health (*Blue Circle Industries plc* v *Ministry of Defence* [1997] Env LR 341).

2.4 OTHER COMMON LAW PRINCIPLES
There are two further common law principles which may enable aggrieved parties to obtain a remedy for water pollution. The first is an extension of the law of nuisance and flows from the principle which entitles the owner of a stretch of riverbank to the natural flow of the river without material interference with its quality (*John Young & Co* v *Bankier Distillery Co* (1893) 20 R (HL) 76). Interdict may be obtained if the aggrieved owner can prove nuisance and damages may be available if loss or harm can be proved. However, the right to object to a certain level of pollution may be lost by prescription after twenty years or by acquiescence on the part of the owner. Material new pollution could still be restrained by interdict (see paragraph 2.2.6).

The second principle involves the servitude of drainage. An owner or occupier may have the right to send drainage in a pipe or river through or by another's property. The owner benefiting from this right may not interfere with the use of the owner through whose property the servitude passes more than is necessary to exercise this right. If, therefore, an aggrieved owner can establish that the use of the right is beyond what is necessary – for example, because the drainage is heavily polluted – he may be able to obtain interdict and if he can establish that the use has caused loss or damage he may be entitled to damages.

However, both these remedies suffer from practical problems of the same nature as are highlighted below in relation to civil actions generally.

2.5 PRACTICAL ASPECTS OF CIVIL ACTIONS AT COMMON LAW

Raising a successful civil action for damages in respect of loss or harm caused by pollution or contamination is likely to be problematic because

— it is necessary to establish that the party raising the action has an interest to sue and that he has suffered actual damage as a result of the polluting activity complained of (see paragraphs 2.2.3–4 and 2.3.2);

— parties who could sue include proprietors of adjoining land which has been damaged by pollutants escaping from the site investigation, or people suffering harm from polluted drinking water, but in each case they would have to be willing to assume the risk of substantial irrecoverable costs (see paragraphs 2.2.4, 2.3.3 and 2.7);

— it is likely to be difficult to prove both fault and the foreseeability of damage at the time of the original wrongdoing (see paragraphs 2.2.3 and 2.3.2);

— it is likely to be difficult to prove causation (see paragraphs 2.2.3 and 2.3.2);

— where large sums are involved, any civil action is likely to be defended vigorously;

— the costs of raising a civil action risk are considerable and in the event of failure the pursuer would be liable to meet not only his own costs but also those of the defender (see paragraph 2.7); and

— where interdict is sought as a remedy it should be noted that a party seeks interdict 'at his peril'. If the court makes, and subsequently withdraws, an order of interdict, the party against whom it is awarded may have a right of recovery of damages in respect of loss arising through the award; such loss is capable of being meaningful, and could, for example, include loss which arises as a result of the sale of a property failing to proceed by reason of the interdict being in place (see paragraph 2.2.7.1).

2.6 CIVIL LIABILITY UNDER STATUTE

2.6.1 Statutory nuisance

To overcome problems such as the need for a pursuer who was willing and able to take action and the non-availability of clean-up remedies, from the middle of the nineteenth century Parliament legislated to impose duties on local authorities to inspect their areas for statutory nuisances and to take action to abate such nuisance. Until recently the applicable legislation was the Public Health (Scotland) Act 1897. This statute was used in an environmental context in *Clydebank District Council* v *Monaville Estates Ltd* 1982 SLT (Sh Ct) 2 where the local authority identified a statutory nuisance consisting of asbestos-contaminated land and served an abatement notice on a developer who had failed to inspect the land prior to purchasing it. From 1st April 1996 the statutory nuisance provisions of the Public Health (Scotland) Act 1897 were replaced by the extension to Scotland of the English and Welsh statutory nuisance provisions contained in Part III of EPA.

Although local authorities have the primary role in abating statutory nuisances, section 82 of EPA provides that an individual may take action in the sheriff court to enforce the abatement of a statutory nuisance.

Statutory nuisance is discussed in detail in Chapter 10.

2.6.2 Statutory liability under waste law

In the area of waste law it is provided that certain acts may produce both civil and criminal liability – for example, breach of section 33 of EPA in relation to the disposal or management of waste without a licence is a criminal offence but the commission of that offence may also give rise to civil liability (see also paragraph 7.10.3). This means that a person harmed by the commission of the offence may sue the party responsible for the offence in a civil court for damages for compensation for the damage, loss or injury suffered. Such an action would require to follow a successful prosecution in a criminal court. If the offence were committed, the pursuer would be required to prove that the damage, loss or injury suffered was caused by the commission of the offence. This is a form of strict liability since there is no need to prove *culpa*.

The availability of this civil remedy under statute does not mean that a person loses his right to sue the party responsible on the basis of the common law of delict.

2.6.3 Statutory liability under nuclear installations law

The Nuclear Installations Act 1965 imposes an express statutory duty on holders of a nuclear site licence to ensure that no occurrence involving nuclear matter causes injury to any person or damage to any property of any person. Liability is strict and applies even where the occurrence is attributable to a natural disaster. There are, however, certain defences including a provision for reduction in compensation where the injury or damage is the fault of the claimant and it should be noted that causation still requires to be proved. This may be very difficult (*Reay* v *British Nuclear Fuels Ltd; Hope* v *British Nuclear Fuels Ltd* [1994] Env LR 320).

Liability is, however, limited to a maximum of £140 million in respect of any one occurrence not including interest and costs. Claims must be made within thirty years of the date of the occurrence. Damages are not recoverable for pure economic loss, such as the fall in value of a house, where the contamination involved does not amount to actual physical damage as, for example, where the presence of radioactive dust in a house amounted to some increased risk to the health of the occupants (*Merlin and Others* v *British Nuclear Fuels Ltd*). However, where radioactive contamination of a property amounts to actual physical damage such that decontamination works are required to be carried out even though there is no risk to human or animal health, economic losses, including the losses associated with the inability to sell the property until the site has been decontaminated, are recoverable (*Blue Circle Industries plc* v *Ministry of Defence* [1997] Env LR 341 (see also paragraph 2.3.5)).

Nuclear installations liability is also discussed at paragraph 11.16.

2.6.4 Statutory liability for land contamination

Part IIA of EPA, which was inserted by EA, establishes a new statutory civil liability régime in relation to land contamination modelled on the statutory nuisance régime. Duties are imposed on local authorities to inspect their land for contaminated sites (and on SEPA in relation to the most contaminated sites known as special sites) and to serve remediation notices (except in certain circumstances) on 'appropriate persons' on whom liability for clean-up is imposed. Liability is principally imposed on the polluter responsible for the contamination but, if that person cannot be found, liability will fall upon the current owner or occupier.

This régime is considered in detail in Chapter 6.

2.6.5 Statutory reimbursement (or cost recovery) actions

Certain environmental statutes provide for SEPA to take remedial and, in some cases, preventive anti-pollution measures and to recover the costs from the polluter by means of civil court actions.

Section 27 of EPA enables SEPA to take reasonable remedial steps where a person has been convicted of an offence under Part I of EPA and to recover the costs of such steps from the person convicted of the offence. However, this power may only be exercised with the written approval of the Secretary of State. If the steps concerned involve going on to or affecting the land of another person, that person's permission is also needed. This power is discussed further at paragraph 9.2.8.

Section 46 of COPA provided for river purification authorities taking preventive or remedial anti-water pollution works and recovering the costs thereof from the person responsible. However, use of that provision was difficult principally because of budgetary constraints. To remedy that situation, EA inserted sections 46A–D into COPA which provide for 'works notices'. These provisions enable SEPA to serve a notice on persons requiring them to carry out specified preventive or remedial works within a stipulated time scale at their own expense. Failure to comply is a criminal offence. If the works are not carried out, SEPA may carry them out and recover any costs or expenses reasonably incurred from the person who failed to carry out the works.

With the introduction of the works notice, SEPA may only use its powers under section 46 where it considers it necessary that the operations are carried out immediately or where, after reasonable inquiry, it has failed to find a person on whom to serve a works notice. This power is discussed further at paragraph 8.4.3.

In waste law a power also exists under section 59 of EPA enabling SEPA or a waste collection authority (WCA) to serve a notice on a person requiring the removal of unlawfully deposited waste within a specified time scale at that person's expense. Failure to comply is a criminal offence and where there is a failure to comply SEPA or the WCA may remove the waste and recover costs from the person who failed to comply with the notice. This power is discussed further at paragraph 7.9.

2.7 COSTS

Costs in all civil actions usually follow success. The unsuccessful party will normally be required to pay the successful party's costs. This can obviously be a major disincentive to taking action. If a party is only partially successful, costs may not be awarded against the unsuccessful party (*R v Secretary of State for the Environment*, ex parte *Greenpeace Ltd* [1994] 4 All ER 352; [1994] Env LR 401). This case also indicates that, in England and Wales at least, costs may be apportioned to reflect the public interest in having certain issues raised in court, even if the action brought by the interest group is ultimately unsuccessful. It is not clear whether Scottish courts would be disposed to act in a similar way.

Legal aid may be available if the pursuer is financially eligible. Even if the pursuer is financially eligible, he must also pass the 'merits' test – namely that there is an arguable case.

The costs of raising a civil action for damages caused by pollution may be substantial. Not only is this area of the law complex and relatively untested (as far as environmental issues are concerned), but there are likely to be particular difficulties in proving quantum of damage or loss. Detailed scientific evidence is likely to be required – for example, in the form of testimony of expert witnesses and in the case of damage flowing from contamination, in the form of site investigation reports.

All these costs would have to be met initially by the party raising the action, but if the action were successful, the pursuer would be able to recover at least part of his costs from the defender. However, full recoverability (especially in the case of a complex action) will almost certainly not be available, and the resulting shortfall may, for practical purposes, be considerable. If, on the other hand, the defender were successful, then the pursuer could be called upon to meet the defender's costs, subject to the restrictions as to recoverability referred to.

If an action were raised simply to obtain an interdict, the costs should in theory be very much less, because there is no need to quantify loss or harm, but only to show that harm or damage is likely to be caused by the action complained of. Nevertheless, the cost of interdict would be capable of rising to a material level, in the event of either party seeking to lead complex scientific evidence or to raise novel and untested legal points.

2.8 Time scale

An interdict can be obtained quickly where the evidence is straightforward. If it appears to the court that harm or damage is likely to result from the action complained of, the court may grant an interim interdict within a very short time scale, even before there has been time to consider all the relevant facts. This gives the person seeking the interdict protection from the alleged harm from the outset and is an essential feature of a remedy whose main aim is to stop an act which is causing harm or to prevent a threatened action which would cause harm. At a later hearing the court will consider the facts in detail, and either withdraw the interim interdict, or grant a final interdict. However, these observations as to time scale should be qualified to the extent that if the evidence led is complex and if the action is fully contested, the length of time it may take to obtain an award of interdict can be considerably extended.

An action for damages may (assuming that it were defended and subject to the comments made above as to time scale for interdict) take much longer to progress. Because of the complexity of the issues and the likely sums involved, most environmental civil litigation in Scotland is likely to be raised in the Court of Session in Edinburgh (see paragraph 2.2.1). Although an expedited form of procedure known as the optional procedure is available in personal injury actions and a recent review of civil procedure in the Court of Session has advocated that this procedure should become the norm for all personal injury actions, it is not available for complex actions, which are likely to include most environmental cases (*Paterson* v *Henry Robb Ltd* 1989 SC 64).

It could take some time, possibly even a number of years, before a conclusion was reached at first instance in the Court of Session. Thereafter the possibility of appeals to the Inner House and the House of Lords may extend the period of litigation for a very considerable period.

2.9 CONCLUSIONS

There are many difficulties associated with civil litigation actions in the context of environmental law under current legal principles, including in particular

— the costs of pursuing court action, which could be considerable, and exposure to the risk of having to bear the costs of the defence of the action (see paragraph 2.7);

— the likely time scale of any action (other, possibly, than proceedings for interim interdict)(see paragraph 2.8);

— the fact that the law has failed to keep pace with modern environmental issues and awareness; and

— the likely complexity of any action (*passim*).

2.10 JUDICIAL REVIEW
2.10.1 What is judicial review?

Judicial review is the means by which aggrieved interested persons can challenge administrative decisions, such as the grant of an environmental licence by SEPA. It should however, be noted that it is not an appeal against the merits of a decision but is essentially a way of reviewing

— whether the authority which took the decision had the power to do so; and/or

— whether the decision was reasonable; and/or

— whether the decision-maker followed the proper procedure (see, eg, *West* v *Secretary of State for Scotland* 1992 SLT 636).

Where alternative remedies exist – for example, statutory appeals procedure – a person would normally be expected to utilise these before seeking judicial review.

Given that persons other than applicants for environmental licences have no statutory appeal rights judicial review is the only means by which third parties such as environmental interest groups or other aggrieved persons may challenge licensing decisions by environmental regulators such as SEPA. An example of this is *Guthrie v Scottish Environment Protection Agency* 1997 GWD 6-244 where the landlord of a landfill site successfully challenged the validity of a modification to his tenant's waste management licence. Persons seeking to challenge such decisions must qualify title and interest in the courts. This issue is discussed further at paragraph 2.10.3.

Where environmental licensing decisions are made on appeal by the Secretary of State, they may, for example, be challenged by the original decision-maker (eg, *R v Secretary of State for the Environment and NC Compton t/a R J Compton & Sons*, ex parte *West Wiltshire District Council* [1996] Env LR 312), by the licence applicant where he is not satisfied by the outcome of the appeal (eg, *Smith Brothers (Hyde) Ltd v Secretary of State for the Environment* [1996] 253 ENDS Report 8-9) or by third parties such as environmental interest groups who object to the granting of the licence.

Judicial review may also be used to challenge the enforcement strategy adopted by regulators or their chosen method of implementation of EC law, although *R v Secretary of State for the Environment*, ex parte *Friends of the Earth Ltd* [1996] Env LR 198 (CA)(which involved an unsuccessful challenge to the Secretary of State's chosen method of implementing EC Directive 80/778/EEC on drinking water quality on the ground that it was illegal in terms of EC law) demonstrates that such a course of action will be very difficult indeed.

2.10.2 The grounds of challenge
The grounds of challenge are broadly the same throughout Great Britain. There are three broad grounds for challenge although there is considerable overlap between them in practice: (a) illegality; (b) irrationality; and (c) procedural impropriety (*Council for Civil Service Unions v Minister for the Civil Service* [1984] 3 All ER 935, especially per Lord Diplock at pp 949–951).

2.10.2.1 Illegality
This ground is relevant where it is alleged that an authority which took a decision did not have the legal power to do so. It is often known as acting *ultra vires* or acting where there is a lack of jurisdiction. Any decision taken without due legal authority which is challenged will be quashed. For example, decisions may be challenged as illegal on the basis that they do not conform to relevant EC laws, as in *R v Secretary of State for the Environment*, ex parte *Greenpeace Ltd*, in which it was held that the government had acted unlawfully in not regarding a requirement of a Euratom directive as binding although in practice it had complied with the requirement.

2.10.2.2 Irrationality
This ground is applicable where it is alleged that a decision is so unreasonable (ie, perverse) that no reasonable authority would have taken it. This ground is usually known as 'Wednesbury unreasonableness' after *Associated Provincial Picture Houses Ltd v Wednesbury Corporation* [1948]

1 KB 233. It is a very difficult test to satisfy, as illustrated by *R* v *Secretary of State for the Environment*, ex parte *Greenpeace Ltd*, where despite the massive public concern, which was apparent from the volume of representations made to him, the Secretary of State was held to have acted rationally in deciding not to hold a public inquiry in relation to the decision to issue authorisations for the disposal of radioactive waste for British Nuclear Fuel's Thermal Oxide Reprocessing Plant (THORP) at Sellafield. The relevant statutory provision gave the Secretary of State discretion to decide whether to hold a public inquiry and provided he had properly applied his mind to the question of whether to hold an inquiry and the relevant considerations (which he had) his decision could not be impugned as being unreasonable.

This ground of challenge also includes matters such as taking into account irrelevant considerations or failing to take into account relevant considerations. For example, a decision taken by SEPA in circumstances where SEPA had not had regard to the statutory guidance issued by the Secretary of State under section 31 of EA (see paragraph 1.3.2.3) would be irrational (and also procedurally improper) since SEPA had not had regard to something which it is bound to have regard to under that Act. However, as long as guidance is considered where that is required, a departure from it is not necessarily irrational since guidance is not binding and does not necessarily cover every situation – for example, *Smith Brothers (Hyde) Ltd* v *Secretary of State for the Environment*, in which an LAPC authorisation holder unsucessfully attempted to challenge conditions to deal with odour nuisance which had been imposed by the Secretary of State on the basis that they did not conform to the relevant guidance. It was held that the Secretary of State could depart from his guidance where circumstances so demanded although he must still have regard to it.

The failure of the Secretary of State to explain why he was departing from an inspector's conclusion that an LAPC authorisation should not be granted has also been held to be irrational (and is also probably an example of procedural impropriety) (*R* v *Secretary of State for the Environment and N C Compton t/a R J Compton & Sons*, ex parte *West Wiltshire District Council*). However, in Scotland, in a planning case, it has been held that cursory reasons for a departure from a reporter's decision can suffice (*London and Midland Developments* v *Secretary of State for Scotland and Dawn Construction Ltd* (IH)1996 SCLR 465.

It is ultimately a matter for the courts which matters are relevant considerations in a decision-making process but the weight to be attached to the considerations is a matter for the decision-maker.

2.10.2.3 Procedural impropriety

This ground is applicable where it is alleged that the procedure expressly laid down by statute was not followed, or that the rules of 'natural justice' (ie, rule against bias and right to a fair hearing) have not been followed, or that a legitimate expectation has been flouted. Where the giving of reasons for a decision is required, the failure to do so will be regarded as procedurally improper and may also be regarded as irrational and/or *ultra vires*.

2.10.2.4 Proportionality

In *Council for Civil Service Unions* v *Minister for the Civil Service*, proportionality, which is a ground of challenge in certain European administrative law systems, was suggested as a new ground of challenge. There are to date no examples of judicial reviews succeeding on this ground although this may change since the statutory guidance issued to SEPA under section 31 of EA (which SEPA must have regard to) indicates that SEPA should 'ensure actions to achieve compliance are proportionate to the objectives concerned'.

2.10.3 Procedure

There is no requirement in Scotland as there is in England and Wales to obtain leave from the court to proceed with a judicial review. However, the person challenging the decision (the 'petitioner') must qualify title and interest (*D & J Nicol* v *Dundee Harbour Trustees* 1915 SC (HL) 7). In England and Wales environmental interest groups have been granted 'standing' to make applications for judicial review (*R* v *HM Inspectorate of Pollution*, ex parte *Greenpeace Ltd* (*No 2*) [1994] 4 All ER 329). It is not clear whether environmental interest groups would be able to establish title and interest so easily in the Scottish courts as they have been able to do south of the border since the issue at stake must be of real rather than general public-spirited concern to the party commencing proceedings (*Scottish Old People's Welfare Council*, Petitioners 1987 SLT 179). However, it is clear that aggrieved licence applicants, or aggrieved regulators, would be able to challenge regulatory decisions made on appeal by the Secretary of State. Furthermore, where a statutory body, such as SEPA, owes a duty to the public, such as a duty to maintain a register of information, individual members of the public have title to sue (*Stirrat Park Hogg* v *Dumbarton District Council* (OH) 1994 SCLR 631; 1996 SLT 1113).

In contrast to the position in England and Wales where judicial review applications must be made promptly and, in any event, within three months from when the grounds for the application arose (*Caswell* v *Dairy Produce Quota Tribunal for England and Wales* [1990] 2 AC 738), in Scotland no time-limit is laid down for presenting a petition for judicial review. However, such petitions should still be presented as promptly as possible otherwise the judge may not be prepared to grant a remedy. This is illustrated by *Swan and Others* v *Secretary of State for Scotland*, Outer House, 11th March 1997; unreported, a challenge to a decision not to require an environmental assessment for a grant-aided afforestation project. In this case the petitioners threatened judicial review proceedings and complained to the European Commission but did not actually commence proceedings, although they knew that planting would follow the Secretary of State's decision and did in fact follow it to completion. This delay personally barred the petitioners from seeking a remedy. Furthermore, since the decision was not challenged timeously and the planting proceeded to completion, the decision was spent and it was academic whether the decision not to require an environmental assessment was valid or not and the courts will not entertain academic questions.

Petitions for judicial review may only be brought in the Outer House of the Court of Session. It is possible to appeal a decision of the Outer House to the Inner House of the Court of Session and thereafter to the House of Lords.

2.10.4 Remedies

It is possible for the court to reduce a decision made or a licence granted (reduction), to force a regulator to take action (order for specific statutory performance or specific implement), to prevent a decision from being taken or being applied (interdict), to declare the rights of parties (declarator) and damages where the petitioner has suffered loss by reason of the action or inaction of a regulatory authority. Interim remedies may also be available where appropriate.

2.11 CRIMINAL LIABILITY
2.11.1 Introduction

A crime may be defined as a wrongful act or omission, the consequences of which are harmful to the community, and which is punishable by the state. In environmental law, many activities have been criminalised, including causing or knowingly permitting certain types of pollution, carrying out various activities without the requisite environmental licence, breaching the conditions of such a licence, failing to comply with various types of administrative notices and obstructing environmental inspectors. Specific offences are considered in detail in the relevant chapters.

Criminal liability in environmental law often involves offences by companies, ie, bodies corporate. It should be noted that it is only in respect of crimes punishable under statute, and where no evidence of malicious intent (*mens rea*) is required, that proceedings may be brought against a body corporate. Furthermore, bodies corporate are vicariously liable for the criminal acts of their employees while acting in the course of their employment (*National Rivers Authority* v *Alfred McAlpine Homes East Ltd* [1994] 4 All ER 286; [1994] Env LR 198).

2.11.2 The prosecution system
2.11.2.1 Public prosecutions

In Scotland, environmental regulators such as SEPA cannot bring their own prosecutions. Instead, if they wish criminal proceedings to be brought against a person, they must send a report to the local public prosecutor, the procurator fiscal, who has discretion as to whether or not proceedings are to be brought. If the procurator fiscal considers the case to be complex, it may be referred to an advocate-depute.

This system has been criticised because it involves the exercise of discretion at two levels. It has also been alleged that procurators fiscal are not conversant with environmental law and do not accord it an appropriate priority (Friends of the Earth Scotland, *Watered Down: Why the Law is Failing to Protect Scotland's Water*, 1994). It has also been criticised on the basis that the environmental regulators lack an appreciation of the rules of criminal evidence, leading to poor reports being sent to the procurators fiscal. By way of contrast, the environmental regulators south of the border bring their own prosecutions using specialist staff and do not need to refer the matter to the public prosecution authorities.

The establishment of SEPA and, as a result, the development of a common reporting system to replace the varied practices of its predecessors, together with guidance issued by the Crown Office to procurators fiscal on prosecuting environmental offences, will no doubt enhance the system.

2.11.2.2 Private prosecutions

Individuals and organisations can also bring prosecutions which are known as private prosecutions. These may be brought if the public authorities refuse or fail to take action. Any penalties imposed following a conviction are exacted by the state.

However, private prosecutions are very rare in Scotland because they cannot be brought without the consent of the Lord Advocate, the government's chief law officer in Scotland. Should the Lord Advocate refuse such consent, the refusal can be reviewed by the Court of Criminal Appeal, but it will not lightly overturn the refusal. It is believed that no private environmental prosecutions have been attempted in Scotland to date.

This may be contrasted with the position south of the border where private prosecution is a live issue as the person bringing the prosecution does not need the consent of the Attorney-General, the government's chief law officer there. Despite this there have been very few successful environmental private prosecutions in England and Wales: *Greenpeace* v *Allbright & Wilson* [1992] 4 LMELR 56; [1991] 3 LMELR 170 being the most notable example. Several actions have failed, including *Anglers Co-operative Association* v *British Coal Corporation* [1993] 227 ENDS Report 44 and *Greenpeace* v *ICI* [1994] 234 ENDS Report 47.

2.11.3 Prosecution procedure

It is entirely within the discretion of the prosecuting authorities as to whether or not they proceed with a prosecution. The decision whether or not to proceed summarily or on indictment is entirely within the discretion of the prosecutor, and will normally depend on the seriousness of the alleged offence. The more serious offences will be prosecuted on indictment where the penalties available are higher.

Summary proceedings, which do not involve trial by jury, may only be commenced in the sheriff court in respect of environmental offences. Proceedings on indictment, which are known as solemn proceedings, involve trial by jury. Proceedings on indictment for environmental offences may be commenced in either the sheriff court or the High Court of Justiciary. An appeal from any of these courts goes to the Court of Criminal Appeal in Edinburgh. There is no further appeal to any other court although, as in civil cases, a reference to the ECJ in Luxembourg is possible (see paragraphs 2.2.1 and 2.12.4).

The court having jurisdiction to try a criminal case will be determined by the place in which the criminal act is alleged to have occurred.

The onus of proof in a criminal action lies with the prosecution and the evidence led must prove 'beyond reasonable doubt' that the offence was committed.

2.11.4 Penalties

2.11.4.1 Fines and imprisonment

The fine levels on summary conviction are often referred to as level 1, 2, 3, 4 or 5. The amounts corresponding to these levels are altered from time to time, but are presently £200, £500, £1,000, £2,500 and £5,000. For some serious offences the highest fine on summary conviction is occasionally stipulated as £20,000. Prison sentences are available for some summary offences.

Penalties on conviction on indictment usually include 'a fine', which means an unlimited fine or a prison sentence, sometimes of up to two years or both. In some cases there is provision for prison sentences of up to five years.

Environmental statutes may provide that where the defender is a body corporate, certain of its officers and/or members (ie, shareholders) may also be liable to prosecution in certain circumstances (see paragraph 2.11.5).

2.11.4.2 Remedial works

Section 26 of EPA also provides that where a person has been convicted of certain specified offences under Part I of EPA, the court may, in addition to, or as an alternative to, other penalties order that person to carry out remedial works (*HM Inspectorate of Pollution* v *Enichem Elastomers* [1994] 238 ENDS Report 40).

2.11.4.3 Sentence deferral

It is possible for a judge to defer sentence to allow the polluter to carry out appropriate remedial works, under the Criminal Procedure (Scotland) Act 1995. The level of penalty imposed will reflect the works undertaken. However, it is not competent for a sheriff to offer a company the inducement of an admonishment rather than imposing a fine on the basis that they make a payment to a charity unconnected with the commission of the offence (*Wilson* v *Transorganics Ltd* [1996] 8 ELM 93; (1996) 55 SPEL 54).

2.11.4.4 Confiscation orders

The Proceeds of Crime (Scotland) Act 1995 make provision for offenders paying a penalty equal to the benefit derived from the offence. This is available in any case on conviction on indictment and also in all cases tried summarily where the maximum penalty is a £20,000 fine which includes a number of the more serious environmental offences.

2.11.4.5 Compensation orders

Under the Criminal Procedure (Scotland) Act 1995 a court may, in addition to, or instead of, imposing a penalty, make a compensation order requiring a person convicted of an offence to pay compensation for any personal injury, loss or damage caused directly or indirectly by the acts constituting the offence. It is not competent to make such an order in certain limited circumstances, such as where the court has deferred sentence. The authors understand that it is SEPA's policy to provide details of any loss, injury or damage caused by an offence in its reports to the procurator fiscal so that compensation orders may be sought where appropriate.

2.11.5 Criminal liability of corporate officers and others

Under section 87 of COPA, section 157 of EPA and section 36 of RSA there are provisions for making corporate officers liable for environmental offences committed by bodies corporate in certain circumstances. Where an offence committed by a body corporate is proved to have been committed with the consent or connivance of, or to have been attributable to any neglect on the part of any director, manager, secretary or other similar officer of the body corporate, that officer as well as the body corporate is guilty of the offence and liable to be punished accordingly. Bodies corporate include not only companies but also local authorities, universities and bodies such as SEPA.

Although the scope of these provisions is clear in relation to directors and company secretaries its scope in relation to 'managers' and 'other similar officers' is much less clear. The fact that an officer is called a manager, even a general manager, is not conclusive (*R v Boal* [1992] 3 All ER 177) and a director of a Scottish local authority department has been held to fall within the intended ambit of such persons under the equivalent provisions in health and safety legislation (*Armour v Skeen* [1976] IRLR 310). What is crucial is the authority which the officer as a matter of fact exercises in the body corporate. To be liable under these provisions the officer must be in a position of real authority such that he is in a position to determine corporate policy (*R v Boal; Armour v Skeen;* and *Woodhouse v Walsall Metropolitan Borough Council* [1994] Env LR 30).

An increasing number of corporate officers have been convicted under these provisions. For example, in *HM Advocate v McBride* 1995 GWD 25-1340 a company director was imprisoned for six months for a waste offence and in *London Waste Regulation Authority v Gray* [1995] 241 ENDS Report 43 a director was imprisoned for eighteen months for depositing chemical waste in a residential street.

COPA, EPA and RSA also extend similar provisions to the members (ie, in most cases the shareholders) of a body corporate which commits an offence where the affairs of the body corporate are managed by those members. These provisions are designed to make parent companies liable for offences committed by subsidiary companies which they control.

2.11.6 Environmental law prosecutions in the UK

Historically, few environmental cases have been brought before the courts in the UK and the penalties imposed have tended to be low and sometimes even derisory. Comparatively few prosecutions have been brought by the environmental regulators for a variety of reasons, including unwillingness to adopt a confrontational stance towards regulated businesses in the belief that more progress could be made by co-operation and education than by confrontation; lack of resources; and the perception that the courts would not impose an appropriate penalty. In addition, perceived problems in the prosecution system in Scotland have probably also reduced the number of cases brought to court although these problems are being addressed (see paragraph 2.11.2.1). The inability of the prosecution to recover costs in criminal cases in Scotland in contrast to the position in England and Wales may also have acted as a disincentive to report cases to the procurator fiscal. From the late 1980s the courts in

England and Wales began to impose heavier penalties in environmental cases, the best-known example being *National Rivers Authority
v Shell (UK) Ltd* [1990] *Water Law* 40 where a fine of £1,000,000
was imposed for pollution of the River Mersey. Heavy penalties continue to be imposed in England and Wales including, for example,
fines totalling £216,000 with £21,000 costs in *Tameside Metropolitan
Borough Council v Smith Brothers (Hyde) Ltd* [1997] 264 ENDS
Report 45 for breaches of conditions in an LAPC authorisation; fines
totalling £175,000 with £35,296 costs for a chemical leak which
devastated a Welsh salmon river in *Environment Agency v Severn
Trent Water* [1996] 259 ENDS Report 38; and an eighteen-month
prison sentence for the unlawful deposit of special waste in *London
Waste Regulation Authority v Gray*. To give an idea of the level of
fines being imposed in English and Welsh cases, the following statis-
tics of National Rivers Authority (NRA) prosecutions may serve as
an example.

Year	Total reported incidents	Category 1 incidents	Successful prosecutions	Total fines	Average fine
1989/90	26,725	n/a	309	£278,409	£901
1990/91	28,652	554	490	£428,415	£874
1991/92	29,524	338	536	£1,051,990	£1,963
1992/93	32,254	362	435	£1,091,025	£2,508
1993/94	34,296	331	423	£1,088,580	£2,573
1994/95	35,291	229	316	£988,625	£3,128
1995/96	35,890	199	318	£904,430	£2,844

(Source: NRA Annual Reports for 1992/93, 1993/94, 1994/95 and 1995/96.)

In contrast fine levels in Scottish environmental cases have remained generally much lower at least until very recently. This suggests that sheriffs in Scotland have not taken these offences as
seriously as their counterparts south of the border. To illustrate this,
the following river purification board prosecution figures may serve
as an example.

RPB	1992/93			1993/94		
	Pollution incidents	Successful prosecutions	Average fine (£)	Pollution incidents	Successful prosecutions	Average fine (£)
Clyde	1,036	11	818	791	12	1,773
Forth	711	17	1,319	622	23	1,061
Highland	271	4	350	283	3	1,333
N East	385	9	3,000	475	1	400
Solway	238	3	275	347	7	429
Tay	289	4	1,750	394	7	1,171
Tweed	151	0	n/a	205	1	1,000
Totals	3,081	48	1,360	3,117	54	1,150

RPB	1994/95			1995/96		
	Pollution incidents	*Successful prosecutions*	*Average fine (£)*	*Pollution incidents*	*Successful prosecutions*	*Average fine (£)*
Clyde	890	7	1,092	763	8	3,106
Forth	634	10	1,455	592	6	1,500
Highland	272	4	500	316	3	3,167
N East	409	1	250	356	4	237
Solway	460	10	6,900	316	3	5,000
Tay	373	2	550	293	4	1,000
Tweed	180	1	500	167	1	0
Totals	3,218	35	2,715	2,803	29	2,183

Although average fine levels have increased considerably, they are still below the average level of fines imposed in England and Wales. The increase is almost solely due to a spate of prosecutions arising out of the construction of the M74 motorway which involved siltation of salmon rivers (eg, *Howdle* v *Miller Civil Engineering* 1995 GWD 12-682 (£40,000 fine for four offences); *Howdle* v *Castelli Girola UK Ltd* 1995 GWD 12-683 (£12,000 fine for a single offence); and *Howdle* v *Castelli Girola UK Ltd* (*No 2*) 1996 GWD 1-46 (£15,000 fine for a single offence).

Although this apparent change in judicial attitudes in relation to water pollution offences is to be welcomed and has indeed been reinforced by Lord Allanbridge's comments in *Caird Environmental* v *Valentine* 1995 SCCR 714, in which he stressed that the courts took the enforcement of water pollution legislation very seriously, and despite the six-month prison sentence handed out to a company director for a waste offence in *HM Advocate* v *McBride*, penalties generally imposed for other environmental offences such as IPC and waste offences remain disproportionately low (*Adam* v *Scottish Hydro-Electric plc*; *Hamilton* v *Scottish Power plc* [1995] 247 ENDS Report 43 – admonishment and £250 fine for breaches of IPC authorisations; *Normand* v *Duffy t/a Spare Batteries* 1995 GWD 25-1341 – £500 fine for the unlawful deposit of special waste). There are recent signs, however, that in these areas also, heavier penalties are beginning to be imposed (eg, *Wilson* v *Buchan Bros Ltd*, Peterhead Sheriff Court, 12th August 1996, unreported – £4,000 fine for unlawful deposit of waste).

2.11.7 Time scales

Section 331 of the Criminal Procedure (Scotland) Act 1975 provided that summary proceedings arising out of statutory contraventions required to be commenced within six months after the contravention occurred unless the statute or order provided otherwise (*Friel* v *Initial Contract Services Ltd* 1994 SLT 1216). In the case of a continuous contravention proceedings required to be commenced within six months after the last date of such contravention and section 331 provided that it was competent in cases of continuous contravention to include the entire period during which the contravention occurred. However, this provision has been replaced by section 136 of the Criminal Procedure (Scotland) Act 1995. Importantly, although this section makes similar provision, its application is restricted to statutory contraventions which are triable summarily only. Given that most environmental offences are triable either summarily or on indictment, the application of this time-bar provision is now much reduced, being confined to those environmental offences committed, for example, under COPA, EPA, RSA and EA which are only triable summarily. In such cases the impact of section 136 is the same as the impact of the former section 331 outlined above. However, the six-month rule does not apply to offences which are triable either summarily or on indictment, in respect of which there now appears to be no time limit.

Although a person cannot be convicted of a statutory offence triable only summarily unless it was wholly or partly committed within six months before the proceedings against him were commenced, evidence may be taken of acts constituting, or contributing to the offence which were committed at any previous time (eg, *Lockhart* v *National Coal Board* 1981 SLT 161).

Proceedings are deemed to be commenced on the date on which a warrant to apprehend or cite the accused is granted, if the warrant is executed without undue delay.

It is difficult to predict the length of time criminal proceedings might take if defended. However, given the potential scientific complexity of the evidence which might require to be led in cases of this kind, an estimate of twelve months or more would not be out of order.

2.11.8 Actions to prevent breach of criminal law

Although criminal prosecutions may provide effective remedies in dealing with environmental offenders, prosecutions may take a long time to prepare and, of themselves, will not necessarily stop their polluting activities. This is where civil remedies in the form of interdicts may assist in either preventing breaches of the criminal law or securing compliance with administrative notices if the criminal law is unlikely to provide an effectual remedy if the notice is breached. Contravention of an interdict is a contempt of court and as such is punishable by heavy penalties which could include imprisonment.

COPA, EPA and RSA now expressly provide that interdicts may be obtained by SEPA to secure compliance with a variety of administrative notices such as the enforcement notice available by virtue of Part I of EPA where SEPA is of the opinion that prosecution would afford an ineffectual remedy (EPA, section 24). The availability of an injunction (the English equivalent of an interdict) under that provision was tested in *Tameside Metropolitan Borough Council* v *Smith Brothers (Hyde) Ltd* [1996] Env LR D4 where it was held that the enforcing authority must demonstrate a serious case to answer, that the court must consider the balance of convenience between the pollution and possible job losses if the injunction were granted; that the enforcement powers in EPA were of recent origin and could therefore not be said to provide an ineffectual remedy; and that it was necessary for the enforcing authority to demonstrate that they had considered the availability of powers such as the court's power to order remedial works to be carried out under Part I of EPA. This decision indicates that it may be very difficult indeed to obtain an interdict under that particular provision, although the court's view that since the enforcement powers in the EPA were of recent origin they could not be said to afford an ineffectual remedy seems misconceived as the section 24 power was enacted by Parliament and presumably intended to be used when appropriate.

However, the availability of interdicts under the above provisions does not cover every circumstance in which such a remedy might be required. For example, there is no express statutory interdict available in circumstances where a person is operating without the requisite environmental licence such as a discharge consent. SEPA may nevertheless have the power to obtain interdicts in such situations by virtue of the general power contained in section 37 of EA, which enables it to do anything which is calculated to facilitate, or is conducive or incidental to, the carrying out of its functions. The government indicated in Parliament that this provision was intended, *inter alia*, to give the agencies the power to obtain injunctions or interdicts although the provision has yet to be tested in the courts.

However, where there is a statutory scheme of regulation which does not expressly include the remedy of interdict, it may be difficult to obtain such a remedy given the decision in *Buckhaven and Methil Magistrates* v *Wemyss Coal Co* 1932 SC 201, which indicated that only the remedies provided for by statute could be sought. However, river purification boards obtained interdicts to prevent ongoing water pollution which constitued an offence even though this was not provided for by statute: see, for example, *Clyde River Purification Board* v *Balfour Beatty Ltd*, although it is not clear in this case whether an interdict was being sought to prevent a breach of the criminal law or a nuisance. Certainly it is the case that if the ongoing pollution constitutes a nuisance, then SEPA may obtain an interdict (*Forth River Purification Board* v *Adam Robertson, The Scotsman*, 7th December 1990). If deemed necessary, a prosecution may follow later.

2.11.9 Costs in criminal actions

In Scotland costs are not recoverable in the event of a successful prosecution. However, by way of contrast, in England and Wales costs may be recovered by the prosecuting agency in the event of a successful prosecution. In *Environment Agency* v *Rhone-Poulenc* [1996] 258 ENDS Report 46, for example, a fine of £50,000 was imposed together with costs of £32,205. In the recent case of *Health and Safety Executive* v *Nuclear Electric* [1995] 248 ENDS Report 46, a fine of £250,000 was accompanied by costs of £138,000.

Legal aid is not available for those wishing to bring private prosecutions. If a private prosecution is unsuccessful, the party bringing the prosecution will usually be required to pay the other side's costs, as Greenpeace found when they had to pay £28,849 in their recent unsuccessful prosecution of ICI (see [1994] 234 ENDS Report 47). ICI had claimed costs of £72,793.

2.12 EC LAW

2.12.1 Introduction

In this section we consider the implementation by member states of EC law and its enforcement by the European Commission and by individuals where there has been a failure to implement the law or a failure to implement it correctly or to comply with it in practice.

For a brief discussion of the European Commission and the European Environment Agency , see paragraphs 1.3.7 and 1.3.8.

2.12.2 Implementation of EC directives

First, it is essential to note that under article 5 of the EC Treaty member states are under a duty to take all necessary steps to meet their obligations under EC law. Secondly, by virtue of the doctrine of supremacy of EC law, member states must always give effect to EC law wherever it conflicts with national laws (*R* v *Secretary of State for Transport*, ex parte *Factortame Ltd* [1990] ECR I-2433; applied in *R* v *Secretary of State for Transport*, ex parte *Factortame Ltd* [1991] 1 AC 603). Furthermore, it is not enough to implement EC law on paper, it must also be implemented in practice.

Directives generally require to be the subject of specific national legislative measures bringing them into force in the country concerned. However, it is the view of the UK government that an equivalent result can be achieved by administrative action alone. However, case-law of the ECJ suggests that administrative action will not always suffice. For example, in *EC Commission* v *Federal Republic of Germany* (C-361/88) [1991] ECR I-2567 it was held that implementation of air quality limit values by means of an administrative circular did not conform to EC law since the limit values were mandatory and accordingly persons who might be affected by the exceeding of such values must be in a position to rely on mandatory legal rules in order to assert their rights.

Directives are binding as to the result to be achieved and therefore member states must achieve the objectives set out in directives within the time frame stipulated. It is not sufficient to make best endeavours to comply with the objectives (*EC Commission* v *UK* (C-337/89) [1992] ECR I-6103 (implementation of Directive 80/778/EEC on drinking water quality) and *EC Commission* v *UK* (C-56/90) [1994] 1 CMLR 769 (implementation of Directive 76/160/EEC on bathing water quality)). Where a member state is found by the ECJ to have failed to implement (or to implement correctly) a directive, it must implement or correctly implement the directive as soon as possible. It has, however, been held by the Court of Appeal in England that questions of practicability enter into the equation of what is possible in this regard in the context of a challenge to the Secretary of State for the Environment's chosen method of securing compliance with the standards in the Drinking Water Quality Directive following the ECJ judgment against the UK noted above (*R* v *Secretary of State for the Environment*, ex parte *Friends of the Earth Ltd*).

2.12.3 Enforcement proceedings by the European Commission

Enforcement proceedings by the European Commission are provided for by article 169 of the EC Treaty. There are three circumstances which may trigger enforcement action by the Commission in relation to directives:

(1) failure to adopt and notify national measures to implement a directive; or

(2) national implementing measures do not incorporate the obligation deriving from EC law fully and correctly; or

(3) national implementing measures are not correctly applied in practice.

Article 169 proceedings involve three stages. First, the Commission sends the member state concerned a letter of formal notice outlining the alleged breach of EC law and giving the member state an opportunity to respond. There must be a reasonable period between sending the letter of formal notice and the next stage, the sending of a reasoned opinion (*EC Commission* v *UK* (C-56/90) in which it was held that a two-year period was quite reasonable). If there is no response or the response is inadequate the Commission will then send the member state a reasoned opinion which contains a more detailed case in relation to the alleged breach. Again the member state is given an opportunity to respond. Finally, if there is no response or the response is still not adequate in the Commission's view, court action will be commenced before the ECJ. The whole process is a lengthy one as *EC Commission* v *UK* (C-337/89) illustrates. The Commission's case must be specific about failure to implement/comply with legislation otherwise the action will fail (*EC Commission* v *Germany* (C-431/92) [1996] 1 CMLR 196).

There are several problems associated with enforcement of the law by the Commission. First, the Commission lacks the resources both in terms of staff and finances to follow up every failure to implement. Secondly, the Commission has in the past at least not necessarily had access to reliable information. Thirdly, the Commission has relied heavily on complaints submitted by individuals or interest groups. This has arguably created a reactive enforcement policy. Finally, as will by now be apparent, article 169 proceedings are very lengthy and there was, until recently, no sanction for non-compliance.

There have, however, been certain developments which may assist in overcoming these problems. These include

— the adoption of Directive 91/692/EEC on the lodging of reports detailing standardised data in respect of environmental directives which should improve the flow of information on the implementation of directives to the Commission;

— the establishment of the EEA by virtue of Regulation 1210/90/EEC to monitor compliance and co-ordinate the collection of data which again should provide the Commission with greater access to more reliable information (see paragraph 1.3.8);

— the introduction of the possibility of sanctions for non-compliance with judgments of the ECJ against member states for non compliance with EC law by the Treaty of European Union which now enables fines to be imposed on member states in certain circumstances (article 171(2)); and

— the stress on the need for more stringent enforcement in the EC's Fifth Action Programme on the Environment.

2.12.4 Enforcement proceedings by individuals

Although this section is primarily concerned with the concept of direct effect (see below), there are various other ways in which individuals may participate in the enforcement of EC law.

In paragraph 2.12.3 it was noted that the Commission has relied heavily on the complaints procedure as the basis of its enforcement efforts. This procedure, developed by the Commission, enables any individual or interest group to present a complaint to the effect that EC law has not been implemented or has not been implemented correctly or is not being complied with in practice. A form is available from the Commission and the complainer should provide the Commission with as much information as possible. Such complaints have, in many cases, led to article 169 proceedings by the Commission.

Individuals also have considerable rights of access to environmental information, partly by virtue of Directive 90/313/EEC on freedom of access to information on the environment. This provision and the Environmental Information Regulations 1992 (SI 1992/3240), which implement the directive in the UK, are discussed in detail in Chapter 4. However, at this point it is worth noting that increased access to information may enable individuals to commence enforcement proceedings themselves before their national courts or to put pressure on the appropriate national environmental regulators to take action.

There is also a very limited possibility of individuals challenging the validity of certain EC legislation where they can demonstrate that it is of direct and individual concern to them, ie, that it affects them above all others, under article 173 of the EC Treaty. Such proceedings must be commenced in the ECJ within two months of the adoption of the measure concerned. In the only environmental case to be brought under this article to date, Greenpeace members resident in the Canary Islands failed to demonstrate that they were directly and individually concerned in relation to a decision of the Commission to grant aid for the construction of a power station in Gran Canaria under Regulation 2052/88/EEC, which provides that matters given such aid must be in keeping with EC law including environmental protection. The power station was authorised without an environmental assessment of the project as required by EC law. The local members of Greenpeace were held not to be directly and individually concerned since they had no interests which were likely to be affected in a different way from other residents in the area (*Stichting Greenpeace* v *EC Commission* (T-585/93) [1995] ECR II-2205).

Another possible opportunity for individuals to enforce EC law may be provided if the draft directive on civil liability for damage caused by waste is adopted by the EC. This draft legislation proposes to give environmental interest groups title to sue in cases where environmental damage is caused by waste. For a more detailed discussion of trends in civil liability, see Chapter 3.

In the remaining part of this section we consider the application of the concept of direct effect in relation to the enforcement of environmental law by individuals.

EC directives provide legal principles which are intended to be incorporated into the law of each member state by national implementing legislation. There is thus an implementation period following the adoption of each directive during which member states have time to produce the relevant implementing legislation. In principle, at the end of this period the directive will be implemented on a national basis in the member state concerned. However, this does not always happen in practice. The following discussion concerns the rights which may be conferred on individuals to enforce directives when they are not implemented at national level, either because the implementing legislation does not accurately reflect the directive or no implementing legislation is enacted, or because they are otherwise inadequately implemented.

It should be noted that where a question regarding the interpretation of an EC directive, such as whether it is directly effective, is raised by a party before any domestic court (criminal or civil), under article 177 of the EC Treaty that court may make a reference to the ECJ for a ruling on the interpretation of the measure in question. Where there is no appeal from a particular court and a question regarding EC law must be answered to enable the court to reach a decision, that court must make a reference to the ECJ.

A directive which thus confers rights upon individuals is said to have 'direct effect', but not all directives qualify under this principle. For direct effect, two criteria must be fulfilled:

(1) the directive's implementing period must have expired, and

— either no national implementing legislation has been produced, or

— the implementing legislation does not correctly reflect the terms of the directive; and

(2) the terms of the directive must be (a) sufficiently clear and precise; (b) unconditional, and (c) leave no room for the exercise of discretion in their implementation by the member state.

If these conditions are fulfilled, it is accepted that directives will confer a right of action on individuals in actions against the state or organs of the state such as public authorities ('vertical direct effect'). The question of which bodies are organs of the state has been answered very broadly and has been held by the courts to include private sector utilities (*Foster v British Gas plc* (C-188/89) [1990] ECR I-3313; [1990] 2 CMLR 833; *Griffin and Others v South West Water Services Ltd* [1995] IRLR 15). In *Guthrie v Scottish Environment Protection Agency* 1997 GWD 6-244 Lord Johnston was of the opinion that the relevant predecessor of SEPA, Lochaber District Council in their capacity as the waste regulation authority which had issued the modified waste management licence, the validity of which was being challenged, were not an agency of government for the purposes of relying on the direct effect of Directive 80/68/EEC on groundwater. This view appears to be wholly misconceived in the light of EC case-law in which it is apparent that all public bodies are to be viewed as agencies of the state (eg, *Marshall* v *Southampton and South-West Hampshire Area Health Authority* (152/84) [1986] ECR 723.

The question of rights of action against other private individuals ('horizontal direct effect') is more complicated. In principle such rights are not available where directives have not been implemented at national level, on the basis that directives are addressed to member states and impose obligations on them (and on all branches of the state) but not upon natural or private legal persons so that there can be no right of action against a body which is not a public authority (*Marshall* v *Southampton and South-West Hampshire Area Health Authority* (152/84)). For a more recent example in an environmental context see *Luciano Arcaro* (C-168/95) [1997] 1 CMLR 179 in which, remarkably, the Italian prosecuting authorities sought without success to establish in the absence of adequate implementing legislation that Directive 83/513/EEC on limit values and quality objectives for cadmium discharges to the aquatic environment was directly effective against a private individual.

There are, however, two possible methods by which individuals can raise actions to counter the unavailability to them of rights under directives. First, the ECJ has developed a principle (known as the Von Colson principle after *Von Colson* v *Land Nordrhein-Westfalen* (C-14/83) [1984] ECR 1891; [1986] 2 CMLR 430) which is based upon article 5 of the EC Treaty, which requires member states to 'take all appropriate measures' to ensure fulfilment of their EC obligations. As the courts are an organ of the member states, they are also under the obligation imposed by the Treaty, and must therefore interpret national law in such a way as to ensure that the objectives of a directive are achieved.

The principle has been seen in operation in the British case of *Litster* v *Forth Dry Dock and Engineering Co Ltd* [1990] 1 AC 546; 1989 SLT 540 in which the relevant directive was held to lack direct effect because the defender was a private party. The pursuer none the less benefited from the directive since the House of Lords held that the UK regulations which implemented the directive had to conform with it. In effect this meant that the court read into the regulations the words which were necessary to enable them to conform with the directive even though this meant construing the regulations in a manner contrary to their apparent meaning.

The Von Colson principle was developed further in *Marleasing SA* v *La Comercial Internacional de Alimentacion SA* (C-106/89) [1990] ECR I-4135; [1992] 1 CMLR 305 where the ECJ held that a national court is bound to interpret national legislation (whether it predates or postdates the directive) in the light of the text and aim of the directive in order to achieve the results envisaged by it.

However, the doctrine cannot be applied to impose upon an individual an obligation required by a directive but not implemented in national law and, in particular, cannot be used to impose or aggravate criminal liability not provided for by national law (*Luciano Arcaro* (C-168/95)).

The second approach to the problem of conflict between EC and national legislation has been to hold member states liable to persons in certain circumstances for losses suffered because of total non-implementation or incorrect implementation of EC law.

Two tests may be identified. The first applies in cases where there is a total failure to implement a directive and is more stringent since directives impose obligations on member states to achieve a particular result which reduces their margin of discretion. In *Francovich* v *Italian Republic* (C-6/90 and C-9/90) [1991] ECR I-5357; [1993] 2 CMLR 66 the provisions of a directive had not been implemented by Italy. As a result of a lack of precision in its terms the directive was held not to be directly effective, but the court took the view that as the member state had failed in its responsibility to enact implementing legislation, the member state was to be liable in damages to individuals prejudiced by its failure to implement the directive, provided (1) the directive conferred rights on individuals; (2) the contents of those rights could be identified from the directive; and (3) there was a causal link between the failure by the member state to implement and the damage suffered by the affected individual.

The second test applies where member states have enacted implementing legislation but that legislation does not adequately implement an EC directive or other measure or is actually directly contrary to the EC law in question. In joined cases *Brasserie du Pêcheur SA* v *Federal Republic of Germany* (C-46/93) and *R* v *Secretary of State for Transport*, ex parte *Factortame Ltd* (C-48/93) [1996] All ER (EC) 301 ECJ, both of which involved the enactment of subsequent national legislation which conflicted with earlier EC law, the ECJ held that member states may be liable for a loss suffered by an individual where (1) the rule of EC law that had been infringed confers rights on individuals; (2) the breach of the rule is sufficiently serious; and (3) there is a direct causal link between the breach of EC law and the individual's loss. If the measure is directly effective, the first criterion should be met. The second criterion is met where the member state had 'manifestly and gravely disregarded the limits on its discretion'. The ECJ said that in assessing whether a breach was manifest and grave the factors which could be considered included:

(1) the clarity and precision of the rule that had been breached;

(2) the measure of discretion which that rule left to the national authorities;

(3) whether the infringement and the loss that it caused had been arrived at intentionally or involuntarily;

(4) whether any error or law was excusable or inexcusable;

(5) any position taken by an EC institution which might have contributed to a member state's so acting; and

(6) the adoption or retention of measures or practices by a member state contrary to EC law.

In *R* v *HM Treasury*, ex parte *British Telecommunications plc* (C-392/93) [1996] All ER (EC) 411 ECJ, a case involving Directive 90/531/EEC on public procurement procedures, the ECJ held that the test from *Brasserie du Pêcheur SA* v *Federal Republic of Germany* (C-46/93) also applied to cases where a member state had incorrectly transposed an EC directive into national law.

The ECJ has indicated a willingness to hold provisions of environmental directives directly effective. In *EC Commission* v *Federal Republic of Germany* (C-361/88), for example, an enforcement action relating to the purported implementation of Directive 80/779/EEC on air quality limit values and guide values for sulphur dioxide and suspended particulates, in which the ECJ held that it was unlawful to implement the directive by means of an administrative circular rather than a mandatory rule since whenever the exceeding of limit values could endanger human health, the persons concerned must be in a position to rely on mandatory rules to be able to assert their rights. This is the closest the ECJ has come to holding that a provision of an environmental directive is directly effective. Limit values in a variety of directives relating to air and water quality seem likely to be directly effective since they are clear, unconditional and leave no discretion to member states in terms of implementation. It also seems certain that those provisions of environmental directives which clearly confer rights on individuals – for example, rights to information or participation in the decision-making process – are directly effective. However, the ECJ has yet to hold that a provision of an environmental directive is actually directly effective. For example, in *Comitato di Coordinamento per la Difesa della Cava* v *Regione Lombardia* (C-236/92) [1994] ECR I-483; [1994] Env LR 281 the ECJ held that a provision of Directive 75/442/EEC on waste (as amended by Directive 91/156/EEC on waste) which requires member states to take necessary measures to ensure that waste is disposed of without endangering human health and without harming the environment was not unconditional or sufficiently precise. Furthermore, in the recent case of *Luciano Arcaro* (C-168/95) doubt was cast by the Advocate General on the potential direct effect of limit values under Directive 83/513/EEC on limit values and quality objectives for cadmium discharges to the aquatic environment. He suggested that since the directive allowed the permitting authority to prescribe more stringent limit values than those laid down in the directive, the authority had considerable discretion and the limit value provisions were not sufficiently unconditional or precise for direct effect to arise, although it should be noted that the ECJ expressly refrained from deciding this point in its ruling.

In Scotland, Lord Coulsfield took the view in *Kincardine and Deeside District Council* v *Forestry Commissioners* 1992 SLT 1180, which concerned Directive 85/337/EEC on environmental impact assessment, that in relation to Annex I projects in respect of which an assessment was mandatory, there might be a strong argument that the directive was directly effective. However, he held that this was not the case in relation to Annex II projects since member states had a wide discretion to decide whether an assessment was required.

2.13 EUROPEAN CONVENTION ON HUMAN RIGHTS AND ENVIRONMENTAL PROTECTION

The European Convention on Human Rights (ECHR), which is administered by the Council of Europe, the European Commission on Human Rights and the European Court of Human Rights based in Strasbourg, is principally concerned with securing basic civil and political rights. For this reason not much consideration has been given to the ECHR as a possible source of remedies for environmental problems as it contains no express environmental provisions. However, in *Ostra* v *Spain* [1995] 7 ELM 49 article 8 relating to privacy and respect for family life was successfully relied upon in an environmental context. It was held that the failure of the relevant national and municipal authorities to deal with pollution could constitute an interference with respect for family life. This is an important development. None the less there is no doubt that the ECHR cannot presently provide a swift and effective remedy, especially in the UK, where it has not been incorporated into domestic law and hence UK legislation cannot be reviewed by the courts as being contrary to the ECHR and individuals must exhaust domestic remedies before taking their complaints to Strasbourg. However, this situation is to change since the new Labour government has announced that it is to introduce legislation to incorporate the ECHR into domestic law in the UK.

2.14 ENVIRONMENTAL REGULATION USING MARKET MECHANISMS

2.14.1 Introduction

In addition to pollution control by means of the common law and administrative regulation by bodies such as SEPA, the government has advocated the use of market mechanisms to promote environmental protection (eg, This Common Inheritance: Britain's Environmental Strategy, Cm 1200, 1990, paragraphs 1.28–1.32; Sustainable Development: The UK Strategy, Cm 2426, 1994, paragraphs 33.9–33.12; Making Markets Work for the Environment (HMSO, 1993)). Market mechanisms are instruments which attempt to influence behaviour in environmentally beneficial ways by altering prices rather than by legal coercion. The rationale for their use is that markets are best placed to find the most cost-effective method of securing environmental protection and will ensure that prices accurately reflect the cost of environmental resources. Market mechanisms are perceived as involving much lower costs than administrative regulation which requires monitoring of emissions and enforcement where appropriate. However, as will become apparent in paragraphs 2.14.2 and 2.14.3, the operation of market mechanisms also requires monitoring and enforcement, so the extent to which they involve lower regulatory costs is perhaps arguable. Market mechanisms may take many forms including (1) taxes, such as the favourable duty on lead-free petrol introduced by the Finance Act 1987 and annual increases in fuel duties of at least 5 per cent above the rate of inflation both of which play a significant role in the government's air-pollution policy; (2) tradeable emission permits, such as the US Clean Air-Act scheme; (3) deposit and refund schemes, such as those operated for bottles; (4) product labelling, such as the EC's Eco-labelling scheme which enables consumers to exercise influence in the market place on the basis of environmental criteria; and (5) civil liability schemes, such as the new contaminated land régime. The adoption of environmental criteria in company purchasing and bank lending policies, whether voluntarily or in response to regulatory developments, is also arguably a market mechanism as is the adoption of voluntary emissions reduction targets by business. However, this discussion will focus solely on two recent developments in the UK: a fiscal measure, the landfill tax (see paragraph 2.14.2), and a new form of market mechanism, producer responsibility for waste (see paragraph 2.14.3).

2.14.2 The landfill tax

SEPA's Draft National Waste Strategy: Scotland – A Blueprint for Progress 1997–2001 (1997) identifies the landfill tax as an economic instrument which will help to bring about a more sustainable approach to waste management. SEPA's finalised national waste strategy is due to be produced by 1998. For a fuller discussion of the role of the national waste strategies, see paragraph 7.1. The objectives of the landfill tax, aside from the obvious objective of raising revenue, are to apply the polluter pays principle by ensuring that landfill disposal is properly priced and also to encourage waste minimisation or reuse and recovery rather than landfill disposal by making the latter less financially attractive.

The Finance Act 1996 provides the framework for the tax which is administered by HM Customs and Excise. The tax is chargeable on disposals of waste at landfill sites made after 1st October 1996 (section 40) and liability to pay falls upon landfill site operators (section 41). The holder of the waste management licence for the site must register with HM Customs and Excise (section 47).

The amount of tax due is calculated on the basis of the weight of waste disposed of. The weight of waste is established by means of a weighbridge or, where none is available, by means of an estimate based, *inter alia,* on lorry size and the materials in the waste. There are two applicable tax rates: £7 per tonne and £2 per tonne for inert or inactive waste which is known as 'qualifying material' (section 42(3)); Landfill Tax (Qualifying Material) Order 1996 (SI 1996/1528).

There are various exemptions from liability to pay the tax set out in section 43 of the 1996 Act. These include the disposal of dredgings from rivers, canals, docks or harbours; naturally occurring material from commercial mining or quarrying operations; and the burial of dead domestic pets in pet cemeteries. In addition, the Landfill Tax (Contaminated Land) Order 1996 (SI 1996/1529) provides that in specified circumstances material from reclamation of contaminated land is exempt. It is understood that this Order is to be reviewed after two years.

By virtue of section 51 of the 1996 Act, tax credits may be claimed in four circumstances:

— where the waste delivered to the site breaches the site's waste management licence conditions and SEPA requires its removal to another site;

— where the waste is temporarily landfilled pending its subsequent removal for reuse or landfilling elsewhere;

— where a customer of the landfill site fails to pay the operator's
charges; and

— where contributions are made to approved environmental bodies.

The last point requires some elaboration. The provision for tax credits for payments to approved environmental bodies is designed to promote sustainable waste management and to remedy the consequences of
past unsustainable waste management. To become an approved environmental body, an organisation must meet certain criteria as regards
its constitution and objects. A private company called ENTRUST has
been established under the 1996 Act to approve environmental bodies
and to ensure that contributions to them are spent on approved objects.
Landfill site operators may reclaim 90 per cent of any payment made to
an approved environmental body, subject to a maximum credit of 20 per
cent of the operator's annual liability to landfill tax.

Whether the landfill tax will achieve its objectives is not yet clear. It
may be that it will result in an increase in fly tipping, ie, unlawful dumping of waste, although the revised Duty of Care Code of Practice, March
1996 (see paragraph 7.3), advises the agencies to give fly tipping a high
priority. The tax may also have been set at too low a level to achieve a
shift towards sustainable waste management practices. Finally, it should
be noted that HM Customs and Excise have produced a set of ten useful information sheets on the tax which are available via their landfill tax
telephone hotline, 0645 128484.

2.14.3 Producer responsibility
Another tool for bringing about a more sustainable approach to waste
management identified in SEPA's draft national waste strategy for
Scotland (see also paragraph 2.14.2) is producer responsibility. Initially
launched as a voluntary initiative to promote waste reuse and recovery
in 1993, legislation to impose producer responsibility obligations was introduced by sections 93–95 of EA.

Although not perhaps a pure market mechanism, producer responsibility is designed (1) to be a business-led approach to achieve waste
reuse, recovery and recycling in the most efficient manner, while ensuring that costs are reflected in decisions on product design and content,
hence implementing the polluter pays principle; (2) to expand the market for recycled material; (3) to act as an incentive to divert more waste
to reuse and recovery; and (4) to act as an incentive on waste producers
to minimise the amount of waste which they produce. It is designed to
involve the lightest regulatory approach which gives the maximum scope
for businesses with producer responsibility obligations to self-certify and
self-assess their obligations and to perform their obligations through
business-run schemes subject to monitoring by SEPA or, in England
and Wales, the Environment Agency.

The framework for producer responsibility is established by sections
93–95 of EA. These sections enable the Secretary of State to make regulations imposing producer responsibility obligations which require pre-

scribed persons to achieve prescribed waste recovery and/or recycling targets. Initially the obligations will relate to packaging and packaging waste only in order to implement the UK's obligations under the EC directive on packaging and packaging waste (Directive 94/62/EC). However, it is likely that the obligations will be extended in future to other waste streams, in particular those included in the EC's priority waste-stream project, ie, chlorinated solvents, used tyres, healthcare waste, end of life vehicles, construction and demolition waste, and waste electrical and electronic equipment.

No regulations may be introduced without prior consultation with bodies or persons representing those whose interests are likely to be substantially affected by proposed regulations (section 93(2)). An extensive consultation exercise was undertaken by the government, involving, *inter alia,* the publication of The Producer Responsibility Obligations (Packaging Waste) Regulations – A Consultation Paper, July 1996, together with draft regulations. The finalised Producer Responsibility Obligations (Packaging Waste) Regulations 1997 (SI 1997/648) ('the 1997 Regulations') came into force on 6th March 1997.

Producer responsibility obligations fall upon 'producers', a term which is defined as those persons who are either manufacturers, converters, packer/fillers, wholesalers, sellers or importers of packaging and packaging materials. Such persons must also (1) own the packaging or packaging materials; (2) supply them to another person in the packaging chain; and (3) handle more than 50 tonnes of packaging or packaging materials annually.

The regulations are being introduced by means of a staged approach, with no business having an annual turnover of less than £5 million or which handled less than 50 tonnes of packaging or packaging waste being subject to any producer responsibility obligations in 1997–1999, while from 1st January 2000, any business with a turnover of £1 million or more and which handled more than 50 tonnes of packaging and packaging materials will be subject to producer responsibility obligations.

A person's obligations may be fulfilled in one of two ways. Either a person may comply individually, which requires registration with SEPA or the Environment Agency, or a person may join a registered compliance scheme. Registration with the Environment Agency is required where a business or a compliance scheme has its registered office or principal place of business in England or Wales and with SEPA where its registered office or principal place of business is in Scotland. Although registration was initially to be required by 25th February 1997, in December 1996 it was announced that the initial registration deadline was to be postponed to summer 1997. The 1997 Regulations provide that registration must take place by 31st August 1997.

Where a business has opted to perform its obligations individually, the amount of packaging and packaging materials which it must recover or recycle are to be calculated as follows:

(1) recovery obligation = amount by tonnage of packaging and packaging material handled × activity obligation percentage × UK recovery target percentage;

(2) recycling obligation (by material) = amount by tonnage of packaging and packaging material (by material) × activity obligation percentage × UK recycling target percentage (by material).

Activity obligations percentages are as follows.

Packaging raw material manufacturing	—	6 per cent
Converting	—	11 per cent
Packing/filling	—	36 per cent
Selling	—	47 per cent
Importing transit packaging	—	100 per cent

The UK recovery and recycling target percentages were initially proposed as

Year	Recovery	Recycling (by material)
1998, 1999, 2000	40 per cent	8 per cent
2001	50 per cent	15 per cent

However, in December 1996 it was announced that the targets were to be revised to include a slower build up to the targets required by the EC directive on packaging and packaging waste in 2001 which would impose a more realistic burden on businesses. The 1997 Regulations targets are as follows.

Year	Recovery	Recycling (by material)
1998	38 per cent	7 per cent
1999	38 per cent	7 per cent
2000	43 per cent	11 per cent
2001	52 per cent	16 per cent

Where a business joins a registered compliance scheme, the scheme will procure achievement of the producer responsibility obligations for all its members. Where the scheme does not procure the performance of the obligations of all its members, the agency with which the scheme is registered may cancel the scheme's registration which would require the members of the scheme either to procure the performance of their obligations individually or to join another scheme.

Businesses complying individually and registered compliance schemes will be required to submit compliance certificates to the relevant agency to demonstrate that they have fulfilled their respective obligations. In order to ensure compliance, the agencies are given monitoring and entry and inspection powers. Penalties for non-compliance include fines and, in the case of individual producers and compliance schemes, deregistration.

Chapter 3

CIVIL LIABILITY FOR DAMAGE TO THE ENVIRONMENT

Civil liability for environmental damage is a much-debated topic. As such, it merits separate consideration. This chapter attempts to explain the background to the debate and to consider possible future developments in respect to civil liability for damage 'caused to the environment' in the wider sense of that phrase.

Consideration is given first to the perceived deficiencies of Scots common law in respect of liability for damage to the environment, then to statutory civil liability provisions and finally to certain international and EU developments.

3.1 COMMON LAW LIABILITY

As discussed in Chapter 2, the common law provides two principal remedies in respect of damage to the environment. These are nuisance and negligence. Ancillary remedies may also be available, such as interdict (forbidding something to be done) and specific implement (requiring something to be done). In the wider context of damage to the environment, it is important to be aware that these remedies have their limitations. This is because, as they have evolved over the centuries, they have done so in relation to many types of damage and are therefore not specific to the question of damage to the environment.

The ability to sustain an action in nuisance or negligence depends ultimately upon questions of loss or damage in the sense of quantifiable and assessable sums of money. To take an obvious example, if my neighbour's activities result in the leaching of damaging substances onto my land, thereby making it unusable, I should have a right of redress against my neighbour in terms of an action of nuisance and my claim will be for the loss or diminution in value of my land. The common law has not yet developed so as to protect the environment *per se*. The loss of a habitat, or the destruction of a species, therefore, is unlikely to be actionable at all unless some form of monetary loss results.

Additionally, common law actions of nuisance and negligence do not, except in certain limited cases, proceed on the assumption that the defender (ie, the person to be made liable) is at fault. It is for the pursuer in such an action to prove this. In the case of a negligence action proof is required that a duty is owed to the pursuer by the party against whom the action is raised, that a breach of that duty has arisen and that the resultant damage was reasonably foreseeable. In an action based on nuisance, it is likewise necessary to show that damage has occurred and additionally necessary to show 'fault' on the part of the defender. In each case, therefore, liability must be proved, on the balance of probabilities, by the party raising the action or seeking the remedy. This distinguishes common law actions from what is often referred to as 'strict liability'. Strict liability is the concept that a person is liable for the results of his actions if it is shown that some act or omission of his caused the resultant damage. It does not matter whether he was at fault or was negligent.

Finally, in respect of common law remedies, it is necessary for anyone raising an action or seeking a remedy to demonstrate that they have both title and interest to sue. That is straightforward where one is dealing with damage to the environment caused by a polluting incident where property is damaged or rendered unfit for its purpose. But in circumstances where it is the 'environment' which has been damaged – for example, the loss of a habitat or the destruction of a species – the question of title and interest to sue is far more complex. A detailed examination of the position in Scotland is outwith the scope of this book (although the subject is touched upon in Chapter 2), but it is by no means clear that, for example, environmental pressure groups or other interested bodies will be able to demonstrate title and interest to sue in respect of environmental damage. Developments in England have certainly suggested that organisations such as Greenpeace are likely to be conceded title and interest to sue, but this cannot yet be taken to be the case in Scotland.

Thus, common law remedies clearly have their place in the context of environmental protection and may indeed be powerful weapons in certain circumstances, but they are necessarily limited in scope and their use must always be assessed by reference to what is actionable and what is not, by reference to what must be proved and by reference to who may sue. In summary, it is not their present function to protect the environment as such, but rather to provide remedies for those who may have suffered loss by virtue of, *inter alia*, damage to the environment.

3.2 Statutory civil liability

A limited number of statutory provisions impose civil liability in respect of environmental damage, but they do so only in respect of particular potentially damage-causing activities. However, such provisions as there are operate on a strict liability basis, ie, they do not require that the party seeking the remedy in damages should prove negligence or fault on the part of the defender. To that extent, they may superficially seem more attractive than common law remedies, but the fact that they cover particular activities considerably limits their scope.

It is not strictly appropriate to consider, under the heading of statutory civil liability, the numerous instances in legislation applicable to Scotland of what may be termed 'regulatory liability'. By this is meant liability which is capable of being imposed by relevant regulatory authorities in respect of clean-up of contamination caused or damage to the environment caused. The relevant aspects of regulatory liability are dealt with in subsequent chapters in the appropriate contexts. Obviously, liability in respect of 'contaminated land' in terms of Part IIA of EPA is an example, but so also is clean-up liability in respect of the pollution of controlled waters as dealt with in sections 46 and 46A of COPA and so on. Each of these provisions, with the possible exception of 'contaminated land' (which is itself to be heavily circumscribed by guidance), is sector-specific rather than general.

3.3 INTERNATIONAL DEVELOPMENTS

Outside the UK, some considerable thought has been given, and is being given, to the imposition of civil liability for damage to the environment. Perhaps the most significant international (as opposed to EU) development has been the Council of Europe Convention on Civil Liability for Damage resulting from Activities Dangerous to the Environment, which opened for signature in 1993 ('the Lugano Convention'). The Council of Europe consists of all EU and European Free Trade Association states and also a number of the former Soviet bloc countries.

The aim of the Lugano Convention is to ensure that 'adequate' compensation is paid for damage caused by activities dangerous to the environment, and further to provide for the prevention and reinstatement of environmental damage. 'Dangerous activities' are defined as operations involving dangerous substances, genetically modified organisms, landfills and other sites for the permanent disposal of waste and a number of other waste disposal and recycling installations, some examples of which are specified in Annex II to the Convention. The definition constitutes an 'open', not a 'closed' list. Damage caused by nuclear matter is specifically excluded, but that is because such damage is regulated by other Conventions, which are given effect to in the UK by the Nuclear Installations Act 1965.

The types of damage for which compensation is available under the Convention include loss of life, personal injury and loss of or damage to property. Additionally, there is liability in respect of loss or damage by virtue of 'impairment of the environment' (other than property loss), but in this case compensation is restricted to the cost of reinstatement measures undertaken or to be undertaken. Despite the limitation, this represents a significant extension beyond standard actionable liability.

The 'environment' is defined so as to include air, water, soil, flora and fauna, as well as 'property which forms part of the cultural heritage' and the 'characteristic aspects of the landscape'. Again, this is a very broad definition and one upon which different people may have different opinions. What is the 'cultural' heritage? Does it include spoil heaps resulting from coal-mining activities? If so, are they also 'characteristic aspects of the landscape'? But yet they may themselves be causing contamination.

The Convention operates on a strict liability basis such that only the causal link between the 'dangerous activity' and the resultant damage need be proved, which means that concepts of negligence and fault are not relevant. The Convention does not, however, envisage retrospective effect, but in practice it is always going to be difficult to demonstrate, in respect of a continuing occurrence, whether it commenced prior to the entry into force of the Convention or not. Liability exemptions include damage caused by acts of war or exceptional natural events as well as, in some circumstances, compliance with regulatory authority directions.

Signatories to the Convention have discretion to set a financial ceiling on civil liability and they may also, instead of adopting the civil liability provisions, replace that liability by a guarantee fund or other financial security mechanism. However, it is also made clear that those who actually carry out dangerous activities must in any event have in place insurance or other financial cover for their liability.

As a general principle, claims for compensation must be lodged within five years of the date upon which the claimant knew or ought reasonably to have known of the relevant damage, but there is a long-stop limitation period of thirty years which bars any claim made more than thirty years after an incident which resulted in damage. In the case of an incident which consists of a series of occurrences or a continuous occurrence this thirty-year period begins from the last occurrence in the series or the end of the continuous occurrence.

The Convention anticipates that environmental interest groups should have certain rights including seeking a court order banning an unlawful dangerous activity or requesting a court order for an operator to take measures to prevent an incident (whether before or after damage has been caused) or to effect restoration. However, any country which ratifies the Convention is entitled to reserve the right not to apply the provisions entitling interest groups to these specified rights of action.

The Convention is significant as a measure which is designed to deal in a relatively wide context with the question of damage to the environment caused by dangerous activities. To that extent, it is considerably broader in scope than any common law or legislative provision presently applicable in Scotland. The UK government has indicated, to date, that it does not intend to ratify the Lugano Convention and it cannot be required to do so by the Council of Europe. The reason for this refusal to ratify can be found in the view of the government that first, the question of damage to the environment is sufficiently catered for in terms of applicable common law principles and legislative measures and secondly, that the Convention would impose an unacceptable burden on business.

However, the Convention still has potential significance in light of considerations of environmental liability at EU level.

3.4 EUROPEAN UNION DEVELOPMENTS

The European Commission has been considering for some time how it should approach the question of liability for environmental damage. Discussions, which began as early as the late 1980s, resulted in the issue of a Green Paper, Remedying Damage to the Environment (COM (93) 47), which was published in March 1993. This consultative document represented the Commission's initial thinking on how civil liability might be used as a tool to implement the principle that the polluter should pay. The Green Paper put forward two possible solutions which are not necessarily mutually exclusive. The first was the introduction of a special civil liability régime in respect of damage to the environment. The second was the setting up of joint compensation funds in circumstances where a civil liability system would not provide a remedy – for example, where the polluter cannot be found or where the polluter is insolvent or indeed where it is not possible to identify the party who was the cause of the pollution. The Green Paper met with a mixed reception, certain member states being opposed to it on the grounds that it imposed further, and arguably unnecessary, burdens on business and other member states on the grounds that if one of its aims was the harmonisation of environmental liability throughout the EU, their arguably stricter liability systems might be imperilled. The debate is not only driven by the 'polluter pays principle' but also by the desire to ensure a level playing field within the EU in order that businesses do not gravitate towards states with a less severe environmental protection régime, thereby saving costs.

In April 1994 the European Parliament passed a resolution to the effect that legislation on liability for environmental damage should be proposed by the Commission.

The Commission subsequently took matters forward by commissioning studies of the environmental liability régimes in place in member states and the economic arguments for and against action at EU level. These studies were released in May 1996. On the economic front, they indicated that any action at EU level should not be retrospective, should not impose joint and several liability and should not impose compulsory liability insurance. However, the economic study also put forward a relatively strong argument for pursuing some form of environmental liability scheme at EU level, although only for specified types of pollution. Perhaps significantly, the studies did not find that differences between national environmental liability régimes were affecting competitiveness – rather they drew attention to the perception that uncertainty about future legislation was a more important factor driving long-term investment decisions than any cost differences.

At present the Commission is considering two options. The first is that the EU should accede to the Lugano Convention (discussed above). The second is that the EU should propose its own directive on the topic of civil liability for damage to the environment. It seems most likely that the Commission will opt for a further round of consultation on these options by way of a White Paper. The timetable for its development and issue is not yet decided. It does, however, appear to be clear that the Environment Commissioner at least is not in favour of arguments that it would be better to do nothing at EU level. As mentioned above, the European Parliament has requested that the Commission take action in respect of environmental liability and it is also one of the threads which runs through the EU's Fifth Environment Action Programme.

It is not clear whether the Commission's current thinking on environmental liability necessarily fits well with all of the provisions of the Lugano Convention, nor is it clear to what extent the EU has power to accede to the Convention. It is thought that any action on civil liability for damage to the environment at EU level will involve adherence to the polluter pays principle, strict, but not retrospective, liability, liability not only for damage to persons or property, but also liability for ecological damage and a widening of access rights to the courts, ie, rights for environmental interest groups. As to the scope of liability, if the approach of the Lugano Convention is followed, liability will be based upon an 'open' list of 'dangerous activities'. However, liability may be based upon all damage to the environment, with specified exclusions, which could result in a much broader scope.

It is highly likely that whatever decision is eventually taken, the resulting discussion, negotiation and implementation will take considerable time thus prolonging the current climate of uncertainty.

In conclusion, European indicators suggest pressures towards a stricter civil liability régime in the future, but the timing, extent and content of that régime is still highly uncertain. Present UK indicators suggest little change to the current liability systems in place.

Chapter 4

ENVIRONMENTAL INFORMATION

4.1 INTRODUCTION

In the past, environmental information was not normally made available to the public. Indeed disclosure of environmental information without the consent of the person supplying it was often criminalised. The government thought that it knew best and that there was no need to inform the public, while business was worried, first, that information would be misinterpreted by activists and would result in vexatious litigation damaging to industry; secondly, that confidential information would become available to competitors; and, lastly, that the costs of providing information would be excessive. As late as 1984 the CBI described the system of water pollution registers introduced by COPA as 'a busybody's charter'. However, in recent years there has been a complete policy reversal resulting in a considerable amount of environmental information becoming publicly available.

This change of policy has resulted from a variety of factors: considerable pressure from 1974 onwards from the Royal Commission on Environmental Pollution; development of government thinking outlined in the White Paper, This Common Inheritance: Britain's Environmental Strategy (Cm 1200, 1990); and European initiatives, particularly Directive 90/313/EEC on freedom of access to information on the environment. This Common Inheritance noted that giving people information puts them in a better position to make their own consumer decisions and to exert pressure for change. Provision of information and giving people an opportunity to make their views known is seen as the best way of stimulating public discussion and earning public confidence in environmental policies. The 1993 White Paper, Open Government (Cm 2290, 1993), also indicated that the government's thinking has moved further towards an open information régime. The purpose of Directive 90/313/EEC is partly to eliminate possible disparities in competition caused by differing laws on the provision of environmental information and partly to improve environmental protection by involving citizens through information provision. More recently the EC has adopted Regulation 880/92/EEC on eco-labelling which will enable consumers to make decisions in the marketplace based on environmental criteria.

Although there are several means by which environmental information is currently made available to the public, this chapter will concentrate on two important ones: first, the extensive system of public registers; and, secondly, the provisions of the Environmental Information Regulations 1992 (SI 1992/3240). The chapter will also briefly consider active dissemination of environmental information by SEPA and the government. Other significant means of providing information, which include labelling of hazardous substances and consumer goods and company reporting, are beyond the scope of the chapter.

Finally, it should be noted that much environmental information is being published on the Internet by SEPA, the Environment Agency, government departments and environmental interest groups. For example, SEPA's site contains copies of materials such as press releases, consultation papers and a guide to environmental information available from SEPA (http://www.sepa.org.uk). Furthermore, the Department of the Environment, Transport and the Regions puts regularly updated air quality monitoring information and drinking water quality information on the Internet at http://www.open.gov.uk/doe/doehome.htm An air quality information archive is also available. Furthermore, Friends of the Earth have put the Chemical Releases Inventory (CRI) on to the Internet (see paragraph 4.2.6). It is likely that the use of the Internet as a means of providing information will be developed significantly in coming years.

4.2 PUBLIC REGISTERS
4.2.1 Introduction
The system of public registers of environmental information is to a large extent modelled on the water pollution registers introduced by COPA, although their implementation was delayed until 1985 largely as a result of CBI pressure. The information which these registers contained included details of discharge consents and also breaches of discharge consents.

The current system of registers extends across the environmental law spectrum. Three types of registers may be identified:

(1) registers containing details of specific environmental licence applications, the licences themselves, conditions contained in such licences, statutory notices served on the licence holder, prosecutions of the licence holder and in certain cases environmental monitoring data – for example, IPC registers;

(2) registers containing brief details of persons required to register particular activities carried on by them – for example, waste carriers; and

(3) contaminated land registers which contain details of remediation notices and associated information.

Planning and litter control registers do not fit neatly into these categories although they do not fall within the scope of this book aside from a brief mention at paragraph 4.2.3. Fuller details of what information is contained in the registers within the scope of this book may be found in the appropriate chapters identified at paragraphs 4.2.2 and 4.2.3.

Inspection of the registers is free but a charge must be paid for copies. Any member of the public may inspect the registers regardless of his motive for doing so (*Stirrat Park Hogg* v *Dumbarton District Council* (OH) 1994 SCLR 631; 1996 SLT 1113). There is no need to show a particular interest to obtain access to the information. Since the introduction of the Environmental Information Regulations 1992 it has become possible to request copies of information held on a register by letter, telephone or in some cases by other means of communication, such as e-mail. This is discussed further at paragraph 4.3.6.

Formerly, a large number of environmental regulators held various registers, but since its establishment SEPA now holds the majority of these registers. The attendant benefits which this concentration of registers brings include the replacement of a variety of administrative practices by a single set of administrative practices, the availability of multiple registers at single contact points and the standardisation of charges for copies from the registers.

4.2.2 Registers held by SEPA

SEPA holds the following registers:

Subject area	Brief summary of information contained	Statute	Further details (if any) in paragraph
Integrated pollution control	IPC authorisations and related information	EPA, s20	9.2.10
Air pollution	Local air pollution control authorisations and related information	EPA, s20	9.2.10
Water pollution	Water quality objectives, discharge consents and related information	COPA, s41	8.4.7
Waste	Waste management licences and related information	EPA, s64	7.5
Radioactive substances	Registrations of keeping, etc, radioactive material; authorisations for accumulation and disposal of radioactive waste and related information	RSA, s39	11.15.1
Waste	Registration of activities exempt from waste management licensing	Waste Management Licensing Regulations 1994	—
Waste	Registration of waste brokers	Waste Management Licensing Regulations 1994	—
Waste	Registration of waste carriers	Control of Pollution (Amendment) Act 1989	—
Contaminated land	Remediation notices and related information in respect of special sites	EPA, s78R	6.5.10

4.2.3 Registers held by local authorities
Local authorities operate registers in relation to:

Subject area	Brief summary of information contained	Statute	Further details (if any) in paragraph
Contaminated land	Remediation notices and related information in respect of all sites except special sites	EPA, s78R	6.5.10
Hazardous substances	Hazardous substances consents and related information	Planning (Hazardous Substances) (Scotland) Act 1997, s27	—
Planning	Applications for planning permission	Town and Country Planning (Scotland) Act 1997, s36	—
Litter	Litter control area orders and related information	EPA, s95	—
Noise	Measurements taken in noise abatement zones	COPA, Part III; Noise Level (Measurement and Registers) (Scotland) Regulations 1982	10.3.4

4.2.4 Registers held by the Secretary of State
The Secretary of State also holds the register which contains details of licences granted in relation to the dumping and incineration of waste at sea and associated information under the Food and Environment Protection Act 1985 and the register which contains details of consents granted in relation to the importation, acquisition and marketing of genetically modified organisms and associated information under Part VI of EPA. However, these subjects fall outwith the scope of this book and are not discussed further.

4.2.5 Exclusion of information from registers
4.2.5.1 Introduction
The following paragraphs are concerned with the grounds for the exclusion of information from the IPC (EPA, section 20), LAPC (EPA, section 20), waste management (EPA, section 64), water pollution

(COPA, section 41) and radioactive substances (RSA, section 39) registers held by SEPA and the contaminated land registers held by SEPA and by local authorities (EPA, section 78R). For the sake of convenience in the following paragraphs SEPA and local authorities are collectively referred to as 'register holders'.

In the case of the above registers it is possible for information to be excluded from the registers on certain limited grounds. These grounds, which have recently been assimilated across the spectrum of such registers, are (1) that it would not be in the interests of national security to disclose the information; and (2) that that information is commercially confidential.

4.2.5.2 National security

In the cases of the registers mentioned at paragraph 4.2.5.1 the Secretary of State may direct that information should be excluded from the register on the grounds that its disclosure would be contrary to the interests of national security (EPA, sections 21, 65 and 78S; COPA, section 42A; and RSA, section 39). A person may also apply to the Secretary of State for a determination of whether information should be excluded on this ground. In such cases the register holder must be notified by the applicant and the information must be excluded from the register until the Secretary of State has determined the application. Information may be excluded for so long as the Secretary of State is of the opinion that its disclosure would be contrary to the interests of national security.

4.2.5.3 Commercial confidentiality

Information may also be excluded from the registers mentioned at paragraph 4.2.5.1 (with the exception of radioactive substances registers under RSA) where an individual or business does not consent to its disclosure and it is commercially confidential in relation to that individual or business (EPA, sections 22, 66 and 78T; and COPA, section 42B). However, information is not regarded as commercially confidential unless there is a determination to that effect by the register holder or, on appeal, by the Secretary of State. In the case of RSA information may be excluded from the register where it would otherwise involve the disclosure of a trade secret (section 39).

In the case of information supplied for the purpose of licence applications, complying with conditions of a licence or complying with a statutory notice requesting information, an application to have the information excluded from the register must be made by the individual or business wishing to have it excluded, otherwise the information will be included in the register. The register holder must make a determination within fourteen days from the date of the application. If the register holder fails to make a determination within fourteen days it is deemed to have determined that the information is commercially confidential.

In other circumstances where it appears to the register holder that any information obtained by virtue of any provision of the relevant legislation might be commercially confidential, the register holder must notify the person to whom or to whose business the information relates that it is required to be included in the register unless excluded on the ground of commercial confidentiality and provide that person with a reasonable opportunity of objecting to the inclusion of the information on the ground that it is commercially confidential and of making representations to justify any such objections. Where such representations are made, the register holder must determine whether or not the information is commercially confidential.

Following the determination (or deemed determination where applicable), the information is excluded from the register for a period of twenty-one days to enable the applicant to appeal to the Secretary of State. Where an appeal is made, the information continues to be excluded from the registers until the appeal has been finally determined or withdrawn.

It should be noted that the Secretary of State has the power to give directions to register holders that specified information or descriptions of information should be included in the registers on the basis of the public interest even though the information may be commercially confidential.

Information is regarded as being commercially confidential if, in relation to any individual or person, its inclusion in the register would prejudice to an unreasonable degree the commercial interests of that individual or person.

Government guidance on IPC illustrates what information might be regarded as commercially confidential. The guidance indicates that 'specific and cogent evidence' is required to substantiate any application for exclusion of information on this ground and provides that such evidence would need to demonstrate that disclosure of the information would negate or significantly diminish a commercial advantage. Such an advantage might relate to preserving the secret of a new process technology, or of a particular raw material or catalyst, or of the capacity of the process, or of some other specific feature which, if made public, might seriously affect a legitimate commercial advantage. However, the guidance stresses that it will not normally be appropriate to withhold information from the register in response to a general claim that disclosure might damage the reputation of an operator and hence his competitiveness. Her Majesty's Inspectorate of Pollution (HMIP) indicated in its 1994–95 Annual Report that it strongly resisted attempts by operators to treat emissions to the environment as confidential.

Information does not remain commercially confidential permanently: it only remains confidential for four years from the date of the final determination that it was confidential. However, if the person who furnished the information wishes it to remain excluded from the register on the ground of commercial confidentiality he may reapply for it to be excluded. The reapplication procedure is the same as for the original application.

4.2.6 Chemical Releases Inventory

The CRI is a non-statutory register held by the Environment Agency providing extensive, although as yet incomplete, information about emissions from the various IPC processes operating in England and

Wales. There is as yet no equivalent for Scotland. It should be noted that the CRI has been published by Friends of the Earth on the Internet at http://www.foe.uk/cri/index.html EC Directive 96/61/EC on integrated pollution prevention and control, which will be implemented through the IPC system in the UK, provides for the publication by the European Commission of an inventory of the principal emissions and sources responsible every three years based on data supplied by member states (article 15(3)). This provision will probably be implemented by putting the CRI on a statutory footing and expanding its scope.

4.3 THE ENVIRONMENTAL INFORMATION REGULATIONS 1992
4.3.1 Introduction
On 31st December 1992 the Environmental Information Regulations 1992 ('the 1992 Regulations') came into force. The 1992 Regulations are designed to implement Directive 90/313/EEC on the freedom of access to information on the environment whose purpose was discussed at paragraph 4.1.

The core provision of the 1992 Regulations is that any relevant person who holds any information on the environment to which the 1992 Regulations apply must make that information available to every person who requests it (regulation 3(1)). The obligation on a relevant person to make available information is a duty owed to the person requesting the information. However, the 1992 Regulations do not apply to all environmental information held by relevant persons: the information must be held in an accessible form (regulation 2(1)(b)), it must not be held for the purposes of any judicial or legislative function (regulation 2(1) (b)) and it must be neither information which is required by statute to be provided on request nor information contained in records which are required by statute to be made available for inspection by every person who wishes to inspect them (regulation 2(1)(c)).

4.3.2 Definitions
The 1992 Regulations apply to information which relates to the environment. This is exhaustively defined to mean information relating solely to

(a) the state of any water or air, the state of any flora or fauna, the state of any soil or the state of any natural site or other land;

(b) any activities or measures (including activities giving rise to noise or any other nuisance) which adversely affect anything mentioned in sub-paragraph (a) above or are likely adversely to affect anything so mentioned;

(c) any activities or administrative or other measures (including any environmental management programmes) which are designed to protect anything so mentioned.

Information includes anything held in records which is defined as including registers, reports and returns, as well as computer records and other records kept otherwise than in a document (regulation 2(4)). In *R* v *British Coal Corporation*, ex parte *Ibstock Building Products Ltd* [1995] Env LR 277, a case on the costs of a judicial review application about whether British Coal had been obliged by the 1992 Regulations to disclose the identity of an individual who had alleged that in 1947 naval munitions were dumped in a disused mineshaft on land which Ibstock Building Products Ltd wished to develop, the parties accepted that the alleged presence of dumped naval munitions in a disused mineshaft was information relating to the state of land in terms of regulation 2(2)(a). More significantly, that case also established that the source of information was capable of being information which related to the state of land because it was necessary to know the source of the information to assess the quality and credibility of the information and accordingly it was held that British Coal had been obliged by the 1992 Regulations to disclose their informant's identity.

The persons subject to the 1992 Regulations are known as relevant persons. Such persons are defined as

(a) all such Ministers of the Crown, government departments, local authorities and other persons carrying out functions of public administration at a national, regional or local level as, for the purposes of or in connection with their functions, have responsibilities in relation to the environment; and

(b) any body with public responsibilities for the environment which does not fall within sub-paragraph (a) above but is under the control of a person falling within that sub-paragraph.

Although the government published a list of more than 200 bodies which it believed would be subject to the 1992 Regulations as part of the consultation process prior to the introduction of the 1992 Regulations, the list was not exhaustive and no definitive list has subsequently been produced. The government's Guidance on the Implementation of the Environmental Information Regulations 1992 (DoE, 1992) indicates that there is no point in providing a definitive list of bodies which are subject to the 1992 Regulations since such a list would change rapidly. The government's advice to bodies is that they must decide whether or not they are subject to the 1992 Regulations. This effectively puts the onus of establishing that a particular body is subject to the 1992 Regulations on the person seeking the information.

The first category of bodies is relatively uncontroversial although it may not be precisely clear which Ministers or government departments have responisibilities in relation to the environment. For example, HM Customs and Excise now have considerable responsibilities in relation to the environment by virtue of their administration of the landfill tax (see paragraph 2.14.2).

The scope of the second category of persons is much less clear. It has been argued (Bakkenist, *Environmental Information: Law, Policy and Experience* (1994)) that every person possessing an environmental licence falls within the second category although that is probably too broad an interpretation of the category. However, it appears possible that utilities may fall within the second category since the test is similar although not identical to the test of whether a person is a branch of the state for the purposes of establishing the EC principle of direct effect (see paragraph 2.12.4). In applying that test it has been held that utilities are branches of the state by virtue partly of the degree of control exercised over the provision of services by public authorities (*Griffin and Others* v *South West Water Services Ltd* [1995] IRLR 15). In relation to the second category, the government's own guidance notes that 'control' is a relationship constituted by statutes, rights, contracts or other means which either separately or jointly confer the possibility of directly or indirectly exercising a decisive influence on a body. The guidance indicates that any private business which is under a statutory duty would be subject to the regulations.

SEPA and the Environment Agency are clearly subject to the 1992 Regulations, and probably fall within the first category of relevant persons although the government's view is that they fall within the second category.

The respondents in *R* v *British Coal Corporation*, ex parte *Ibstock Building Products Ltd* expressly did not concede that they were subject to the 1992 Regulations although for the purposes of that case they did not pursue that contention in order to shorten proceedings.

4.3.3 Practical arrangements for complying with duty

The 1992 Regulations do not lay down precise arrangements whereby each relevant person is to supply information requested. Instead they lay down a skeleton framework of arrangements and it is likely that as a result of this different public authorities will adopt detailed arrangements which may vary considerably. It is not clear whether this scheme adequately implements the obligation contained in the relevant provision of Directive 90/313/EEC which states that 'Member States *shall define the practical arrangements* under which such information shall be made available' (article 3(1)) (emphasis added), and it is understood that Friends of the Earth have made a complaint to the European Commission in relation to this issue.

Importantly, a person does not need to demonstrate any interest in the information concerned. Every person is entitled to environmental information which may be withheld only on the grounds set out in the 1992 Regulations.

Relevant persons must respond to requests for information as soon as possible and not more than two months after the request was made (regulation 3(2)). It is not yet clear whether a holding letter within the two-month period would constitute a valid response. If a response to a request for information contains a refusal to make information available such a refusal must be in writing and must specify reasons for the refusal (regulation 3(2)). General case-law on giving reasons indicates that the decision-maker must give proper and adequate reasons which deal with the substantial questions in an intelligible way (*Wordie Property Co Ltd* v *Secretary of State for Scotland* 1984 SLT 345).

Given that it is only relevant persons who are subject to this duty, bodies which take the view that they are not relevant persons could also accordingly take the view that they are not subject to the above duties in relation to responding to requests for information. The person requesting information could only challenge this approach by means of judicial review.

The person requesting the information may be charged by the relevant person for costs reasonably attributable to the supply of information and the supply of any information may be made conditional on the payment of such a charge (regulation 3(4)). The establishment of SEPA has led to standardisation of charges in relation to information which it holds. Prior to the establishment of SEPA there was widespread variation in charges applied in relation to information held on registers: the Scottish Consumer Council and Friends of the Earth Scotland Report, Come Clean! Public Access to Information about Local Authority Air Pollution Control (March 1993), identified a range of charges between 5p and £5 a page for photocopies from LAPC registers. SEPA now charges 10p per side for copies of documents.

Information need only be made available in such form and at such times and places as may be reasonable (regulation 3(5)). This is likely to be interpreted as meaning during normal working hours which register holders regard as the reasonable time to allow access to public registers.

Any statutory provision or rule of law which restricts or prohibits disclosure of information which is inconsistent with the requirements of the 1992 Regulations is disapplied (regulation 3(7)). Thus, it will only be possible to restrict disclosure on grounds which are consistent with the grounds set out in the 1992 Regulations (see paragraph 4.3.4).

4.3.4 Grounds for non-disclosure of information

The grounds for non-disclosure which a member state might employ are exhaustively set out in the directive. The UK government has chosen to implement all the available grounds in the 1992 Regulations (regulation 4).

A distinction is drawn in the 1992 Regulations between information which is capable of being treated as confidential, in which case such confidentiality may provide a ground for non-disclosure, and information which must be treated as confidential, in which case no disclosure is possible.

Information *may* be treated as confidential if and only if it is

— information relating to matters affecting international relations, national defence or public security;

— information relating to, or anything which is or has been the subject-matter of, any legal or other proceedings (whether actual or prospective);

— information relating to the confidential deliberations of any relevant person or to the contents of any internal communications of a body corporate or other undertaking or organisation;

— information contained in a document or other record which is still in the course of completion; or

— information relating to matters to which any commercial or industrial confidentiality attaches or affecting any intellectual property.

In *R v British Coal Corporation*, ex parte *Ibstock Building Products Ltd* it was held that the information sought was not confidential on the first of these grounds since there was no evidence that the presence of munitions allegedly dumped in mineshafts in 1947 was a matter which affected national defence or public security, especially as the Ministry of Defence did not take up the matter. It was also held that the second of these grounds relating to prospective legal proceedings did not apply as a planning application was not a legal or other proceeding and its existence did not mean that there was a prospective appeal which the court clearly regarded as falling within the definition of a legal or other proceeding.

In *R* v *London Borough of Tower Hamlets*, ex parte *Tilly* [1996] Env LR D23, the applicant sought leave for judicial review to challenge a decision not to disclose a report of a study which found high levels of volatile organic compounds around the News International plant in London on the basis that it was still in the course of completion. On a renewed application to the Court of Appeal it was held that leave for judicial review would have been granted so that consideration could be made for production of the report had a copy of the final report not been made available to the applicant in the meantime.

Information *must* be treated as confidential and hence not disclosed at all if and only if

— it is capable of being so treated and its disclosure in response to a request would contravene any statutory provision or rule of law or would involve a breach of any agreement;

— the information is personal information contained in records held in relation to an individual who has not given his consent to its disclosure;

— the information is held by the relevant person in consequence of having been supplied by a person who –

— was not under, and could not have been put under, any legal obligation to supply it to the relevant person;

— did not supply it in circumstances such that the relevant person is entitled apart from the 1992 Regulations to disclose it; and

— has not consented to its disclosure; or

— the disclosure of the information in response to that request would, in the circumstances, increase the likelihood of damage to the environment affecting anything to which the information relates.

The respondents in *R* v *British Coal Corporation*, ex parte *Ibstock Building Products Ltd* also argued that the information could not be disclosed on the basis that it was personal information contained in records held in relation to an individual who had not given his consent to its disclosure. However, the court rejected this argument holding that the records held by the respondents were not records held in relation to the individual informant.

In addition, a request for information may be refused in cases where the request is manifestly unreasonable or is formulated in too general a manner (regulation 3(3)).

The 1992 Regulations do not authorise a refusal to make available information on the ground that it is held with other information which is subject to the confidentiality exception unless it is incapable of being separated from the other information for the purpose of making it available (regulation 4(4)).

4.3.5 Remedies

Directive 90/313/EEC provides that a person who considers that his request for information has been unreasonably refused or ignored, or has been inadequately answered by a public authority, may seek a judicial or administrative review of the decision in accordance with the relevant national legal system (article 4). The 1992 Regulations do not make any express reference to this article but it is clear that judicial review would be available – for example, to compel performance of the duty to supply information or to challenge unreasonable charges imposed for the supply of information. Given the costs involved in judicial review, this is not a particularly accessible remedy and is likely to be used only where considerable economic interests are at stake, as in *R v British Coal Corporation*, ex parte *Ibstock Building Products Ltd*. For aggrieved individuals an alternative remedy may be available through the offices of the Parliamentary ombudsman or local ombudsman depending on whether the person refusing to supply information is a central or local government body.

Although the former government proposed the establishment of a new tribunal to deal with complaints relating to environmental information, at the time of writing no legislation has been introduced to set it up.

4.3.6 Relationship of the 1992 Regulations with existing rights to information

There are already considerable existing rights to information on the environment based on the system of registers discussed at paragraphs 4.2.1–4.2.5. The 1992 Regulations do not apply to information which is required, in accordance with a statutory provision, to be provided on request, nor to information contained in records which are required, in accordance with a statutory provision, to be made available for inspection by every person who wishes to inspect them (regulation 2(1)(c)). This covers information held on registers. Where there is an existing right to information under any statutory provision, such as is the case with the existing register system, the 1992 Regulations require that the arrangements made by any relevant person for giving effect to the requirements of that provision must be such as to secure that every request for information which is made for the purposes of that provision is responded to as soon as possible and no later than two months from the date of the request, that any refusal must be in writing and must specify reasons therefor and that no charge made for making the information available exceeds a reasonable amount (regulation 5). This is to ensure that arrangements for existing rights to information comply with the requirements in the 1992 Regulations. This means that whereas some information relating to the environment was previously made available simply by having registers open to inspection, the information contained in these registers must now also be available on request for a fee to cover, for example, administration, photocopying and postage.

4.4 ACTIVE DISSEMINATION OF INFORMATION

Directive 90/313/EEC also requires member states to disseminate general information on the environment and suggests that this may be done by the periodic publication of descriptive reports. To this end both the Environment Agency south of the border and SEPA published *State of the Environment Reports* in 1996. SEPA's report contains information on the state of air, land and water in Scotland and also provides an outline of the issues confronting the environment, including climate change, acid rain, waste management and radioactivity. An edited version of this report is available via SEPA's website (http://www.sepa.org.uk).

Furthermore, government action on the environment throughout the UK is also regularly publicised through the annual follow-up reports to the 1990 White Paper, *This Common Inheritance*, which indicate the extent to which earlier commitments are being met and which also set new targets. These reports include a section on Scotland.

Finally, EA also places SEPA under a statutory duty to produce an annual report on its activities for the Secretary of State who must lay a copy before Parliament and arrange for its publication. This provision should lead to the publication of a considerable amount of environmental information and will be an improvement on previous reporting practice in Scotland where not all the previous environmental regulators were subject to statutory reporting duties. Although the river purification boards were under such a duty and produced good quality annual reports on their activities, HMIPI was not under such a duty and although it did produce two reports on its activities covering the periods 1987–88 and 1988–92, these reports were produced some time after the periods concerned had ended which meant that the information that they contained was far from current and hence not particularly useful.

4.5 ACCESS TO INFORMATION HELD BY THE EC

Directive 90/313/EEC on the freedom of access to information on the environment does not apply to environmental information held by the EC (see paragraph 4.3). However, Decision 94/90/EC provides for access to such information, by adopting a Code of Conduct on public access to Commission and Council documents. Under this provision there is a mandatory ground for refusing access to a document, including protection of the public interest, and a discretionary ground to protect the institution's interest in the confidentiality of its proceedings. In *World Wide Fund for Nature (UK)* v *EC Commission* (T-105/95) [1997] Env LR 242 it was held that although the decision contains obligations voluntarily assumed by the Commission, it is capable of conferring legal rights on third parties which the Commission is obliged to respect; that the Commission must, when relying on a mandatory ground, indicate to which subject-matter the documents relate, and, in particular whether they relate to inspections or investigation of possible breaches of the law (the case involved an investigation into a possible breach of EC law). The Commission cannot rely on a blanket refusal and must, when relying on the discretionary ground, refer to the categories of the documents in question and provide adequate reasons for refusing access to them.

Chapter 5

PLANNING, POLLUTION CONTROL AND WASTE MANAGEMENT

5.1 INTRODUCTION

'The Town and Country Planning system and the statutory environmental protection regimes are separate but complementary in that both are designed to protect the environment from the potential harm caused by development and operations, but with different objectives' (PAN 51, Planning and Environmental Protection, paragraph 1).

Although one of the main aims and objectives of the planning system is to protect the environment, it is often seen as a separate area of regulation from environmental law. However, the planning system does have a role to play in environmental law, not least because many potentially polluting developments will require both planning and environmental consents.

In the planning system, the environmental effects of a proposed development have always been a material consideration. As statutory regulation of emissions and waste management becomes more sophisticated, there is an increasing potential for overlap between planning and other statutory systems. These issues are considered further below.

5.2 THE PLANNING SYSTEM: AN OUTLINE

The planning system controls the use of land, primarily through the requirement for planning permission. The statutory provisions are contained in the Town and Country Planning (Scotland) Act 1997. Since 1st April 1996, the planning authority for each area has been the new unitary council.

Planning permission is required for 'development' of land, defined as the carrying out of building, engineering, mining or other operations in, on, over or under land, or the making of any material change of use of any buildings or land (section 26).

Where planning permission is required, an application must be submitted to the local authority in advance of commencement of development. Notice of the application must be served on the owner, any lessee under a lease with at least seven years to run, and the tenant of any agricultural holding within the application site, and on neighbours. An advertisement in a local newspaper may also be required. Recipients of a notice and other members of the public can submit representations to the local authority in connection with the proposed

79

development. The local authority will then consult various statutory and other bodies on the proposed development. The views of consultees and others who submitted representations must be taken into account when the application is determined. In the first instance, applications are generally determined by the elected councillors for the area, although officials may have delegated powers to decide some applications.

An application for planning permission must be determined in accordance with the development plan unless material considerations indicate otherwise (section 25). The development plan consists of the approved structure plan and adopted local plan for the area (section 24). The structure plan deals with strategic matters and broad statements of policy, which are applied by detailed land use policies contained in the local plan.

In determining a planning application, the authority must also take into account any guidance issued by the Scottish Office, such as a national planning policy guideline (NPPG), circular or planning advice note (PAN).

A grant of planning permission will usually be subject to conditions.

Once a planning permission has been granted, it cannot be varied or revoked unilaterally by the planning authority without creating liability to pay compensation.

Where development is commenced without a planning permission, or in breach of its terms, the planning authority have the discretion to use their enforcement powers.

The following publications provide useful information: Collar, *Planning* (W. Green/Sweet & Maxwell, 1994); Henderson and O'Carroll, *Town and Country Planning in Scotland* (Hillside, 1994); McAllister and McMaster, *Scottish Planning Law* (Butterworths, 1994).

5.3 Material considerations

The jurisdiction of the planning authority is determined by the material considerations arising from the proposed development. Apart from the classic definition restricting material considerations to land use factors (*Stringer* v *Minister of Housing and Local Government* [1971] 1 All ER 65, per Cooke J), guidance from the courts on the extent of material considerations has been limited to a case-by-case basis. However, it is possible to draw some broad conclusions.

5.3.1 Environmental effects

The environmental effects of a proposed development are a material consideration. Factors such as loss of amenity, visual impact, dust, noise, smell and fumes, are relevant to the decision whether to grant planning permission.

The Environmental Assessment (Scotland) Regulations 1988 (SI 1988/1221, as amended), require environmental assessment for any project specified in Annex I, including crude oil refineries, major chemical and steel works, aerodromes with runway lengths over 2,100 metres, and the permanent storage or final disposal of radioactive and other toxic waste. Annex II projects require environmental assessment if the planning authority consider that the proposed development is likely to give rise to significant environmental effects.

Environmental assessment involves gathering information and reporting on the environmental effects of the proposed development. The result of this process is the submission of an environmental statement which reports on the likely significant effects of the proposed development on human beings, flora, fauna, soil, water, air, climate, the landscape, the interaction between these effects, material assets, and the cultural heritage.

Even if the proposed development does not fall within the terms of the 1988 Regulations, the planning authority have a general power to request further information to enable them to determine the application (Town and Country Planning (General Development Procedure) (Scotland) Order 1992 (SI 1992/224), as amended, article 13).

5.3.2 Contamination
Contamination, or the potential for it, is a material consideration (PAN 33, Development of Contaminated Land, paragraph 6). Where a site is contaminated, the planning authority must decide whether the proposed development could give rise to unacceptable risks to health or the environment, and, if so, what restrictions could/ should be imposed to reduce those risks. A grant of planning permission may be subject to conditions designed to ensure that the proposed development will not expose future users or occupiers of the site to hazards associated with contamination.

5.3.3 Pollution
The likelihood of pollution as a result of the proposed development can be a material consideration. The environmental impact of emissions to atmosphere is a material consideration, but it is also a material consideration that there is a stringent régime under EPA for preventing or mitigating that impact and for rendering any emissions harmless (*Gateshead Metropolitan Borough Council* v *Secretary of State for the Environment* [1994] 1 PLR 85; [1995] JPL 432).

The planning authority should only be concerned with health and pollution fears insofar as these fears can be detrimental to existing or future uses of neighbouring land, such as 'clean' industries, tourism and farming. However, the planning application cannot be determined on the basis of the worst-case scenario without some form of risk assessment exercise being conducted to determine the likelihood of that situation occurring (*Envirocor Waste Holdings* v *Secretary of State for the Environment* [1996] JPL 489).

5.3.4 Waste management
All statutory authorities, including planning authorities, are required to

— ensure that waste is recovered or disposed of without endangering human health or harming the environment; and

— establish an integrated and adequate network of disposal installations, enabling waste to be disposed of at one of the nearest appropriate installations (Waste Management Licensing Regulations 1994 (SI 1994/1056), regulation 19, Schedule 4).

5.4 OVERLAP OF PLANNING, POLLUTION CONTROL AND WASTE MANAGEMENT POWERS

Where planning permission and pollution control/ waste management consents are required for a proposed development there is potential for overlap between the statutory roles of the planning authority and SEPA. This is acknowledged in EPA which provides that the grounds for refusal of a waste management licence can include serious detriment to amenity, but only if no planning permission has been granted for the development (section 36(3)), presumably because in granting the planning permission the likelihood of detriment to amenity will have been taken into account.

This leads to the question of which matters are properly the concern of the planning authority, and which should be dealt with by SEPA. To answer this question it is necessary to look at both the law and Scottish Office policy.

5.4.1 Law

As a matter of law, planning powers may be exercised by the planning authority notwithstanding the existence of more specific statutory powers, provided a planning purpose is being served. For example, the likely creation of litter from a proposed hot-food takeaway may be a relevant planning consideration because it could affect residential amenity, notwithstanding that it is dealt with by other legislation (*City of Aberdeen District Council* v *Secretary of State for Scotland* 1993 SLT 1325).

In upholding a decision by the Secretary of State to grant planning permission for a clinical waste incinerator, the court held that the environmental impact of emissions to atmosphere is a material planning consideration. However, it is also a material consideration that there is a stringent régime under EPA for preventing or mitigating that impact. The Secretary of State was therefore entitled to be satisfied that, having regard to the existence of EPA controls, a residual difficulty or uncertainty was capable of being overcome so that there was no reason to refuse planning permission. Whether that point had been reached was a question for the judgment of the decision maker in each individual case (*Gateshead Metropolitan Borough Council* v *Secretary of State for the Environment*).

Although the planning authority are required to consult certain bodies such as SEPA and take into account their views on the proposed development, they are not obliged to follow their views, which have to be weighed together with the other material considerations. Thus it was not unlawful to grant planning permission for a development which breached an NRA policy embargo caused by problems with the sewerage system (*Ynys Mon Borough Council* v *Secretary of State for Wales* [1993] JPL 225).

5.4.2 Scottish Office policy

The long-established Scottish Office policy is that planning controls should not duplicate other statutory controls (eg, NPPG 10, paragraph 17). This is more restrictive than the legal position. Although planning authorities are not obliged to comply with Scottish Office policy, in practice there is general compliance, due in part to the fear of losing an appeal to the Secretary of State following a refusal of planning permission.

NPPG 10, Planning and Waste Management, advises on how planning authorities should deal with potentially polluting developments.

— Planning authorities should not substitute their own judgment on pollution control issues for that of SEPA, which has the relevant expertise and statutory responsibility for that control.

— Planning authorities should consult SEPA.

— The dividing line between planning and pollution control is not always clear but the planning system should

— focus on whether the development itself is an acceptable use of the land rather than the control of the processes or substances involved;

— regulate the location of the development and the control of operations in order to avoid or minimise adverse effects on the use of land and on the environment; and

— secure restoration to a condition capable of the agreed after-use.

PAN 51, Planning and Environmental Protection, provides the legislative background to environmental protection and provides advice to help planning authorities avoid duplicating the more specific environmental protection régimes. It stresses the need for liaison and consultation between planning authorities and regulatory bodies. It acknowledges that, on occasions, the protection of the environment will require more than one means of control to be applied.

The planning system also deals with general pollution issues such as traffic emissions (see, for example, NPPG 8, Retailing, and the draft NPPG, Transport and Planning).

5.4.3 Planning appeal decisions

Incinerator proposals have been rejected by the Secretary of State for Scotland and the Secretary of State for the Environment on the grounds of detriment to regeneration strategy, the risk of tainting of products of nearby food factories, and the periodic odorous and obnoxious emissions which could only be cured by a higher chimney which would be a major intrusion into the skyline.

Unsuccessful arguments against development, and therefore non-material considerations, have included unsubstantiated fears of health hazard, a lack of need in circumstances where no comprehensive review had been undertaken of other disposal options and sites, the likelihood of existing landowners relocating, and potential land users being discouraged.

5.4.4 Conclusion: role of planning powers

There are four questions which planning authorities should seek to answer for potentially polluting developments.

(1) Whether the development is capable of being designed and operated in a manner which is reasonably likely to be authorisable under the pollution control legislation.

(2) Whether the development presents such a level of risk to neighbouring land uses (including people, water resources on or under the ground, commercial operations and natural systems) – either through the nature of the source of the risk or the sensitivity of the receptor – that it is an inappropriate use of the land.

(3) Whether, if the risk to neighbouring land uses cannot be allayed by reference to objective or accepted standards, the development would harm the current use of the land or prejudice the planning authority's aspirations for its future use as set out in the development plan.

(4) Whether there is a global, national or local need sufficient to outweigh any important planning objections on pollution grounds, and, if so, whether there is a reasonable alternative to the proposal which would cause lesser pollution impacts (DoE Research Study, Planning, Pollution and Waste Management (1992), p 29).

The law and Scottish Office guidance suggest two scenarios.

(1) The development is acceptable in land use terms and planning permission can be granted, with concerns about emissions and other pollution left to the pollution control agency.

(2) Despite the potential grant of a pollution control consent or waste management licence, the development is unacceptable on land use grounds and planning permission is refused.

However, it seems likely that a third situation will frequently arise, where the planning authority are satisfied that the development is broadly acceptable in land use terms, but residual fears regarding pollution remain, and the authority are unwilling to accept assurances from SEPA that any potential for pollution can be controlled.

5.5 TIMING OF APPLICATIONS

Where a project requires several different statutory consents, it is always necessary for the developer to consider the order in which consents should be sought.

There is a prohibition on the grant of a waste management licence until planning permission has been obtained (EPA, section 36(2)), but this would not prevent applications for both consents being submitted simultaneously.

NPPG 10 suggests that applications for planning and pollution control consents should be submitted in parallel, to avoid delay and to enable conditions to be taken into account in each decision. This presumably envisages that each authority would be aware of the full details of the project and share concerns with the other authorities. The details of the project could be adjusted to resolve planning and pollution control concerns, and the consents could be granted. The difficulty is that changes in the project to satisfy one agency might be unacceptable to the other. For example, SEPA might require the height of an incinerator chimney to be increased, but the resultant visual impact may be unacceptable to the planning authority.

A practical answer might be to submit an application for planning permission while discussing details of the project with SEPA. The planning authority will consult SEPA, and can grant permission if they indicate that a pollution control consent would be likely to be granted for the project. Any subsequent changes to the project made following discussions might require changes to the planning consent. However, this will probably be preferable to undertaking the work required to submit parallel applications, thereby incurring considerable expense, without any guarantee that a planning permission will be granted.

Chapter 6

CONTAMINATED LAND

6.1 INTRODUCTION

In this chapter we consider the law relating to contaminated land, with particular reference to the 'contaminated land' powers contained in Part IIA of EPA. However, it must be appreciated at the outset that these new powers are not by any means all that the law has to say on the topic of contaminated land. They are intended to be available for use in respect of the worst cases of land contamination and the definition of 'contaminated land' in Part IIA, as refined by the guidance, is appropriately restricted. It follows from this that other statutory provisions and common law principles will still be relevant in respect of contaminated land in a broader sense than the statutory definition for the purposes of Part IIA of EPA.

It should also be noted that the new powers contained in Part IIA of EPA are only available where land is not suitable for its current use. Therefore, the issue of land contamination where a change of use is proposed is not dealt with in Part IIA. Instead, it will be addressed as part of the planning process (see Chapter 5).

Although there is a definition of 'contaminated land' for the purposes of the Part IIA provisions, there is no generally accepted definition of contaminated land in the broader sense. It can probably be said, however, that contaminated land is land which has been affected by noxious or polluting matter to a material extent. Depending on the nature of the noxious or polluting matter, the mere fact of its existence may be sufficient to found liability in respect of certain statutory provisions. However, generally speaking, to give rise to legal liability, the land must not only be affected by noxious or polluting matter, but there must also be actual, or threatened, harm or interference with property, health or the environment generally. We expand upon the relevant statutory and common law provisions at paragraph 6.3.

It should also be noted that the issue of contaminated land is usually most relevant in respect of historic contamination and particularly relevant to derelict and vacant sites. Where land contamination occurs during the course of ongoing activities, the process of identifying the polluter and making him pay is generally straightforward. For example, if the operator of an industrial site spills contaminants at that site which subsequently enter into a river, then the offence of polluting controlled waters will have been committed in terms of Part II of COPA. If, in addition, fish in that river are killed by virtue of the entry of contaminants, the owners of the fishing rights may have a claim in respect of negligence or nuisance against the operator under common law. There may also be liability in respect of breaches of any necessary consents required to operate the facility. Not all cases are as straightforward, of course, in that it is sometimes difficult to prove that the damage complained of was caused by the contamination, particularly in circumstances where it migrates over a distance.

In the case of historically contaminated land, however, the problems are very much magnified. The polluter may no longer be identifiable. There may be many causes of the contamination, attributable to many previous polluters. There is then the risk of a conflict between the 'polluter pays principle' and the principle that those affected or harmed by land contamination should be able to seek legal redress. It is for this reason that owners and occupiers of contaminated land may become liable, even though they did not cause the contamination in the first place. Their 'wrong' is to allow the consequences of the contamination to continue such that harm to property, persons and, in some cases, the environment, is caused.

Inevitably, the result is a compromise. There is no legal principle which states that contaminated land, in itself, must be remediated. The reason is obvious. If that were so, the costs of decontamination would be enormous and there is no possibility of the economy bearing these all at once. On the other hand, it is now appreciated more fully that land contamination (and particularly historic land contamination) of a more serious nature must be addressed and that the general law must be able to respond by providing rights and remedies in respect of the problems which may arise.

6.2 HISTORY
6.2.1 EPA, section 143
The first steps to deal with the problem of contaminated land were taken by virtue of the enactment of section 143 of EPA. This section (which was never brought into force and is to be revoked) provided for the setting up of registers of land put to contaminative uses. These registers would simply have noted that particular land had been put at some time in the past, or presently, to a particular use taken from a list of uses identified as giving rise to a risk of land contamination. The original list of uses was lengthy and would have resulted in the designation of relatively large areas of land as potentially contaminated. The registers would not have indicated whether land was in fact contaminated, but merely that it had been put to a particular use. Additionally, there was no provision for the removal of land from the registers. This proposal was heavily criticised by industry and the property market and as a result, the government put forward a revised proposal containing a much reduced list of contaminative uses. However, the basic principle remained the same and there was a similar degree of criticism.

6.2.2 Decision to consult
In March 1993 the government announced that the issue of contaminated land would be subjected to a wide-ranging review and in March

1994 it issued two very similar Consultation Papers, one for England and Wales, Paying for Our Past: The Arrangements for Controlling Contaminated Land and Meeting the Cost of Remedying Damage to the Environment, and the other for Scotland, Contaminated Land Clean-Up and Control. These papers set out the existing legal régime which was available to deal with land contamination and drew the tentative conclusion that, if properly used and implemented, the existing law was capable of dealing with most cases of land contamination. The authors of the Consultation Papers were clearly aware of the danger which would result from the application of any principle that contaminated land generally required to be remediated, partly because of the obvious cost implications, but partly also because of the difficulty in deciding to what standard contaminated land should be remediated where that land was not presently being put to any use and where no future use was yet proposed. It was also noted in the papers that in certain circumstances the owners and/or occupiers of contaminated land might be made liable in respect of that contamination. This was not considered inappropriate, given the much greater awareness of environmental issues in the present day.

6.2.3 Outcome of the consultation exercise
In November 1994 the government published the outcome of the contaminated land consultation exercise again by means of separate, though very similar, papers for England and Wales, Framework for Contaminated Land, and Scotland, Contaminated Land Clean-Up and Control: Outcome of Review. It adhered to the general statement contained in the Consultation Papers that the present mix of statutory and common law powers was generally sufficient to deal with the issue of land contamination and did not require any major overhaul. Three major points did, however, emerge from the outcome of the consultation exercise:

(1) remediation should be procured by the operation of the market and in accordance with the 'suitable for use' principle;

(2) serious land contamination problems should be dealt with in an orderly manner, such that the economy can cope;

(3) a special power is required for sites which pose an immediate and serious threat, ie, sites which are not suitable for their current use.

The first of these points is in many ways the most important. The government does not intend to interfere with market principles in order to achieve more remediation of contaminated land than the market itself considers can be effected. The 'suitable for use' principle, which is a vital part of the new 'contaminated land' powers, is the principle that the remediation of contaminated land should be carried out in a cost-effective manner and to a standard which makes that land suitable for its proposed future use and not for any use whatsoever. Where a future use is proposed, it will fall within the ambit of planning legislation and associated guidance and any necessary remediation should be achieved within that framework and not within Part IIA of EPA (see, generally,

Chapter 5). Part IIA of EPA is only relevant where land is not suitable even for its current use.

By way of comparison, remediation to a 'suitable for any use', or multifunctional, standard has been tried in other jurisdictions, but is perceived to have two major drawbacks. The first is that it can be seen as a waste of resources to remediate land which is to be used for, say, retail development to the standard required for residential development. The second is that there is no such thing as an objectively ascertainable 'perfect' standard of remediation – standards evolve, usually by way of improvement, such that remediation to present-day standards might well be considered unsuitable in the future. This problem has already emerged in respect of land remediation projects carried out in the 1970s and 1980s.

The special power in respect of sites which pose an immediate and serious threat is now contained within the contaminated land provisions of Part IIA of EPA, as discussed at paragraph 6.4.

6.3 LEGAL LIABILITIES (EXCLUDING PART IIA OF EPA)
6.3.1 Introduction
In this section we consider the legal liabilities which may arise in respect of contaminated land other than in terms of the powers contained in Part IIA of EPA. These fall into the two principal categories of criminal and civil liability. Civil liability may usefully be subdivided into statutory civil liability, including clean-up powers, and civil liability arising under common law principles.

6.3.2 Criminal liability
Criminal liability in respect of contaminated land can arise not only where there are ongoing activities (which may, or may not, require a licence, authorisation, permit or consent) but also, and importantly, where no activities are being carried on at all.

The principal heads of criminal liability are as follows.

— Liability in respect of deposits of waste on land in circumstances where there is no waste management licence in force (see section 33 of EPA, discussed at paragraph 7.8.2). It is important to note that if there is a waste management licence in force in relation to the relevant land, then liability can also result from a breach of the provisions of that licence. Additionally, and equally importantly, any contamination which results from the carrying on of the activities licensed by the waste management licence or from a breach of the licence conditions is to be dealt with wholly within the scope of the waste management licensing régime set out in Part II of EPA, ie, the new contaminated land powers in Part IIA of EPA are not to be applied.

— Liability in respect of unconsented discharges to controlled waters (see section 30F of COPA, discussed at paragraph 8.4.6).

— Liability in respect of carrying on a process subject to IPC or LAPC without authorisation, in terms of section 23 of EPA, discussed at paragraph 9.2.8.

6.3.3 Statutory civil liability and clean-up powers and relationship with Part IIA

The following provisions may be applicable in contaminated land situations.

— Liability for removal of unlawful deposits of waste in terms of section 59 of EPA, discussed at paragraph 7.9. Again, it is important to note that in circumstances where the section 59 powers are available for use, they must be used and a remediation notice in terms of the new contaminated land powers may not be served.

— Liability for clean-up or compliance with a works notice in respect of pollution of controlled waters (see section 46A of COPA, discussed at paragraph 8.4.3). There is no provision to the effect that if these powers are available for use they must be used to the exclusion of the new contaminated land powers (except in limited circumstances as set out in section 78J(2) of EPA, discussed in the penultimate paragraph of paragraph 6.4.3) which contrasts with the situation applicable in terms of the powers contained in section 59 of EPA. It is not wholly clear how this matter is to be resolved in practice.

— Clean-up powers in respect of breach of the IPC or APC provisions of Part I of EPA (see section 27 of EPA, discussed at paragraph 9.2.8). In this case, if contamination is caused by such a breach, the service of a remediation notice in terms of the new contaminated land powers is again precluded.

— Statutory nuisance in terms of Part III of EPA as discussed at Chapter 10. We mention statutory nuisance in this context to point out that section 79(1A) and (1B) of EPA (not yet in force) specifically state that nothing shall constitute a statutory nuisance to the extent that it consists of, or is caused by, any land being in a contaminated state. The phrase 'contaminated state' is defined more broadly than 'contaminated land' in terms of the new contaminated land powers. Land is in a 'contaminated state' if, by reason of substances in, on or under the land, it is in such a condition that (a) harm is being caused or there is a possibility of harm being caused or (b) pollution of controlled waters is being, or is likely to be caused. It follows from this that not only are the statutory nuisance powers not available in situations which fall within the definition of 'contaminated land' for the purposes of the Part IIA provisions, but that they are also unavailable for use where land is simply in a 'contaminated state'. The use of the statutory nuisance provisions in contaminated land situations is therefore precluded.

— Although not strictly a matter of statutory civil liability, it should be noted that the new contaminated land powers are not available for use to the extent that the contamination in question is attributable to any radioactivity possessed by any substance (EPA, section

78YC); however, this is specifically stated in EPA to be subject to review.

6.3.4 Civil liability under common law
The two main common law principles which may be applicable in cases of contaminated land are as follows.

— The law of nuisance, discussed at paragraph 2.2. In cases of nuisance, liability depends upon proving (a) that the harm suffered was 'more than tolerable'; (b) fault; and (c) that the harm was reasonably foreseeable.

— The law of delict, discussed at paragraph 2.3. Liability here depends upon proving a duty of care, breach of that duty of care and that there is resultant harm that is reasonably foreseeable. Its use in the context of historically contaminated land is far from straightforward. It may be difficult to establish by whom any duty of care is owed, whether there has been a breach of that duty of care and, in particular, it may be difficult to demonstrate the necessary casual link between that breach and the damage alleged to be suffered.

6.4 Contaminated land provisions of Part IIA of EPA
6.4.1 Introduction
The policy background to the new contaminated land powers is outlined in paragraph 6.2. It is vital that these powers be understood against that policy background and in particular against the background of the 'suitable for use' principle. The powers are loosely based upon the régime applicable to statutory nuisances, but are much more complex. The statutory provisions are only part of the equation. In many ways, they are a framework. Much of the detail, and particularly the relationship with the 'suitable for use' principle, is to be found in government guidance on the exercise of the powers. At paragraph 6.4 we give an overview of the content of the statutory provisions and comment on the liability structure, and at paragraph 6.5 we examine the terms of government guidance and regulations available at the time of going to press.

The new powers are not yet in force, and the relevant guidance and statutory instruments have not yet been issued or made. The guidance and the statutory instruments (discussed below in draft form) may therefore change and the text must be read in this light. It is thought unlikely that Part IIA will be commenced before the end of 1997.

It needs to be remembered that the contaminated land powers are intended to be used in respect of sites which pose an immediate and serious threat and are not intended to be available for what may be described as 'ordinary' contaminated land situations. For a brief overview of the relevant interfaces between the contaminated land powers and other statutory powers, see paragraph 6.3.

6.4.2 Summary of the statutory provisions
The following is a summary of sections 78A–78YC of EPA. Where guidance or regulations (by way of statutory instrument) are relevant, the paragraph of the text in which they are mentioned is marked with '**G**' or

'**R**' as appropriate. The provisions which constitute the essential framework are marked with '**E**'. See also Appendix 2, which attempts to summarise the essential framework in the form of a flow chart.

— '[C]ontaminated land' means land which 'appears to the local authority [ie, the Council] in whose area it is situated to be in such a condition, by reason of substances in, on or under the land, that significant harm is being caused or there is a significant possibility of such harm being caused; or pollution of controlled waters is being, or is likely to be, caused' (section 78A(2)).

— The questions of what harm is to be regarded as 'significant', whether the possibility of significant harm being caused is 'significant' and whether pollution of controlled waters is being, or is likely to be, caused are to be determined in accordance with guidance issued by the Secretary of State (section 78A(5)) **(G)**.

— In determining whether any land appears to it to be contaminated land, the local authority must also act in accordance with guidance with respect to the manner in which that determination is to be made (section 78A(2))**(G)**.

— '[H]arm' is defined as 'harm to the health of living organisms or other interference with the ecological systems of which they form part and, in the case of man, includes harm to his property' (section 78A(4)).

— A duty (not a power or a discretion) is imposed on local authorities to inspect their areas in order to identify contaminated land and also to identify whether any such land identified is required to be designated as a 'special site' (section 78B(1)) **(E)**.

— In performing their duty to inspect, a local authority shall act in accordance with guidance issued for the purpose (section 78B(2))**(G)**.

— Broadly, a 'special site' is a site where the contamination is serious in the sense that 'serious harm' or 'serious pollution of controlled waters' would or might be caused by it rather than just 'harm' or 'pollution' – however, the Secretary of State has prescribed descriptions of land which require to be designated as special sites (section 78C(10) and (8))**(R)**.

— The significance of special sites is that although it is for the relevant local authority to identify them, it will be for SEPA to act as 'enforcing authority', once they have been designated (section 78A(9)).

— Once contaminated land, including a special site, has been identified, it must be designated as such. Notice of designation of contaminated land, including special sites, must be given by the local authority to (1) SEPA, (2) the owner of the land, (3) any occupier of the land, and (4) each person who appears to the authority to be 'an appropriate person' (sections 78B(3) and 78C(1), (2)). After designation, there must (except in cases of emergency) be a consultation period of three months before any further action is taken (section 78H(3)) (**E**).

— The purpose of the three-month period is, in effect, to permit relevant parties to discuss what remediation is required (section 78H(1)). If voluntary remediation is commenced, and continues, then the authority must postpone the service of a 'remediation notice' (section 78H(5)(b)).

— The next step in the procedure is the service of a 'remediation notice' by the enforcing authority, that is, either the local authority, or SEPA in the case of special sites. There is a duty (not a power or a discretion) to serve such a notice, subject to the three-month consultation period and to the provisions of section 78H(1), (5) (**E**).

— In serving a remediation notice an enforcing authority may only require to be done those things which they consider reasonable, having regard to (a) cost, and (b) the seriousness of the harm, or the pollution of controlled waters, in question (section 78E(4)).

— Additionally, in determining what is to be done by way of remediation, the standard of remediation, and what is reasonable for the purposes of section 78E(4), the enforcing authority shall have regard to guidance issued for the purpose (section 78E(5))(**G**).

— A 'remediation notice' is a notice specifying what is required to be done by way of remediation and the periods within which it is required to be done (section 78E(1)) (**E**).

— A remediation notice may be served only on an 'appropriate person' and that term is defined as 'any person, or any of the persons, who caused or knowingly permitted the substances, or any of the substances, by reason of which the contaminated land in question is such land, to be in, on or under that land' or, if (a) no such person has been found or (b) more specifically, if no such person has been found in relation to whom the things to be done by way of remediation are 'referable' to substances which that person caused or knowingly permitted to be present in, or under the contaminated land in question, then on 'the owner or occupier for the time being of the contaminated land in question' (section 78F(2)–(5)) (**E**).

— The definition of 'appropriate person' is such that more than one person may fall within the definition. In such cases, the enforcing authority must determine, in accordance with guidance issued for the purpose, whether any, and if so which, appropriate person is to be treated as not being an appropriate person (section 78F(6)) (**G**).

— Further, where there are two or more appropriate persons, they shall be liable to bear the cost of compliance with a remediation notice in proportions determined in accordance with guidance issued for the purpose (section 78F(7)) (**G**).

— There are special provisions in respect of liability for contaminating substances which escape from land to other land. Put broadly, if a person has caused or knowingly permitted substances to be in, on or under land, that person is also taken to have caused or knowingly permitted them to be on other land to which they appear to the enforcing authority to have escaped and thus to be an appropriate person in respect of that other land. Additionally, if a person purchases (ie, becomes the owner) or becomes the occupier of contaminated land, that person is not to be made liable for the previous escape of contamination to other land except to the extent that he caused or knowingly permitted that escape – he will not be absolved of liability, however, for continuing or future escapes (section 78K(1), (5)).

— Any party upon whom a remediation notice is served must comply with it and if he does not, a criminal offence is committed with a maximum penalty on summary conviction, where the premises are industrial, trade or business premises, of a £20,000 fine, with provision for a further daily fine of one-tenth of that amount thereafter, and where the premises are not industrial, trade or business premises, of £5,000 with similar provision for a further daily fine (section 78M(3), (4)) (E).

— In specified circumstances (for example, failure of an appropriate person to comply with a remediation notice or to carry out voluntary remediation in terms of a written agreement with the enforcing authority to that effect) the enforcing authority (whether a local authority or SEPA) are entitled to carry out the necessary remediation works themselves (section 78N(1)).

— In circumstances where the enforcing authority carry out the necessary remediation works themsevles, they are entitled to recover the costs of so doing from the relevant appropriate persons, with an obligation to have regard to (a) hardship which such recovery may cause, and (b) guidance issued on cost recovery by the Secretary of State (section 78P(2)) (G).

— In England, but not in Scotland (for no ascertainable good reason), there is provision for the service of a charging notice over the land itself to secure the recovery of costs from the owner of the land but only where the owner caused or knowingly permitted the contamination (section 78P(3)–(13)).

— Provision is made for appeals against the service (within twenty-one days of service) of remediation notices (to the sheriff court if served by a local authority and to the Secretary of State if served by SEPA (special sites)) and for the grounds of appeal to be set out in regulations (section 78L(1), (4)) (R) (E).

— Registers are to be kept by local authorities and SEPA of, *inter alia*, remediation notices, special site designation notices, notifications given to the authority or SEPA of what is claimed to have been done by way of remediation and other particulars to be prescribed in regulations (section 78R(1)). These registers do not include designation notices in respect of contaminated land which is not a special site. These should, however, be available in terms of the Environmental Information Regulations 1992 (public access to environmental information) **(R)** **(E)**.

One of the most significant features of the new régime is that local authorities are put under a duty to inspect their areas and that once land has been designated as contaminated land and the three-month consultation period has expired and the provisions of section 78H have been satisfied, enforcing authorities are under a duty to serve a remediation notice. These matters are not, therefore, within the discretion of local or enforcing authorities – for a case in point in connection with similar duties under the statutory nuisance régime, see *R* v *Carrick District Council,* ex parte *Shelley* [1996] Env LR 273.

6.4.3 The liability structure
The basic structure is that liability to comply with a remediation notice will be imposed upon

— the causer or knowing permitter of the contamination;

— if that person or persons cannot be 'found', or cannot have 'referred' to them the things to be done by way of remediation, the owner or occupier for the time being of the contaminated land in question.

Looking at each of the relevant concepts and categories in turn:

— The question of who 'causes' contamination is likely to take as its starting-point a whole series of cases on causation in the environmental law context, primarily dealing with water pollution offences. It is clear that the concept of 'cause' is to be given an ordinary and commonsense meaning, to be arrived at by looking at the facts of the case. Causation does not entail knowledge or fault – it will be sufficient that one has acted or set actions in motion so as to bring about a result, namely contamination. This is clear from House of Lords authority in *Alphacell* v *Woodward* [1972] AC 824 and *National Rivers Authority* v *Yorkshire Water Services Ltd* [1995] 1 All ER 225 and from Scottish authority in the case of *Lockhart* v *National Coal Board* 1981 SLT 161. See also the further discussion at paragraph 8.4.6 (but in the context of water pollution, which is a different régime).

— The concept of 'knowingly permitting' is more difficult to pin down. There may be a role for constructive knowledge, in that a complete failure to inquire as to the state of particular land where there is likely to be a contamination problem could be regarded by the courts as amounting to 'knowingly permitting'. What seems clear, however, is that if a person does become aware of a contamination problem on land, and does nothing about it, that person will be a 'knowing permitter'. Scottish authority for this proposition can be found in the realm of statutory nuisance (see *Clydebank District Council* v *Monaville Estates* 1982 SLT (Sh Ct) 2). See also the cases on 'knowingly permitting' referred to, albeit in the context of a different regulatory régime (water pollution) at paragraph 8.4.6. Two things follow from this: first, a polluter may be a knowing permitter, indeed he is likely to be such, and secondly and very importantly, an owner or indeed an occupier may also be a knowing permitter.

— An 'appropriate person' must be 'found' before he can be made liable and, similarly, an owner or occupier is liable if that person has not 'been found'. The guidance suggests that for a person to be 'found' (in the context of being made liable), that person must be alive or in existence, so that if, for example, the causer or knowing permitter is identified but is dead, or in the case of a company, liquidated or dissolved, no person has in fact been found, thus leading to owner or occupier liability. It is by no means clear that this suggestion is correct in dictionary definition terms and the use of the word 'found' has been the subject of considerable criticism.

— The referability of the things to be done by way of remediation to substances which a person caused or knowingly permitted to be present in, on or under the contaminated land in question is important (see section 78F(3)). If a remediation notice requires the removal of substance A, it cannot be served on a person who caused or knowingly permitted substance B to be present. In effect, if no person can be found who caused or knowingly permitted substance A to be present, then owner or occupier liability results. Likewise an 'appropriate person' can only be made liable for remediation in respect of those substances which he caused or knowingly permitted to be present, and not in respect of other substances. Joint and several liability can only therefore occur where there are (a) two or more 'appropriate persons' who are (b) linked to (or 'referable' to) the presence of particular substances in, on or under the land.

— The legislation defines 'owner' as a person for the time being entitled to receive or who would, if the land were let, be entitled to receive, the rents of the land in connection with which the word (ie, 'owner') is used and states that this includes a trustee, factor, guardian or curator, but does not include a creditor in a heritable security not in possession of the security subjects (section 78A(9)). Clearly, this includes a landlord, as well as an 'outright' owner.

— There is therefore limited protection for lenders who have securities over land or an interest in land (eg, a standard security/mortgage) but only for so long as they are not in possession of the subjects of their security. Lenders will need to be careful before taking a decision to call up or otherwise enforce securities, because once they do so, they are capable of being caught by the definition of 'owner' if, for example, they are deemed to have entered into possession because the borrower has abandoned the security subjects and delivered the keys to the lender. Lenders may also be 'causers' or 'knowing permitters' but not, it is thought, if they exercise merely the normal banking degree of oversight of their customers' affairs.

— There is no protection for trustees, factors, guardians or curators who will therefore have to consider their position very carefully in relation to the estate under their management.

— The term 'occupier' is not defined in the legislation, but clearly includes a tenant under a lease, or a licensee under a licence to occupy. What is relevant is the degree of control exercised over the land. It has been held in Scotland that receivers can be 'occupiers' in *Lord Advocate* v *Aero Technologies Ltd (In receivership)* 1991 SLT 134, which concerned the Explosives Act 1875. However, see below for specific protection afforded to insolvency practitioners generally.

— There is limited protection for owners and occupiers (but only in circumstances where they are not also causers or knowing permitters) in relation to land which is contaminated land by virtue of pollution of controlled waters being, or being likely to be, caused (but not in relation to the 'significant harm' limb of the definition of 'contaminated land'). In these circumstances, an owner or occupier may not be served with a remediation notice (section 78J(2)). The purpose of this provision is to avoid imposing additional liability in the circumstances of water pollution on owners or occupiers beyond that which they may have in terms of section 46 or 46A of COPA (clean-up of water pollution and 'works notices' in relation to water pollution). In other words, liability will not attach in terms of Part IIA of EPA in addition to the liability which may attach under these provisions of COPA.

— There is protection for persons acting as insolvency practitioners (administrators, receivers, liquidators, trustees in sequestration, etc) in that they are not to be made personally liable to bear any part of the cost of carrying out remediation works unless the contamination in question is a result of any act or omission made by the insolvency practitioner 'which it was unreasonable for a person acting in that capacity to do or make'. There is similar relief from prosecution (section 78X(3), (4)).

6.5 DRAFT GUIDANCE AND DRAFT REGULATIONS IN RELATION TO PART IIA OF EPA

6.5.1 Introduction

As already discussed, much of the detail of the contaminated land provisions is to be found in guidance issued by the government. In effect, the guidance sets out how the powers are to be used, covering almost every stage of the process from identification of contaminated land to cost recovery from 'appropriate persons'. In many cases, the guidance is not guidance to which local authorities and SEPA must 'have regard', but rather guidance 'in accordance with which' they must act. This leaves little leeway for the exercise of discretion save, probably, in the limited circumstance where compliance with the guidance would produce an absurd result. The aim is to ensure consistency of approach by the use of 'statutory' guidance, which in fact requires to be laid before Parliament before it can take effect.

At paragraph 6.4.3 we indicated individual areas in respect of which guidance is issued by use of the letter 'G', and at paragraphs 6.5.2–6.5.6 we consider that guidance in overview. The guidance considered is the draft guidance issued by the government in September 1996.

We also indicated at paragraph 6.4.3 areas in respect of which regulations (by statutory instrument) are to be made by use of the letter 'R' and at paragraphs 6.5.7–6.5.11 we consider these Regulations in overview. The regulations considered are the draft regulations issued by the government in November 1996. It is possible that these may be made as one compendious set, rather than separately.

In understanding the guidance, the importance of the 'suitable for use' approach cannot be overemphasised. The definition of contaminated land and the guidance are stated by the government to be consistent with this approach and are to be taken as relating only to the current use of the land, which means that consideration of the impact of contamination on future or proposed uses must not be taken into account in deciding whether or not particular land requires to be remediated in accordance with the new provisions.

6.5.2 What is contaminated land? (statutory guidance)

In assessing whether or not land is contaminated, local authorities must adopt a scientific approach, based on identification and risk assessment. They are to have regard to the standard environmental audit terminology of source, receptor and pathway. The source is the potential pollutant – for example, the presence on land of a substance with potential to cause harm. The receptor is the presence of some thing which could be harmed by the source. The pathway is the means whereby the receptor could be exposed to the source. Any land which is to be designated as contaminated must have a source/receptor/pathway relationship, which the guidance refers to as a 'pollutant linkage'. It is vital to be aware that there may be more than one pollutant linkage in respect of particular contaminated land. From this it also follows that different persons may be 'appropriate persons' in respect of separate pollution linkages.

The definition of 'contaminated land' is contained in section 78(A)(2) and is set out in full at paragraph 6.4.2, as is the definition of 'harm' contained in section 78A(4).

Before land may be designated as contaminated under the new provisions (a) harm must be 'significant' or (b) where significant harm is not actually being caused, there must be a 'significant' possibility of significant harm being caused or (c) pollution of controlled waters must be being caused or (d) pollution of controlled waters must be likely to be caused.

Harm is to be regarded as significant in the following circumstances and only the following circumstances:

(1) in humans, death, serious injury, cancer or other disease, genetic mutation, birth defects, or the impairment of reproductive functions;

(2) irreversible or other substantial adverse change in the functioning of

a habitat notified, declared or designated under the Wildlife and Countryside Act 1981;

(3) structural failure or substantial damage to buildings, substantial damage to be regarded as occurring when any part of the building ceases to be capable of being used for the purpose for which it is or was intended;

(4) death, disease or other physical damage to livestock (including wild animals which are the subject of shooting or fishing rights) or crops kept, reared or grown on the land in question or other land such that there is a 'substantial loss' in their value, ie, a substantial proportion (with a benchmark of 10 per cent) of the livestock or crops is no longer fit for the purpose for which they are intended.

This list is tightly drawn and is clearly intended to catch only the worst, or most ecologically damaging, contamination.

Consideration of whether the possibility of 'significant harm' being caused is 'significant' must have regard to the same test of 'significant harm' but will require an added degree of risk assessment, again scientifically based. In general terms, however, the more severe the harm, the greater its degree, the shorter the time scale for it to occur, or the greater the vulnerability of the receptor, the more likely it is that the possibility of significant harm being caused will be significant.

Various combinations of each of these factors will need to be considered by local authorities. For example, the possibility, albeit perhaps slight, that an explosion could take place, causing serious injury to humans, would probably be regarded as a significant possibility, not so much because of the probability of its occurring, assuming that to be low, but rather because, if it did occur, the number of receptors affected would be high.

Land is also contaminated in circumstances where 'pollution of controlled waters is being, or is likely to be, caused'. In those cases, there is no need to consider the significant harm or significant possibility of significant harm tests. Instead, local authorities are to have regard to the same test as would be applied by the relevant water pollution authority (SEPA) when it is acting under the legislation which is relevant to the pollution of controlled waters, ie, COPA. This is intended to avoid a different approach being adopted by local authorities as to what constitutes pollution of controlled waters from that which is adopted by SEPA.

Pollution of controlled waters by substances emanating from contaminated land is a potentially serious problem and one which occurs not infrequently. The tests which require to be applied in order to reach a decision as to whether pollution of controlled waters is being, or is likely to be, caused, may result in more land being designated as contaminated land under these heads than under the more difficult and complex heads of 'significant harm' or 'significant possibility of significant harm'. To give one example, if leachate is reaching controlled waters from land, and is having a serious effect on water quality, that would suggest that the land is 'contaminated land' within the terms of Part IIA of EPA. 'Controlled waters' does not just mean rivers, lochs and ponds, but also includes groundwater, the pollution of which is a problem in parts of Scotland.

6.5.3 Inspection of their area by a local authority (statutory guidance)

A duty is imposed upon local authorities in section 78B(1) to cause their areas to be inspected from time to time for the purpose of identifying contaminated land and of enabling the authority to decide whether any contaminated land requires to be designated as a special site. The guidance makes the following points in connection with this duty:

— the overall aim should be to adopt an approach which will be proportionate to the seriousness of any actual or potential threat;

— a 'rational and ordered' approach is to be taken to the identification of contaminated land;

— local authorities are to prepare, adopt, publish and implement a 'formal written strategy' for the inspection of their areas. That strategy is to set out arrangements and procedures for consideration of the possibility of land being contaminated, the response to information or complaints from members of the public, businesses and voluntary organisations, and the response to information from other statutory bodies, including SEPA;

— the strategy is to be published within fifteen months of the issue of the guidance;

— the local authority are to send a copy of their strategy document to SEPA;

— the strategy must contain appropriate time scales for the inspection of different parts of their area in order to ensure that pressing and serious problems are located soonest;

— the strategy must incorporate procedures for the consideration of new information and for the review of assumptions made and information previously used;

— in developing their strategy, a local authority must reflect local circumstances including, in particular:

— available evidence that significant harm or pollution of controlled waters is being caused;

— the extent to which information on land contamination is already available;

— the history, scale and nature of industrial or other activities which may have caused contamination in different parts of the local authority's area;

— the extent to which remedial action has already been taken by the relevant authority or others to deal with land contamination;

— the extent to which other regulatory authorities are likely to be considering the possibility of harm being caused or the likelihood of any pollution of controlled waters being caused in particular parts of the relevant authority's area.

These provisions require a far more wide-ranging exercise to be carried out than was envisaged by the government in the EPA proposals for registers of land put to contaminative uses. In those circumstances all that was necessary was to identify from historical records and other information whether or not land had, at some stage in the past, been put to a particular use from within the list of uses provided for the purpose. In the circumstances of 'contaminated land', not only will it be necessary to ask those questions, and to answer them, but also (a) to consider in each particular case, whether there is an appropriate source, receptor, pathway relationship, and (b) whether, if there is, significant harm is being caused, or there is a significant possibility of significant harm being caused, or pollution of controlled waters is being, or is likely to be, caused. All this must be done within the framework of a written strategy. Local authorities are therefore required to take a proactive role which is essentially the same as that which would be undertaken by an environmental consultant asked to investigate a site for the purposes of, for example, a sale transaction.

Section 108 of EA (discussed at paragraph 1.5) confers wide powers of entry to premises, for inspection and sampling, on various pollution control authorities for the purposes of exercising or performing their functions under specified legislation including Part IIA of EPA.

The guidance states that before a local authority decide to exercise their powers to inspect particular land, they should be satisfied as to the likelihood of a particular pollutant linkage being present on that land. The objectives of exercising the rights of inspection should be to obtain sufficient information to

— determine that the land in question appears to be contaminated land; or

— be reasonably satisfied that the land in question is not contaminated land.

At least seven days' notice of the proposed entry to premises must be given (except in cases of emergency) to the person who appears to the local authority to be in occupation of the relevant premises. The guidance contains special provisions for involving SEPA (and in the case of a nuclear licensed site, the NII) in the carrying out of the inspection of the land in circumstances where, if it were to be identified as contaminated land, it would require to be designated as a special site.

After an inspection (if thought necessary) has been carried out, the local authority must consider whether or not the relevant land should be designated as 'contaminated land'. In carrying out that exercise, they must act in accordance with the statutory guidance discussed at paragraph 6.5.2. They should prepare a written record of the determination, which should include a summary of the evidence upon which it is based and of the scientific assessment of that evidence. The particular pollutant linkage or linkages providing the basis for the determination must be specified with reference to the three relevant elements, ie, source, pathway and receptor. The local authority may only determine that land is 'contaminated land' on the basis of the four grounds contained in the definition of that term. Broadly speaking, the authority should aim to be satisfied, on the balance of probabilities and in light of all the relevant evidence and an appropriate scientific assessment, that the relevant ground of the definition is satisfied. However, in circumstances where they are considering whether or not there is a 'significant possibility' of significant harm being caused, they must carry out their risk assessment according to appropriate authoritative and scientifically based guidance on such risk assessments provided they are satisfied that such guidance is relevant to the circumstances in question.

It is very clear that any determination that land is 'contaminated land' must be carefully, clearly, logically and scientifically made in order to fall within the terms of the guidance. It is a ground of appeal against any subsequently served remediation notice that contaminated land has not been designated in accordance with the statutory guidance issued for that purpose.

6.5.4 Remediation (non-statutory guidance)

This guidance concerns (a) what the enforcing authority (SEPA or the local authority) may do or require to be done by way of remediation of contaminated land, (b) to what standard, and (c) what is to be regarded as reasonable in the context of an enforcing authority only being able to require to be done by way of remediation that which they consider reasonable having regard to (i) cost, and (ii) the seriousness of the harm, or the pollution of controlled waters, in question.

In the context of this guidance, it is important to note that remediation, as defined for the purposes of Part IIA of EPA, includes

— assessment of contaminated land or waters affected by that land;

— the carrying out of works for the purposes of preventing or minimising or remedying or mitigating the effects of significant harm, or pollution of controlled waters, or their restoration to their former state; and

— post-works monitoring.

This definition is broader than the ordinary usage of the term, which covers only the second of the above points.

On the standard of remediation, the guidance points out that the objective is to secure (so far as possible) the result that the land is 'suitable for use' in the context of its present use, which is the same thing as saying that it will no longer be contaminated land within the definition of that term. In achieving this, the 'best practicable technique' should be used. In considering what represents the 'best practicable technique' for remediation, the enforcing authority must consider:

— what is reasonable (on which see further below);

— what is effective in achieving the aim of remediation;

— what is 'durable' in maintaining that effectiveness;

— what is practicable;

— what is efficient in achieving the above results with the minimum resources.

In assessing what is reasonable in terms of remediation, the enforcing authority must carry out a cost-benefit analysis, ie, a remediation action will be regarded as being reasonable to the extent that an assessment of the costs likely to be involved and the resulting benefits demonstrate that the benefits are worth incurring the costs. At this point in the process, the identity or financial standing of any person who may be required to pay for a remediation action is not a relevant factor in determining whether the costs are reasonable. It only becomes a relevant factor in deciding whether or not the enforcing authority can require that person to meet all or part of the costs, on the guidance in relation to which see further paragraph 6.5.6. Additionally, all real costs which might be incurred should be taken into account, whether or not they are actually going to be incurred. By this it is meant that the carrying out of the cost-benefit analysis is not to be affected by the nature of the person who may be liable to carry out the relevant remediation works or by resources available to that person, such as the ability to carry out such works by use of its own personnel or equipment. On the other hand, it appears that enforcing authorities must ignore costs which may be regarded as purely environmental, such as any residual harm or pollution of controlled waters which may be caused by the continued presence of any substances once remediation has been carried out.

It is a necessary condition of an action being reasonable that there is no alternative action which would achieve the same purpose to the same standard for a lower cost.

What is reasonable must have regard not only to cost, as discussed above, but also to the seriousness of the harm, or the pollution of controlled waters, in question. That process will involve a further degree of risk assessment by reference, for example, to the nature and importance of the relevant receptor and whether the effects on that receptor or receptors would be irreversible.

On what is to be done by way of remediation, the enforcing authority must have regard to the overall aim of ensuring that the 'contaminated land' in question should become 'suitable for use', ie, should no longer be 'contaminated land' within the definition of that term. This is to be achieved by means of the 'best practicable technique'. The action to be taken must also be 'reasonable', as discussed above.

If a remediation notice is to be served, that notice must specify the remediation action which is required in order to achieve, within the limits of what is reasonable, the required standard. It is accepted that a remediation notice, where phased works are required, will not be able to specify every remediation action required. It appears that it will be sufficient to make it clear that what is specified in the remediation notice is specified on the basis of information available at the time of its preparation.

As mentioned above, 'remediation' for the purposes of Part IIA of EPA includes assessment, actual works and post-works monitoring. The guidance categorises these, respectively, as assessment action, remedial treatment action and monitoring action.

Assessment action should be carried out only where it is for the purpose of obtaining information on the condition of the relevant land or waters which is needed to obtain more detail about a particular significant pollution linkage or to enable technical specifications or design of remedial treatment action to be established or, in certain limited circumstances, after remediation has been carried out.

Remedial treatment action should be carried out only where it is necessary to achieve a standard of remediation described in the guidance.

Monitoring action should be carried out only where it is for the purpose of providing information on any changes which might occur in a source, pathway or receptor where that source, pathway or receptor was identified previously as part of a significant pollution linkage and where it is necessary to consider whether any further remedial treatment might be required as a consequence of any such change.

Three things may perhaps be drawn from this part of the guidance. The first is the importance of the cost-benefit analysis to be carried out. The second is that remediation may deal only with those matters which have resulted in the land being 'contaminated land' and not with other 'lesser' pollutants as well (unless this should be done on a purely voluntary basis). The third is that the aim of remediation is to do no more than to make the land suitable for its current use. Remediation of land in the context of future or proposed uses should be regulated by means of the planning process.

6.5.5 The exclusion from, and apportionment of, liability for the remediation of contaminated land (statutory guidance)

This section of the guidance deals with the issues which are raised by section 78F(6) and (7) of EPA. The first issue is guidance on circumstances in which, where there are two or more persons who are 'appropriate persons', any of them is to be treated as not being an appropriate person ('exclusion'). The second issue is guidance on how the costs of any remediation are to be apportioned where there are two or more appropriate persons ('apportionment').

Appropriate persons fall into two categories. The first category is those who 'caused or knowingly permitted' the circumstances to arise by virtue of which land is or became contaminated land. The second category is those who are 'owners or occupiers' of the relevant land. The second category of person is liable if no person can be found who falls within the first category. The enforcing authority must first identify who falls within these categories. This part of the guidance is crucial because around it will focus all arguments as to how many people should be liable to bear the costs of remediation and also the question of the proportions in which they will be so liable.

The aim of the liability exclusion part of the guidance is to reduce the population of appropriate persons, having regard to considerations not only of what is fair in all the circumstances but also to the undesirability of too large a population of appropriate persons. The more appropriate persons there are, the greater the risk of complex liability disputes arising such that the legislation will simply fail to achieve the desired aim of returning badly contaminated sites to suitability for their current use.

The guidance seeks to achieve this aim by being highly detailed and by being prescriptive in its terms. However, it is worth pointing out that the act of excluding somebody from liability is just as likely to give rise to challenge by those who are left within the population of appropriate persons.

Enforcing authorities will therefore need to be extremely careful in applying this part of the guidance in a transparent manner if they are to avoid their actions being challenged by aggrieved parties.

Before considering the guidance as it deals with exclusion and apportionment, it should be noted that where two or more persons are responsible for all or part of the costs of a remediation action, have agreed the basis on which they wish to share such costs, are not in dispute about such agreement and have notified the agreement to the enforcing authority, then the enforcing authority should determine exclusion and apportionment in such a manner as to give effect to the agreement, except in circumstances where the agreement would increase the share of costs to be borne by a person who would benefit from a limitation on recovery of remediation costs under the hardship provision or under the cost recovery guidance, in which case the enforcing authority are directed to disregard the agreement.

The guidance on which of two or more appropriate persons are to be treated as not being an appropriate person (ie, 'exclusion') works, in summary, in the following way.

6.5.5.1 An enforcing authority must have regard in relation to each piece of contaminated land, to the pollutant linkages which have been identified, ie, the source, receptor, pathway relationship. For each piece of contaminated land, there may be one of these, or there may be more than one. If a pollutant linkage results in land being identified as contaminated land, it is called a 'significant pollutant linkage'. For each significant pollutant linkage, the authority must identify the appropriate persons. Obviously it is possible that one group of people may be the appropriate persons for one pollutant linkage and another group may be the appropriate persons for another.

6.5.5.2 Clearly, if only one person is found who is the appropriate person for a particular pollutant linkage, then that person alone will be liable under the contaminated land provisions. It may also be the case that the appropriate person who is found may not be the causer or knowing permitter of the relevant pollutant linkage – for example, because the causer or knowing permitter cannot be found. In that case, the appropriate person will be the owner or occupier.

6.5.5.3 If, however, more than one appropriate person, being the causer or knowing permitter of each pollutant linkage (a 'Class A person') is found then a series of tests must be applied with a view to determining whether any of the appropriate persons selected (ie, causers or knowing permitters) can be excluded from the 'Class A liability group'. Financial circumstances are irrelevant to this process. The tests are as follows, and must be applied in the following order.

— *Excluded activities test.* This test is designed to exclude those who have been identified as having caused or knowingly permitted land to be contaminated land solely through having carried out certain actions. The fact that these actions are mentioned for the purposes of this test must not be taken to imply that these actions necessarily amount to 'causing or knowingly permitting', but rather that if they do, exclusion from liability will in any event be justified. All members of the relevant liability group are to be excluded if they are such members solely by reason of one or more of the following activities:

— providing financial assistance to another person by means of making a grant or loan, giving a guarantee, giving an indemnity, investing in a body corporate or providing any other financial benefit;

— withholding financial assistance as specified above;

— carrying out any action necessary for the purpose of underwriting an insurance policy, but not including any intrusive investigation where that investigation is itself the cause of the significant pollutant linkage;

— providing legal, financial, engineering, scientific or technical advice to another person in relation to an action or omission by reason of which that other person has been held to have caused or knowingly permitted the presence of the relevant pollutant, or for the purpose of assessing whether the land might be contaminated land or for the purpose of establishing what might be done to the land by way of remediation, but subject again to the intrusive investigation exception referred to above;

— entering into and performing a contract with another person where that other person knowingly took over responsibility for the proper disposal of the relevant pollutant and did so at a time before the relevant pollutant came to be on the land in question;

— creating a tenancy in favour of another person;

— granting a licence of land, but only if granted by the owner of the land, and not in circumstances where the person granting the licence operated the land as a site for waste disposal or storage at the time of the grant of the licence;

— issuing any statutory permission, licence or consent;

— carrying out an action or series of actions required of an employee, service provider or goods provider under the terms of an employment contract, a contract for services or a contract for the provision of goods (including subcontracts), but subject to certain specified exceptions among the more significant of which is the fact (much criticised) that directors, as opposed to other employees, are not protected.

These are significant exclusions. Without them, many people who ordinarily deal in or are involved, however tangentially, in relation to contaminated land might need to consider their position very carefully, as might their insurers.

— *Payments made for remediation test.* If an appropriate person has made a payment to another appropriate person (a) voluntarily or (b) in the course of a legal action or (c) as part of a contract for the transfer of ownership of the relevant land, in each case sufficient for the purpose of carrying out remediation on the land, and that remediation has not been carried out effectively, but if it had been, the land would not have been identified as being contaminated land, then the person who made the relevant payment will be excluded from the liability group.

— *Sold with information test.* Where a site has been sold on arm's length terms or let on a long lease (in excess of twenty years) by one appropriate person to another appropriate person and it can be demonstrated that the seller (or lessor) provided sufficient information which would reasonably allow the purchaser (or tenant) to be aware of the presence on the site of the relevant pollutant, then the seller (or lessor) is to be excluded from the liability group. Permission from the seller to the purchaser to carry out its own survey should normally be taken as a sufficient indication that the purchaser has the necessary information 'in transactions since 1990 between large commercial organisations' (a loose and much-criticised phrase). However, the seller must not have misinterpreted the implications of the relevant pollutant to the purchaser, nor may the seller have any further connection with the land after the sale. (This is an extremely important test as it means that those who sell or lease land may be wise to disclose any relevant or potentially relevant contamination problem in the hope – but not the certainty – that they may avoid liability in the future.)

— *Changes to substances test.* This test applies where a first substance is present on the land, but is affected by the presence of a second substance, which second substance is a necessary catalyst in bringing about the relevant chemical reaction or biological process which creates the significant pollutant linkage, in which case the members of the liability group other than those who were responsible for the entry of the second substance on to the land are to be excluded, *unless* such chemical reaction or biological process was reasonably foreseeable.

— *Escaped substances test.* This test applies where the relevant pollutant is solely present as the result of an escape from other land on to the affected land and where (a) one or more members of the liability group have caused or knowingly permitted that pollutant to be on that other land and (b) one or more members of the liability group caused or knowingly permitted the escape of that pollutant from that other land, and (c) that pollutant escaped solely because of the actions or omissions of those who caused or knowingly permitted its escape, in which case there are to be excluded all appropriate persons who were not actually responsible for the actual escape from the other land.

— *Introduction of pathways or receptors test.* Where an appropriate person has carried out a relevant action or made a relevant omission either as part of causing or of knowingly permitting the presence of the pollutant in a significant pollutant linkage and it appears that the pollutant linkage would not have been significant if the relevant action or omission had not been carried out or made (in effect because the action or omission introduces a new pathway or receptor), then all appropriate persons are to be excluded who did not carry out a relevant action or make a relevant omission. 'Relevant action' means (a) carrying out building or engineering works and/or (b) making a change in the use of the land for which a grant of planning permission is required. 'Relevant omission' means (i) failing in the course of a relevant action to take a step which would have ensured that a significant pollutant linkage was not brought into existence as a result of that action and/or (ii) unreasonably failing to maintain or operate a system installed for the purpose of reducing or managing risk associated with the presence of the pollutant in the relevant pollutant linkage.

6.5.5.4 It is important to be aware of the overriding requirements of the Class A liability group exclusion process. First, the exclusion process should be undertaken separately in respect of each significant pollution linkage. Secondly, the tests must be applied in their order. Thirdly, no test should be applied if its application would result in the exclusion of all the members of the liability group. Fourthly, groups of companies are in effect to be treated as the same person so that no test should be applied so as to exclude a company if another company is also a member of the liability group and at the same time is a member of the same group of companies as the first company.

6.5.5.5 Appropriate persons who are such by virtue of being 'owners or occupiers' of the contaminated land in question are referred to in the guidance as 'Class B persons'. Just as with Class A persons, it is possible that there may be more than one appropriate person and there is likewise a test which must be applied with a view to determining when any of the Class B appropriate persons can be excluded from the Class B liability group. The purpose of this test (and there is only one) is to exclude from liability those who do not have an interest in the capital value of the land in question. Therefore, the enforcing authority should exclude any owner or occupier who either occupies the land under a licence which has no marketable value or is liable to pay a rent equivalent to the full market rent for the land in question and who otherwise holds no land ownership interest in the land in question.

6.5.5.6 There is a general requirement on enforcing authorities to ensure that anyone who might benefit from either an exclusion from liability or an apportionment of liability is aware of the relevant guidance, in order to give them the opportunity to make appropriate representations. There is also a requirement on the enforcing authority to make reasonable endeavours to consult those who may be affected either by exclusion from liability or apportionment of liability. In doing this, they should not seek to obtain information beyond what it is reasonable to seek having regard, in particular, to the costs of obtaining such information. In deciding upon a particular exclusion or a particular apportionment, the authority should act on the basis of the balance of probabilities. It is made clear that the burden of providing an enforcing authority with further information which may be necessary to establish an exclusion or an apportionment should rest with the person who wishes to benefit.

If enforcing authorities are to avoid their actions being challenged (by way of appeal against a subsequent remediation notice), they must adhere to the consultation provisions in a fair and transparent manner. If they do so, it is helpful that the burden of providing the authority with any further information is shifted to the person wishing to benefit either from the exclusion or the apportionment. It will subsequently be difficult for a person who has simply failed to provide information to make a successful appeal.

It also needs to be remembered that those who may be affected by an exclusion or an apportionment will include those who remain liable as well as those who are relieved from liability. Above all, however, an enforcing authority must be able to justify their actions on the basis of the balance of probabilities, that is, upon the basis of a judgment that it is more likely than not that the circumstances permitting exclusion or apportionment exist or do not exist. The guidance does not appear to require that the enforcing authority issue a written determination to all those who may be affected by a decision to exclude from liability or to apportion costs (although there is a requirement to send a copy of a remediation notice to all those who were consulted prior to its service – see paragraph 6.5.9). Clearly, however, affected parties will need to be advised of the decision and it is likely to be desirable to make it clear what the grounds are for reaching that decision. In any event, enforcing authorities would be well advised to maintain clear internal records of how they have gone about the exclusion or apportionment process, so that all relevant information is to hand in the event of a subsequent appeal.

The guidance on how the costs of remediation to be carried out by the identified appropriate persons are to be apportioned between or among them (ie, 'apportionment') works, in summary, as below.

6.5.5.7 As previously noted, if two or more appropriate persons, whether they are causers or knowing permitters or owners or occupiers, agree between themselves the basis upon which they wish to bear the cost of remediation and they so advise the enforcing authority in writing, then the enforcing authority are to act upon that agreed basis unless the effect of the agreement is to increase the cost to be borne by a person who would benefit from a limitation on recovery of remediation costs under the hardship provision contained in section 78P(2)(a) or the guidance on cost recovery, in which case the agreement is to be disregarded.

6.5.5.8 Where the above is not the case, and in respect of appropriate persons who are members of a Class A liability group (ie, are causers or knowing permitters), the enforcing authority are to seek to obtain necessary information in order to assess the relative degree of responsibility of each member of the liability group for the presence of the relevant significant pollution linkage and to apportion the costs on the basis of those degrees of responsibility. If appropriate information is not available or cannot be obtained, then the costs are to be apportioned equally among the Class A liability group.

In assessing relative degrees of responsibility the enforcing authority are directed to have regard to specific factors including:

— the nature of each person's involvement with the relevant significant pollutant linkage;

— whether that person could reasonably have been expected to know at the time of such involvement the nature of the significant pollutant linkage and the seriousness of the harm, or pollution of controlled waters;

— whether that person had the ability at the time of such involvement to take steps to prevent or control the presence of the significant pollutant on the land, or to remove it, and had a reasonable opportunity to do so.

6.5.5.9 In respect of appropriate persons who are members of a Class B liability group (ie, owners or occupiers), the costs must be apportioned as follows:

— where the remediation action for which a Class B liability group is responsible clearly relates to a particular area of the land affected by the significant pollution linkage, liability should be apportioned among the members of the Class B liability group who own or occupy that particular area of land;

— where the above does not apply, liability should be apportioned among all of the members of the Class B liability group in proportion to the capital values of the affected land (including those of any buildings or structures on the land). Capital value should be estimated on the basis of available information but disregarding the existence of any contamination and in relation to the date immediately before the authority first served a notice designating the relevant land as 'contaminated land'.

6.5.5.10 It needs to be remembered that the costs apportionment discussed above is carried out not only with respect to separate liability groups (Class A or Class B) but also in relation to separate significant pollution linkages. In some circumstances, however, a remediation action may be referable to two or more significant pollution linkages where, for example, that one action represents the best way of dealing with each of the relevant significant pollution linkages. There is therefore a need, in those circumstances, to apportion the costs among, rather than within, the relevant liability groups. The guidance refers to this situation as a 'shared action'. The guidance sets out complex rules for apportioning liability in such circumstances.

6.5.6 Recovery of the costs of remediation of contaminated land by enforcing authorities (non-statutory guidance)

Section 78P(1) provides that enforcing authorities may carry out necessary remediation works themselves and seek to recover their reasonable costs incurred in so doing from the appropriate person or from the relevant appropriate persons in the relevant proportions (ie, as determined by the guidance referred to at paragraph 6.5.5).

In cases where enforcing authorities carry out the works themselves they are to have regard first to hardship which the recovery may cause to the person from whom the cost is recoverable and secondly to guidance issued by the Secretary of State for the purposes of the relevant subsection (in this case section 78P(2)).

Dealing first with hardship, the term is not defined in Part IIA of EPA. The guidance refers to the meaning contained in the Oxford English Dictionary of 'hardness of fate or circumstance, severe suffering or privation'. The guidance also mentions injustice, suffering and anxiety as well as severe financial detriment. Assistance could be derived by enforcing authorities from eligibility criteria applying to housing renovation grants and indeed to other statutes with a hardship criterion with a view to deciding in what circumstances the hardship test should be applied.

The guidance sets out certain general principles in relation to cost recovery. It reminds enforcing authorities that costs may only be recovered from those who are appropriate persons, ie, those who remain in the liability loop after application of the exclusion and apportionment tests set out in the mandatory guidance on that subject. Additionally, if an enforcing authority should waive or reduce recovery of remediation costs, then they become responsible for those costs and none of them may be reallocated to other appropriate persons. In deciding whether to recover their costs an enforcing authority should consider the degree and nature of responsibility of the relevant appropriate person for the circumstances which have led to the land in question being 'contaminated land'. In deciding whether to waive or reduce the recovery of costs, the authority should aim for an overall result which is 'as just, fair and equitable as possible to all who may have to meet the costs of remediation, including national and local taxpayers'.

Except where hardship applies, an enforcing authority should seek to recover costs in full. They should adopt the same approach to consideration of cost recovery irrespective of whether the appropriate person is a public corporation, a limited company (public or private), a partnership or an individual operating as a sole trader. This is a further provision in the guidance designed to avoid any deep-pocket approach being taken. It is stressed that a different approach may be appropriate in the case of a charity or a private individual not carrying on a profession or trade. However, business closure or insolvency in the case of small or medium-sized enterprises should be given sympathetic consideration in circumstances where full recovery would cause the enterprise to become insolvent and thereby result in a greater cost to the local economy than would be incurred if the enforcing authority were to bear the costs of remediation themselves. The aim, therefore, in these cases, is to recover as large a portion of the cost as is consistent with the ability of the enterprise to continue to exist.

The guidance then considers separately Class A persons (ie, causers or knowing permitters) and Class B persons (ie, owners or occupiers). This is, of course, subject to the general principles outlined above.

Dealing with Class A persons, the guidance states that the enforcing authority should be more ready to recover where Class A persons caused or knowingly permitted the presence of the significant pollutant in the course of carrying on a business than where they were not carrying on a business. Sympathetic consideration to waiving or reducing the recovery of costs should be given if, *inter alia*, the following should apply:

— the appropriate person demonstrates, again to the satisfaction of the enforcing authority, that he would have been excluded from liability by virtue of the exclusion tests but for the fact that one or more persons were not found to have caused or knowingly permitted the presence of the significant pollutant; or

— the appropriate person demonstrates, again to the satisfaction of the enforcing authority, that his potential share of the costs which are being considered for recovery would have been less, by virtue of the guidance on apportionment, but for the fact that one or more persons were not found to have caused or knowingly permitted the presence of the significant pollutant.

If the application of both the general principles and the above provisions is not sufficient to enable an enforcing authority to decide whether or not to waive or reduce recovering of remediation costs, the authority should take into account whether it was reasonably foreseeable at the time when the appropriate person caused or knowingly permitted the significant pollutant to be present, that significant harm or the pollution of controlled waters could arise. Specifically, if the best practicable means are used in order to minimise the risk of such harm or pollution the authority should give sympathetic consideration to waiving or reducing recovery. The content of, and compliance with, regulatory consents will be particularly relevant in demonstrating what was and was not foreseeable. It is stressed that such cases should be exceptional.

Dealing with Class B persons, it is first stated that the enforcing authority should be more ready to recover from such persons who could reasonably be expected to be aware of the presence of pollutants than from those who could not.

Additionally, the enforcing authority should be more ready to waive or reduce recovery of costs where a Class B person can demonstrate to the satisfaction of the authority that it took such steps as could be reasonably expected 'at the time of purchase' (an important qualification) to establish, prior to acquiring the land, the presence of any pollutants and was none the less unaware of the significant pollutants now identified or their extent. In determining such a case, the enforcing authority should consider, provided appropriate data is made available to them, whether the price paid on the purchase reflected, in whole or in part, its contaminated state or whether it was the full market value for uncontaminated land. The authority should also bear in mind that the steps which might reasonably expect to be taken would be different depending on the nature of the transaction – for example, whether it was a commercial sale/purchase, the purchase of a private dwelling or the inheritance of property.

112

In particular, the authority should waive or reduce recovery of remediation costs where an appropriate person is an owner-occupier of a dwelling on land which he did not know and could not reasonably have been expected to have known, was adversely affected by the presence of the significant pollutants when he purchased the house, unless the financial circumstances of the owner-occupier would enable him to meet 'easily' the remediation costs in question.

An enforcing authority should also take into account whether the costs of remediation are likely to exceed the value of the land in its current use and with any existing planning permission after the required remediation has been carried out. In this context, 'value' means the value that the land would have on the open market, disregarding any possible blight arising from the contamination. In circumstances where that value would be less than the costs of remediation, the authority should give sympathetic consideration to waiving or reducing recovery of costs to the extent that the costs of remediation are greater than that value. It must, however, take into account any off-setting increase as a result of the remediation in the value of nearby land which is in the same ownership or occupation.

Finally, it is noted that the authority should consider waiving or reducing recovery where trustees are held liable for remediation costs. Generally, the aim should be to recover as much as, but no more than, the amount that can be made available from the trust to cover those costs. However, for charitable trusts, a greater reduction may be appropriate.

6.5.7 The Contaminated Land (Special Sites) Regulations (draft)

The categories of land which must be designated special sites under and in terms of the new contaminated land powers are set out in a draft statutory instrument (ie, delegated legislation as opposed to guidance), the Contaminated Land (Special Sites) Regulations. For a site to be a special site, it must first of all be contaminated land and therefore must satisfy all the tests referred to earlier in this chapter. It must also be a site in respect of which 'serious' harm or 'serious' pollution of controlled waters is being, or is likely to be, caused (see section 78B(1)). The purpose of the draft regulations is to indicate which categories of contaminated land, once having satisfied the tests, must be designated as special sites and therefore subject to SEPA control as the enforcing authority. It is, however, for local authorities to designate special sites but only after requesting, and having regard to, the advice of SEPA (see section 78C(3)).

The following types of contaminated land will require to be designated as special sites:

— contaminated land which is affecting various categories of controlled waters, including those which are used for the supply of drinking water for human consumption and those which are being affected by dangerous substances as defined in the EC Groundwater Directive (80/68/EEC);

— contaminated land (or land adjacent to or adjoining such land to which substances have escaped from the original land) on which a process which requires an IPC authorisation in terms of Part I of EPA is being or has at any time been carried out and, additionally, land upon which the purification or refining of petroleum or the manufacture of explosives has been carried out;

— land in, on or under which certain specified substances, as set out in Schedule 1 to the draft regulations, are present and which have led to that land being designated as contaminated land (consisting of dangerous and polluting solvents);

— land comprising, including, or forming part of a site in respect of which a nuclear site licence under the Nuclear Installations Act 1965 is in force (eg, nuclear power stations);

— land which is contaminated land by reason of waste acid tars which are or were stored on that land in lagoons or bunds;

— land occupied for the purposes of the Ministry of Defence.

It should be stressed again that land must first of all be contaminated before one has regard to the draft regulations in deciding whether or not the enforcing authority is to be SEPA rather than the relevant local authority.

6.5.8 The Contaminated Land (Appeals) Regulations (draft)

The draft Contaminated Land (Appeals) Regulations set out the grounds upon which an appeal may be made against a remediation notice. We have touched upon one or two of these grounds in earlier parts of this chapter. There are seventeen grounds of appeal including *inter alia*:

— that the appellant is not an appropriate person;

— that some other person should also have been served with notice as an appropriate person;

— that the enforcing authority did not act in accordance with guidance as to the exclusion of relevant appropriate persons;

— that the proportion of the cost stated in any remediation notice to be borne by the appellant was not determined in accordance with guidance;

— that the whole or any part of the land described in the notice as contaminated land was wrongly identified as such by the local authority and that they failed to act in accordance with the guidance issued for that purpose;

— that the enforcing authority have unreasonably failed to be satisfied that appropriate things are being done or will be done by the appellant by way of remediation without service of a notice;

— that a requirement of the notice is unreasonable having regard to the cost likely to be involved and the seriousness of the harm or pollution of controlled waters in question.

It is entirely appropriate that, given the complexity of the legislation and indeed of the guidance, parties have clear and distinct rights of appeal against the actings of enforcing authorities when remediation notices are served. The apparently comprehensive nature of the grounds of appeal again demonstrates that enforcing authorities must act extremely carefully and thoroughly before they take the step of serving a remediation notice. If they do not their decisions are liable to be appealed against and they will have to produce, in court, detailed evidence to prove that they did in fact act in accordance with relevant guidance.

6.5.9 The Contaminated Land (Form and Content of Remediation Notices) Regulations (draft)

Section 78E of EPA requires a remediation notice to contain the following:

— what is to be done by way of remediation;

— the period within which it must be done;

— the proportion of the costs of remediation which each person is to bear where there are two or more appropriate persons.

The draft Contaminated Land (Form and Content of Remediation Notices) Regulations specify additional information which each notice is to contain, primarily with a view to achieving clarity in the sense of affected parties being able to ascertain all necessary information as to how the relevant enforcing authority arrived at their decision and who else may be affected by it.

The draft regulations require, *inter alia,* the following to be specified in addition to the information set out above:

— the location and extent of the relevant land;

— brief particulars of the significant harm, or pollution of controlled waters, by reason of which the relevant land is contaminated land;

— the main substances by virtue of which the relevant land is contaminated land;

— whether the enforcing authority consider the person on whom the notice is served to be an appropriate person by reason of causing or knowingly permitting the land contamination, or by virtue of ownership or occupation of the relevant land;

— brief particulars of the reasons for the decision of the enforcing authority that the person served with the notice is an appropriate person, which shall show how any relevant guidance has been applied;

— brief particulars of the reasons for the decision of the enforcing authority as to remediation action required by the person on whom the notice is served, which shall show how any relevant guidance has been applied;

— brief particulars of the reasons for the decision of the enforcing authority on cost apportionment, which shall show how any relevant guidance has been applied;

— the name and address of any person whose consent is required under section 78G of EPA (right of entry) before anything required by the remediation notice may be done;

— details of the enforcing authority, an individual contact within that authority, and the date of the notice;

— that failure without reasonable excuse to comply with any requirements of the remediation notice is an offence;

— that the person on whom the remediation notice is served has a right to appeal and how, where, within what period and on what grounds such an appeal may be made.

The remediation notice must be copied to the following persons, except in the case of imminent danger of serious harm, or serious pollution of controlled waters, being caused:

— any person whose consent is required under section 78G of EPA (right of entry) before anything required by the notice may be done;

— any persons who were consulted before service of the notice;

— SEPA, if the local authority are the enforcing authority;

— the local authority, if SEPA is the enforcing authority.

Again, the details and prescriptive nature of these draft regulations make it vitally important that enforcing authorities are able to justify the actions they have taken and the decisions they have reached at each stage in the process of identification of contaminated land, identification of appropriate persons, exclusion of appropriate persons, apportionment of costs and what ought to be done by way of remediation. Failure to include such information in a remediation notice will constitute a ground of appeal against that notice.

6.5.10 The Contaminated Land (Remediation Registers) Regulations (draft)

Section 78R(1) makes reference to public registers in connection with the new contaminated land régime and, in addition to the matters specified in that section, states that the registers will also contain such particulars as may be prescribed by regulations. The draft regulations prescribe, *inter alia*, the following matters for inclusion in the relevant registers:

— a statement as to the location, extent and estimated area of the contaminated land in question;

— a statement as to the contamination and its effects;

— the date of any notice designating the land as a special site and a statement as to which head of the Contaminated Land (Special Sites) Regulations (see paragraph 6.5.7) the land so designated falls under;

— the date of a remediation notice served by an enforcing authority;

— the date of a remediation declaration (for which, see section 78H(6) of EPA) prepared and published by the enforcing authority;

— the date of a remediation statement (for which, see section 78H(7) of EPA) prepared and published by a responsible person;

— the date of notification of claimed remediation which has been given to the enforcing authority and details of that remediation;

— notices of appeals and of their determinations;

— details of convictions in respect of offences under section 78M;

— copies of reports and documents relating to the contaminated land, whether prepared by or on behalf of the enforcing authority or any other person.

It is clear, therefore, that the registers will contain detailed information in respect of land which has been designated as 'contaminated land' and in respect of which remediation action has been taken. It should be noted, however, that statements as to what has been done by way of remediation and reports prepared in connection with land contamination and remediation will not in any sense be warranted by enforcing authorities – they will simply be on the register by way of information. This is understandable, as it would be extremely difficult (in liability terms) for enforcing authorities to confirm that a site had a clean bill of health. In any event, the standard of remediation is to ensure that the site in question becomes suitable for its current use, which does not mean that further remediation will not be required if the site is to be put to a different use in the future. At best, all that an enforcing authority are in a position to do is to indicate that they are satisfied with what has been done by way of remediation in the sense that they are no longer continuing enforcement action.

The draft regulations also provide that, where the enforcing authority are a local authority, the registers are to be kept at their principal office and where the enforcing authority are SEPA, the registers are to be kept at its office for the area in which the contaminated land in question is situated.

6.5.11 The Contaminated Land (Compensation) Regulations (draft)

There is one final set of regulations to be introduced pursuant to Part IIA of EPA. The Contaminated Land (Compensation) Regulations (draft) deal with a point which arises out of section 78G of EPA, which provides that a remediation notice may require an appropriate person to do things by way of remediation, notwithstanding that that person is not entitled to do those things. This covers, for example, the requirement to have access to neighbouring land for the purpose of monitoring. Section 78G provides that third parties must grant the appropriate person such rights as are necessary for that person to implement the remediation notice in question. It further provides that compensation must be paid by the appropriate person to the person who grants the necessary rights in accordance with regulations to be made.

The draft Regulations, therefore, deal with the following:

— the period within which an application for compensation must be made (twelve months from the date of the grant of the relevant right);

— the person to whom application for compensation must be made (the appropriate person to whom the right was granted); and

— the manner in which an application for compensation shall be made (in writing).

The heads under which compensation may be claimed include depreciation in value by virtue of the grant of the relevant interest, loss and damage incurred by virtue of the grant of the right or its exercise, and reasonable valuation or legal expenses incurred by the grantor of the right.

There is provision for disputes as to the amount of compensation to be determined by the Lands Tribunal for Scotland.

6.6 CONCLUSION

Inevitably, this chapter has concentrated on Part IIA of EPA. This is partly because the powers are new, but primarily because they are extremely complex. It is too early to express any firm view as to how Part IIA will, once commenced, operate in practice. It may be that its principal value will be to bring about a greater amount of voluntary remediation of the worst cases of contaminated land. The three-month consultation period which must elapse following designation of land as 'contaminated land' seems clearly intended to point in this direction. So also does the very fact of the complexity of the powers, the guidance and the statutory instruments. One thing is clear, however. It is not enough simply to enact legislation of this nature – the real threat of enforcement must be present and for that to be the case, the task of identifying and designating contaminated land throughout the UK must be carried out, because it is only then that the remediation stage (voluntary or otherwise) is reached.

Finally, it must be stressed again that the powers contained in Part IIA of EPA are intended to deal with the worst cases of contaminated land and are drafted accordingly. Other statutory régimes, as discussed, remain available to deal with less serious cases of land contamination and, even in serious cases, must in certain circumstances be used to the exclusion of the new powers. Likewise, the provisions of the common law remain available to deal with land contamination as a private matter. In other words, the Part IIA régime is the apex of an enforcement pyramid, and is by no means the UK's sole answer to the vexed question of land contamination.

Chapter 7

WASTE ON LAND

7.1 INTRODUCTION

This chapter considers the topic of waste on land, which is regulated by
Part II of the Environmental Protection Act 1990 (EPA), and
regulations, guidance and codes of practice issued thereunder. Put
broadly, Part II of EPA regulates the deposit, treatment, keeping and
disposal of waste. It does this in the usual manner of 'command and
control' legislation, by making the deposit, treatment, keeping or disposal of waste an offence, save in circumstances where it is permitted by
virtue of a waste management licence.

Waste is a highly significant environmental topic, because a very large
amount of it is produced and because it can cause significant harm to
the environment, which means that its disposal needs to be appropriately regulated and its production appropriately reduced. By way of
example, the City of Glasgow produces about 250,000 tonnes of household waste annually, while in 1994 Scotland as a whole produced about
2,400,000 tonnes of household waste, roughly 16,000,000 tonnes of
'controlled waste' (see paragraph 7.2), and an estimated 36,200,000
tonnes when agricultural waste, mining and quarrying waste, sewage
sludge disposed of to land, offshore waste brought onshore, and radioactive waste are added. These are very large quantities and are very
much the product of the consumer or 'throw-away' culture in which,
until recently (but not always so historically) waste was perceived as
something to be discarded rather than recycled, let alone minimised in
production terms. Until 1972 there was no regulation of waste disposal
in the UK except through the law of nuisance and the planning system.
The Control of Pollution Act 1974 (COPA), which introduced a waste
disposal licensing régime, was a very significant step forward, so much
so that the first EC directive on waste (75/442/EEC) was based on it.
The 1974 Act régime has now been replaced by EPA, Part II. Despite
these advances in regulatory protection, the UK system of waste disposal
continues to be very much based on the landfilling of waste in suitable
sites throughout the country. In Scotland, it is estimated that about 88
per cent of 'controlled waste' went to landfill in 1994. Until recently,
there have been few measures designed to encourage waste minimisation
at the production stage (although the principle of BATNEEC (best
available techniques not entailing excessive cost) which informs integrated pollution control (IPC) in terms of Part I of EPA is a notable
exception), or to encourage recycling or recovery of waste. However, the

introduction of the landfill tax under the Finance Act 1996 and producer responsibility for packaging waste in terms of sections 93–95 of EA and associated regulations, represent market mechanisms which are intended, in the former case, to make landfill more expensive (and therefore less attractive) and, in the latter case, to reduce the amount of waste which is simply thrown out, without reuse and recovery operations being considered. For a brief discussion of each of these measures, see paragraphs 2.14.2 and 2.14.3. Further legislative measures are likely, for example in valuation to used vehicles, where an EU directive is under discussion. Additionally, some industry sectors have adopted voluntary targets for recycling – for example, in relation to newsprint (a 40 per cent target by 2000) and lead-acid batteries (a 90 per cent current target). Other sectors are likely to follow suit.

The European Union has arguably been more active in the field of waste. The principal directive on waste is Directive 75/442/EEC, as amended by Directive 91/156/EEC. Waste policy at EU level is based on the principle that waste has a special propensity to damage the environment. The following policy hierarchy has been adopted:

— waste reduction/minimisation;

— reuse;

— recovery;

— safe disposal.

The aim is to minimise waste streams and also, and significantly, to ensure that waste is disposed of as near as possible to its place of arising, so that it does not require to be transported either from one member state to another, or across long distances within a member state. The EU hierarchy has been adopted by the UK – see, for example, Scottish Office Environment Department Circular 10/94 issued on 19th April 1994, Environmental Protection Act 1990: Part II – Waste Management Licensing – The Framework Directive on Waste. That circular also makes it clear that regulation should be proportionate to the risks involved and the benefits to be obtained. This should not be interpreted as suggesting that costs should be cut or minimised – rather it is a principle which must be applied having regard to the legislation in force and to the EU waste hierarchy.

Additionally, national waste strategies are to be drawn up for England and Wales, and Scotland, in terms of section 44A and B of and Schedule 2A to EPA. These national strategies will replace existing local waste disposal plans previously made under the 1990 Act. The responsibility of drawing up the national waste strategy for England and Wales rests with the Secretary of State whereas in Scotland it rests with SEPA. A draft plan has been issued for England and Wales, Making Waste Work.

SEPA issued its draft national waste strategy for Scotland, A Blueprint for Progress 1997–2001, in March 1997.

A Blueprint for Progress summarises the governing principles of the national waste strategy for Scotland as set out in Schedule 2A to EPA:

— waste shall be disposed of without endangering human health or harming the environment;

— establishment of an integrated and adequate network of disposal facilities taking account of the best available techniques not entailing excessive costs, ensuring self-sufficiency within the European Community and the UK and adopting the proximity principle in waste disposal to minimise the transportation of waste;

— encouragement of the reduction and prevention of waste production and its harmfulness through developing

— clean production technologies;

— the technical development and marketing of products which minimise the impact of the production, use and final disposal on the environment;

— the development of appropriate techniques for the final disposal of dangerous substances in waste destined for recovery;

— encouraging the recovery of wastes by means of recycling, reuse or reclamation with a view to extracting secondary resources or energy from waste.

It will be clear that this set of governing principles closely follows the waste hierarchy. In developing its strategy for waste management, SEPA will encourage use of the best practicable environmental option and BATNEEC in any given situation. Having set out the policy background, A Blueprint for Progress considers current waste management practice from the Scottish point of view, noting a number of significant issues:

— heavy reliance on the landfill of waste and a lack of waste incineration facilities;

— a lack of reprocessing infrastructure within Scotland causing difficulties for the recycling, with or without energy recovery, of waste;

— the fact that Scotland is a net exporter of special waste, because of the lack of suitable disposal sites in Scotland;

— a projected major increase in the disposal of sewage sludge to land in Scotland, given that disposal to sea must cease at the end of 1998 in accordance with the Urban Waste Water Treatment (Scotland) Regulations 1994 (SI 1994/2842);

— a need to address rural disposal, in the sense of balancing the economics of the use of larger sites against the economics of transporting waste across a larger distance to such sites.

The draft strategy then notes that change in waste management activities may be effected by various means, which are listed as

— economic instruments (eg, the landfill tax);

— regulation (ie, broadly, Part II of EPA considered in this chapter);

— the planning system (which must be informed by sustainable development and the waste hierarchy);

— information and research (the provision of sound information about sources, amounts and types of controlled and other wastes and the manner in which they are disposed of, as also support of the development of new technologies in the waste management industry);

— producer responsibility (both legislative, in terms of sections 93–95 of EA (packaging waste, etc), and voluntary – for example, newsprint, batteries, used vehicles, etc);

— IPC (EPA, Part I, considered in Chapter 9); and

— integrated pollution prevention and control (in terms of the EC directive on that topic, also considered in Chapter 9).

SEPA proposes to develop its waste strategy, in co-operation with key players, by the setting up of five task groups covering the areas of (1) waste regulation; (2) planning and development; (3) data collection and use; (4) building on the waste hierarchy; and (5) promoting, integrating and developing the strategy. The first and last of these will be developed by SEPA internally. The second, third and fourth will be developed by the involvement of representatives not only from SEPA, but also from industry, local authorities, government and other interested parties who can bring relevant expertise.

It is proposed that the strategy will be finalised by summer 1998 which will allow, broadly, a twelve-month period for each of the task groups to consider its specific area.

A Blueprint for Progress notes that the English national waste strategy, Making Waste Work, sets out indicative targets and confirms that SEPA adopts these meantime, but wishes to assess them in a Scottish context. The particular targets which are referred to in Making Waste Work, and which are adopted by SEPA meantime, include the following:

— to reduce the proportion of controlled waste going to landfill to 60 per cent by 2005;

— to recover 40 per cent of municipal waste by 2005;

— to recycle or compost 25 per cent of household waste by the year 2000;

— to ensure that 40 per cent of domestic properties with a garden carry out composting by the year 2000;

— to ensure that all waste disposal authorities cost and consider the potential for establishing central composting schemes by the end of 1997;

— to provide easily accessible waste recycling facilities for 80 per cent of households by the year 2000;

— to compost 1,000,000 tonnes (presumably reduced proportionately for Scotland) of organic waste per annum by 2001.

SEPA's draft national waste strategy is not by any means a carbon copy of the English strategy and this is to be welcomed. It is SEPA's clear aim properly to take account of specific Scottish circumstances and to consult widely on the strategy as it evolves. The Scottish strategy, and the English strategy, as they proceed towards implementation, should enable the UK to make up a considerable degree of lost ground in respect of waste minimisation, reuse and recovery in comparison to certain EU member states.

At EU level, a draft directive on the landfill of waste (the original version of which was thrown out by the European Parliament) has now been resuscitated and seems likely be adopted in the reasonably near future. Although many of its provisions are already reflected in Part II of EPA, it will nevertheless have a significant impact on the landfilling of waste in the UK, if adopted in its present form. This is because it will seek to ban the co-disposal to landfill of putrescible and inert wastes within a period of five years from its coming into force. Co-disposal of these types of waste is standard UK practice, so this measure, if adopted, will require significant change, at a practical level, in this country.

As already mentioned, the régime contained in Part II of EPA replaced the waste disposal régime contained in COPA. EPA is significantly more stringent than the 1974 Act. In particular, EPA introduced

— tougher penalties for offences;

— the duty of care as respects waste;

— stricter requirements for the granting of waste management licences, in particular the concept of the 'fit and proper person';

— the removal of the ability of licence holders to surrender their licences at will;

— increased public access to information by the expansion of public registers of waste management licences.

Most of the operative provisions of Part II of EPA were brought into force on 1st May 1994, although the duty of care as respects waste contained in section 34 was brought into force on 1st April 1992, as was the offence of treating, keeping or disposing of controlled waste in a manner likely to cause pollution of the environment or harm to human health contained in section 33(1)(c).

As is often the case with environmental legislation, much of the detail is to be found in regulations, of which the most important are the Waste Management Licensing Regulations 1994 (SI 1994/1056), as amended, and the Special Waste Regulations 1996 (SI 1996/972), as amended. Again as discussed, EC directives have also had a major impact and the definition of 'waste' for the purposes of Part II of EPA is taken directly from the EC Framework Directive on waste (75/442/EEC), as amended by the EC Waste Directive (91/156/EEC). Likewise, the provisions of EPA relating to 'special waste', and the Special Waste Regulations 1996, are designed to implement the EC Hazardous Waste Directive (91/689/EEC).

Government guidance and circulars are also highly significant in this area. The Scottish Office Environment Department Circular 10/94, issued on 19th April 1994, contains a detailed examination of the waste management licensing régime, together with an attempt to explain the significance of the revised definition of 'waste', following the European legislation. Scottish Office Circulars 13/96 and 26/96 explain the operation of the Special Waste Regulations 1996. Waste Management Paper No 4, The Licensing of Waste Management Facilities, issued by the Department of the Environment, provides guidance on waste management licences and on the 'fit and proper person' test for the granting of such licences, while Waste Management Paper No 26A, Landfill Completion, deals with the monitoring and aftercare of closed landfills. A code of practice, issued in March 1996, provides guidance on the duty of care as respects waste, replacing an earlier code of practice issued in 1991.

The net effect of these various changes has been to make the regulation of waste a complex and technical subject, far more so than was the case even five years ago. This chapter presents an overview of the subject.

7.2 WHAT IS 'WASTE'/WHAT IS 'CONTROLLED WASTE'?

As previously mentioned, Part II of EPA operates on the basis that it is an offence to deposit, treat, keep or dispose of waste without an appropriate licence. The first question which needs to be considered, therefore, is what is regulated by Part II of EPA. To answer this, we must first consider the meaning of 'waste'.

Section 75(2) of EPA, as amended, defines waste as

> '[A]ny substance or object in the categories set out in Schedule 2B to this Act which the holder discards or intends or is required to discard; and for the purposes of this definition—
>
> — "holder" means the producer of the waste or the person who is in possession of it; and
>
> — "producer" means any person whose activities produce waste or any person who carries out pre-processing, mixing or other operations resulting in a change in the nature or composition of this waste.'

For a Scottish case in which it was held that a sub-contractor could be a producer of waste (in circumstances where that sub-contractor was engaged to remove asbestos lagging from pipes, the main contract being to replace a heating system), see *Gotech Industrial and Environmental Services Ltd* v *Friel* 1995 SCCR 22.

On the face of it, therefore, one would expect Schedule 2B to EPA to contain a definitive list of what constitutes 'waste'. However, although Schedule 2B (for which see Appendix 3) contains a series of numbered paragraphs which refer to items which would normally be regarded as waste, it ends with a paragraph making reference to 'any materials, substances or products which are not contained in the above categories'. In other words, the list in Schedule 2B is very wide and contains much which is not actually waste. The important part of the definition, therefore, is the reference to a substance or object (on the Schedule 2B list) 'which the holder discards or intends or is required to discard'.

This definition follows the definition of waste contained in the EC Framework Directive on waste, as amended by the EC Waste Directive (the Waste Framework Directive). In the Scottish Office Environment Department Circular 10/94, guidance is given on the government's view of the test for whether or not an item is waste. This is contained in Annex 2 to the circular. It needs to be remembered that this circular simply represents the government's view on how the Waste Framework Directive definition is to be interpreted. Ultimately, the question of what is waste is a matter for the courts.

Annex 2 of Circular 10/94 suggests that the crucial question to be asked in order to determine whether or not a substance or object has been discarded is 'has the substance or object been discarded so that it is no longer part of the normal commercial cycle or chain of utility?' If the answer is no, then it would suggest that the item in question is not waste – the example is given in the circular of glass bottles which are subject to a deposit which is refunded when they are returned by their holder. The circular goes on to distinguish this from the collection of glass bottles in bottle banks, in which case they are being discarded as 'waste'.

The above is an overview – the circular considers many nuances and variants on this theme. One of the areas where there can be considerable debate as to whether or not a substance is waste is that of by-products from industrial processes. It is often very difficult to determine whether these are waste or not, particularly if market conditions in respect of their disposal (ie, whether a price is paid or not) should fluctuate such that in certain circumstances they fall outwith the commercial cycle or the chain of utility. What is of primary significance, however, is the intention of the holder or the producer of the relevant substance or object and not whether or not a price is paid. The fact that a present or even a subsequent possessor of that substance or object may sell it on (whether having subjected it to some process in the meantime or not) does not preclude it from being waste. To that extent, previous UK case-law which has focused on the intention of the producer or holder is likely to remain of relevance, as this is of equal relevance having regard to the European-inspired definition of waste.

For English cases based on previous legislation, see *Long v Brooke* [1980] Crim LR 109, where it was stated that the character of the relevant material must be looked at from the point of view of the person discarding it, a view which was also taken in the case of *Berridge Incinerators v Nottinghamshire County Council*, QBD, 14th April 1987; unreported. In Scotland, see the case of *H L Friel & Son Ltd v Inverclyde District Council* (IH) 1994 SCLR 56. Circular 10/94 draws attention to two decisions of the ECJ on waste, namely *Vessoso and Zanetti* (C-206/88 and C-207/88) [1990] ECR I-1461 and *E Zannetti and Others* (C-359/88) [1990] ECR I-1509 – both these cases were based on the interpretation of Directive 75/442/EEC and again take the approach that waste must be assessed by having regard to the intention of the producer or holder.

Reference should also be made to the ECJ cases of *Euro Tombesi and Others* (joined cases C-304/94, C-330/94, C-342/94 and C-224/95 [1997] All ER (EC) 639). In these cases, the court delivered an opinion on the meaning of 'discard' in the Waste Framework Directive. The most important question which came before the court was whether or not a waste producer which sells unwanted residues can be said to be discarding them. The court observed that the definition of waste extends not only to substances or objects which are actually disposed of, but also to substances or objects which are to be recovered, ie, the word 'discard' encompasses both meanings. The result is that the EC waste legislation applies to objects or substances even in circumstances where they have a commercial value and are to be further used but where they must first be subjected to a specialised recovery operation. The fact that transactions involving such material may be treated as sales in the accounts of the discarder is immaterial. In this respect, the case-by-case analysis which is suggested by Circular 10/94 as being necessary appears to constitute a proper interpretation of the EC legislation.

The question of when waste ceases to be waste is also relevant and capable of being difficult to determine. It should be the case that once waste has been subjected to a process of recycling or reconstitution, such that it once again falls within the chain of utility, the product resulting from the recycling or reconstitutive activity will no longer be waste – see *Kent County Council* v *Queenborough Rolling Mill Co* [1990] Crim LR 813.

This definition of waste is not the only definition of significance for the purposes of Part II of EPA. It is also necessary to consider the definition of 'controlled waste' which is contained in section 75(4). This states that 'controlled waste' is 'household, industrial and commercial waste or any such waste'. Household, industrial and commercial waste are defined in sections 75(5)–(7) respectively and also by virtue of the Controlled Waste Regulations 1992 (SI 1992/3303) and the Waste Management Licensing Regulations 1994, which amend the 1992 Regulations. Scottish Office Circular 24/92 contains an explanation of the Controlled Waste Regulations 1992. The reason that these definitions are significant is that, for the purposes of Part II of EPA, we are only concerned with 'controlled waste' and not with all waste. In other words, for the purposes of the requirement to have a waste management licence one must ask the following questions.

— Is the item 'waste' in terms of the definition of that term contained in section 75(2), ie, does it fall within the categories set out in Schedule 2B to EPA and is it an item which the holder (ie, the producer or the person in possession) discards or intends or is required to discard?

— If it is waste, is it also 'controlled waste', which question must be answered by reference to section 75(5)–(7) and the 1992 Regulations, as amended.

The topic of 'special waste' which is a further, and important, subcategory is considered at paragraph 7.6.

It follows from the fact that 'controlled waste' is a sub-set of 'waste' that not all waste which falls within the scope of the section 75(2) definition is subject to control in terms of Part II of EPA. In addition, even the definition of 'waste' in section 75(2) is not exhaustive in that the EC directive from which the definition is taken excludes at article 2(1)(a) 'gaseous effluents emitted into the atmosphere' and also, at article 2(1)(b), five categories of waste in circumstances 'where they are already covered by other legislation'. These five categories are radioactive waste, waste resulting from prospecting, extraction, treatment and storage of mineral resources and the working of quarries, specified agricultural wastes, waste waters (with the exception of waste in liquid form) and decommissioned explosives. It is the view of the UK government that each of these five specified areas is (generally) subject to appropriate legislative control by virtue of other provisions. For example, radioactive waste is dealt with by RSA (for which, see Chapter 11) and mineral waste in terms of town and country planning legislation and the Mines and Quarries (Tips) Act 1969. There are, however, certain mismatches in that, for example, not all agricultural waste is exempt from the control required by the EC directive, whereas all waste from agricultural premises is outside the definition of 'controlled waste' because of section 75(7) of EPA. These anomalies will require to be corrected so that the Waste Framework Directive may be properly implemented.

The result is that the waste streams which are regulated by Part II of EPA, although significant and important, do not represent by any means a majority of the waste which is produced in this country. Consideration of mineral and quarry waste and agricultural waste is outside the scope of this book, but on agricultural activities generally, see the very helpful code of Good Practice for the Prevention of Environmental Pollution from Agricultural Activity issued in July 1997 by the Scottish Office Agriculture, Environment and Fisheries Department

7.3 THE DUTY OF CARE AS RESPECTS WASTE

In addition to introducing a new waste management licensing régime, Part II of EPA also introduced the concept of a duty of care as respects waste. This is contained in section 34 of the Act. Section 34(1) imposes a duty on any person who imports, produces, carries, keeps, treats or disposes of controlled waste or, as a broker, has control of such waste to take all such measures applicable to him in that capacity as are reasonable in the circumstances

— to prevent any contravention by any other person of section 33 of EPA (the offence of treating, keeping, disposing of or depositing waste without a licence);

— to prevent the escape of the waste from his control or that of any other person; and

— on the transfer of the waste to secure

— that the transfer is only to an 'authorised person' or to a person for authorised transport purposes; and

— that there is transferred such a written description of the waste as will enable other persons to avoid a contravention of section 33 and to comply with the duty under section 34(1) as respects the escape of waste.

The duty does not apply to an occupier of domestic property as respects the household waste produced on that property. The 'authorised persons' to whom transfers of waste are permitted are defined in section 34(3) as follows:

— a waste collection authority (local councils);

— any person who is the holder of a waste management licence under section 35 of EPA;

— any person to whom dection 33(1) of EPA does not apply by virtue of regulations under section 33(3) (exemptions from the requirement to have a waste management licence, for which see the Waste Management Licensing Regulations 1994, regulations 16 and 17, and Schedule 3);

— any person registered as a carrier of controlled waste under section 2 of the Control of Pollution (Amendment) Act 1989;

— any person who is exempt from the requirement to register as a waste carrier by virtue of regulations under section 1(3) of the Control of Pollution (Amendment) Act 1989; and

— a waste disposal authority (local councils).

The purpose of section 34, which came fully into force on 1st April 1992, is to impose a degree of responsibility on all parties in the waste chain for the ultimate fate of that waste. Putting this in practical terms, it is not sufficient simply to dispose of waste to a person who collects it without making some reasonable inquiry as to whether that person is an 'authorised person' and without also providing an appropriate written description of the waste so that those who may have to deal with it further down the waste chain may know what they are dealing with.

Section 33(7) provides that a code of practice may be prepared and issued for the purpose of providing guidance on how to discharge the duty of care imposed by section 34(1). A code of practice was first issued by the Department of the Environment, the Scottish Office and the Welsh Office in December 1991, and a revised code was issued in March 1996. It contains detailed practical guidance on the duty of care and its ramifications and should be required reading for all involved in the waste chain. Significantly, section 34(10) provides that the code of practice is admissible in evidence and that if any provision appears to the court to be relevant to any question arising in proceedings it shall be taken into account in determining that question.

Breach of the duty of care is a criminal offence by virtue of section 34(6). The penalty for such a breach is a fine not exceeding the statutory maximum on summary conviction and, on conviction on indictment, a fine.

It should also be noted that although the duty of care and the related code of practice require appropriate written descriptions of waste to accompany any transfer of that waste, these provisions are significantly tightened in questions which concern 'special waste', for which, generally, see paragraph 7.6.

There have been a considerable number of prosecutions in respect of breaches of the duty of care, most of which have involved either failure to produce transfer notes in respect of waste or failure to provide adequate written descriptions of waste. On the former see *Surrey County Council* v *Alan Greenwood & Co (Transport)* [1996] 258 ENDS Report 46 and *Avon County Council* v *David Rowland, t/a Abba Skips* [1994] 233 ENDS Report 45. For the latter, see *Leicester County Council* v *Simons Construction Ltd* [1993] 226 ENDS Report 45; *Surrey County Council* v *Kingston NHS Trust* 1995, unreported; *Shropshire County Council* v *Severn Trent Water* [1995] 250 ENDS Report 45; and *West Yorkshire Waste Regulatory Authority* v *DuPont* [1996] 252 ENDS Report 45.

Penalties imposed in England and Wales would appear to be increasing from a relatively low starting-point, such that fines of £1,000 or over are relatively common. In Scotland, there are only two reported cases on breach of the duty of care as respects waste. In the first of these, *PF (Stonehaven)* v *James Gauld* [1993] 220 ENDS Report 39, no penalty was imposed and in the second, *Normand* v *Duffy, t/a Spare Batteries* 1995 GWD 25-1341, the duty of care charge was dropped (and a fine of £500 imposed for disposal of special waste without a licence).

7.4 WASTE MANAGEMENT LICENCES

7.4.1 General

The deposit, treatment, keeping or disposing of controlled waste or knowingly causing or knowingly permitting any of the foregoing without a waste management licence is an offence in terms of section 33(1)(a) and (b) of EPA. It is also an offence, whether or not there is a waste management licence in force, to treat, keep or dispose of controlled waste in a manner likely to cause pollution of the environment or harm to human health – see section 33(1)(c). The requirement to have in place a waste management licence does not apply, however, in cases prescribed in regulations made by the Secretary of State in terms of section 33(3) of EPA. There is a substantial range of activities which are exempted from the requirement to have a licence (but not from the duty of care) and for these, reference should be made to the Waste Management Licensing Regulations 1994, in particular regulations 16 and 17 and Schedule 3. The principal purpose behind the various exemptions is to have regard (in terms of section 33(4) of EPA) to the expediency of excluding from the controls imposed by waste management licensing the following:

— any deposits which are small enough or of such a temporary nature that they may be so excluded;

— any means of treatment or disposal which are innocuous enough to be so excluded; and

— cases for which adequate controls are provided by another legislative provision.

The various exemptions available are further explained in Annex 5 to the Scottish Office Environment Department Circular 10/94. It should be noted that, in many cases, the exemption (ie, details of it) must be registered with SEPA.

7.4.2 Application procedure

Sections 35 and 36 deal with the requirement to obtain a waste management licence. Section 35(1) explains that a waste management licence is a licence granted by a waste regulation authority (in Scotland, SEPA) authorising the treatment, keeping or disposal of any specified description of controlled waste in or on specified land, or the treatment or disposal of any specified description of controlled waste by means of specified mobile plant. In the case of a licence relating to the treatment, keeping or disposal of waste in or on land, that licence must be granted to the person who is in occupation of the land, and in the case of a licence relating to the treatment or disposal of waste by means of mobile plant, to the person who operates the plant. It is further provided that a licence shall be granted subject to such conditions as appear to SEPA to be appropriate.

It should be noted, in terms of section 35(4), that conditions may be imposed upon the holder of the licence which may require that person to enter upon the premises of some other person – for example, for monitoring purposes – and that there is provision in section 35A of EPA for compensation to be paid to any third party who is obliged to grant the necessary rights – for example, of access – as also provision for prior consultation with any such third party in terms of section 36A of EPA.

Section 36 requires any application for a waste management licence to be made on a form provided for the purpose by SEPA, accompanied by such information as SEPA may reasonably require and by payment of the prescribed fee for the application (which is dependent upon the activities to be licensed and the type and quantity of waste involved). Section 36(2) makes clear that no licence may be issued unless an appropriate planning permission for the proposed use of the land is in force. In practice, this means that to the extent that no relevant planning permission is in force, an application for planning permission will need to be made at the same time as the application for a waste management licence. The local authority, as planning authority, will liaise with SEPA and vice versa in relation to both applications and they will be taken forward in tandem, but it must be remembered that the actual grant of planning permission will have to precede the grant of the waste management licence. Care should be taken by applicants and the regulatory authorities involved to avoid duplication as between planning and pollution controls on which, generally, see Chapter 5.

Importantly, section 36(3) provides that a waste regulation authority to which an application for a waste management licence has been duly made shall not reject the application provided they are satisfied that the applicant is a 'fit and proper person' (discussed at paragraph 7.4.3) except where they are satisfied that his rejection is necessary for the purpose of preventing pollution of the environment, harm to human health, or serious detriment to the amenities of the locality (although this last is not applicable where there is a planning permission in force).

Before issuing a waste management licence SEPA must refer the proposal to the appropriate planning authority and to the Health and Safety Executive and consider any representations which either of these bodies should make (section 36(4)) and must also, where any part of the land to be used is land which has been notified under section 28(1) of the Wildlife and Countryside Act 1981 (ie, sites of special scientific interest) refer the proposal to Scottish Natural Heritage and likewise consider any representations which it may make (section 36(7)).

SEPA is deemed to have rejected an application for a waste management licence if, within four months from the date of receipt of the application, it has neither granted a licence nor notified the applicant that the application has been rejected, except in circumstances where SEPA and the applicant agree upon a longer period (section 36(9)).

7.4.3 The 'fit and proper person' test

The most significant innovation introduced by Part II of EPA in respect of the grant of waste management licences is the 'fit and proper person' test for applicants, which is referred to in section 36(3) of EPA. Section 74 expands upon this concept as does Waste Management Paper No 4. Section 74(3) provides that a person shall be treated as not being a fit and proper person if it appears to SEPA

— that he or another 'relevant person' has been convicted of a 'relevant offence';

— that the management of the activities which are or are to be authorised by the licence is not or will not be in the hands of a technically competent person; or

— that the person who holds or is to hold the licence has not made and either has no intention of making or is in no position to make financial provision adequate to discharge the obligations arising from the licence.

There are thus three limbs to the fit and proper person test. The first is conviction of a relevant offence, the second is technical competence and the third is adequate financial provision. It should be noted that as regards conviction of a relevant offence, SEPA may, if it considers it proper to do so in any particular case, treat a person as a fit and proper person notwithstanding that there has been a conviction in respect of a relevant offence (see section 74(4)). There is no such leeway in respect of the other two limbs of the test.

7.4.3.1 Relevant offences

Section 74(6) makes provision for regulations to prescribe the offences which are 'relevant offences' for the purposes of section 74(3)(a); this has been done in terms of regulation 3, as amended, of the Waste Management Licensing Regulations 1994. The relevant offences include not only the offences contained in Part II of EPA, but a whole raft of offences under other legislative provisions, including statutory nuisance, water pollution, IPC and the landfill tax (the last added by the waste Management (Miscellaneous Provisions) Regulations 1997 (SI 1997/351)). It is not therefore necessary that the conviction should have been in respect of a waste disposal site - any relevant conviction must be taken into account. Chapter 3 of Waste Management Paper No 4 contains further guidance

131

and should be consulted by applicants and SEPA. For example, it is made clear that where a relevant offence has been committed by a body corporate, the regulatory authority should have regard to whether, if that offence had been committed by an individual, it would have been spent by virtue of the Rehabilitation of Offenders Act 1974 (there being no similar provision for offences committed by bodies corporate). The Waste Management Paper also makes clear that the number of relevant offences which have been committed must be taken into account, as also the nature of the offence and the gravity of the offence. Particular regard should be paid to offences which involve controlled waste.

The relevant offence part of the fit and proper person test also applies to circumstances where another 'relevant person', ie, someone other than the applicant, has been convicted of an offence. This is expanded upon in section 74(7) and is designed to impute offences committed by other persons to the licence applicant. For example, if the licence applicant was a director, manager, secretary or other similar officer of a body corporate and that body corporate was convicted of a relevant offence, then the offence committed by the body corporate will be imputed to the licence applicant. There is a similar provision in respect of offences committed by employees in the course of their employment and offences committed by business partners of the applicant where the offence was committed in the course of the partnership business. However, it is made clear in Waste Management Paper No 4 that SEPA should, in assessing whether the applicant is a fit and proper person, have regard to whether any relevant offence was actually committed by the applicant or whether it was imputed to him or it by virtue of section 74(7) of EPA. Perhaps strangely, the 'relevant person' provisions do not cover all connected situations which might arise – for example, they do not impute offences committed by one body corporate in a group of companies under the same ultimate control to other bodies corporate in the same group. The scope for avoiding the need to disclose relevant offences is not as limited as it might be.

7.4.3.2 Technical competence

The technical competence criteria are to be found in regulation 4 of the Waste Management Licensing Regulations 1994. This provides that a person is technically competent in relation to specified types of facility (listed in a table after regulation 4) to the extent that he holds the certificate of technical competence appropriate to that type of facility. The certificates are awarded by the Waste Management Industry Training and Advisory Board, which was created in 1990 with a view to developing the necessary qualifications. For obvious reasons, these qualifications are conferred upon individuals, rather than upon bodies corporate and it will be necessary for the applicant, in circumstances where it is not an individual or where he is an individual but not a technically competent person, to demonstrate to SEPA that the management of the relevant facility will be in the hands of a person with appropriate technical competence. There are transitional provisions exempting specified facility managers from the need to satisfy the technical competence test at, and for a specified time after, the date at which the Waste Management Licensing Regulations 1994 were brought into force (ie, 1st May 1994).

The technical competence requirement is also expanded upon in Waste Management Paper No 4, Chapter 3 and represents a significant step forward in the transformation of an industry previously perceived as low-tech.

7.4.3.3 Adequate financial provision

The third limb of the 'fit and proper person' test requires an applicant for a waste management licence to make 'financial provision adequate to discharge the obligations arising from the licence'. EPA is silent on the content of 'adequate financial provision', but guidance has been issued under section 74(5) in the form of the latter part of Chapter 3 of Waste Management Paper No 4. In practice, satisfaction of the financial provision part of the fit and proper test is likely to be the most complex aspect of any application for a waste management licence. The reason for the test is to attempt to avoid the difficulties which may emerge where licences for waste disposal have been granted, but the licence holder may not have the financial means to comply with licence conditions dealing with, for example, remedial or corrective action or with appropriate monitoring and aftercare after tipping has ceased. These problems can be particularly acute in the case of landfill sites where income is generated while the site is operational, but ceases upon its being completely filled. The obligations under the relevant licence do not then cease – indeed, the monitoring and aftercare obligations only apply with full effect at that time and there is therefore a legitimate concern on the part of regulatory authorities that those who are granted licences should have made financial provision adequate to discharge these liabilities, some of which may be very long term.

A problem with the concept of adequate financial provision lies in the tension which arises between, on the one hand, the strong suggestion in Waste Management Paper No 4 that financial provision must be assessed on a case-by-case basis (having regard to the site, to specific licence conditions, and to the operator in question) and, on the other hand, the understandable desire on the part of regulators to impose some form of financial provision, at least for long-term licence obligations, which will be proof against the insolvency of the licence holder.

Waste Management Paper No 4 draws distinctions between the following aspects:

— financial standing generally;

— specific licence conditions imposing corrective or remedial action; and

— post-closure monitoring.

As regards financial standing generally, the concern of SEPA will be to ensure that there are funds available for the development and operation of the facility in respect of which a waste management licence is required. It is stated in this context that no realistic applicant for a licence should have difficulty in providing evidence that he is either of sufficient substance or has made appropriate plans to obtain external funding to meet the immediate obligations of the licence.

As regards specific licence conditions imposing corrective or remedial action (eg, the failure of containment systems at the site), Waste Management Paper No 4 envisages provision for such events being made by way of insurance, self-insurance or a specifically negotiated bank overdraft facility. The problem at this stage lies in how one assesses the likely costs which might be incurred if corrective or remedial action has to be carried out. On one view, if the facility is appropriately designed, then the risk of such corrective or remedial action should be very substantially reduced and therefore any assessment of costs should be made on that basis and not upon an assumption that corrective or remedial work will require to be carried out.

As regards post-closure monitoring, this is an even more problematic area. Particularly in respect of commercial landfill sites, post-closure monitoring may not commence for twenty to thirty years after the grant of the relevant licence. How therefore is the regulatory authority to be certain that funds will be available at that time to discharge the obligations? Waste Management Paper No 4 suggests the use of bonds, escrow accounts, trusts or, possibly, a mutual fund. For a commercial landfill site, the use of a trust fund may well make sense in that money may be put into such a fund while the facility is operational and then used after it has closed and has ceased to be income-generating. Such a mechanism is also proof against the insolvency of the operator.

However, whether such mechanisms are appropriate for landfill sites which are being operated as part of an on-site remediation project of short duration may well be a different question. There is, as yet, no settled practice in relation to what is or is not adequate financial provision and it is suggested that, given the number of different variables involved, there probably should not be. It should be noted, however, that the Environment Agency in England has moved towards suggesting the use of trust funds as a norm.

7.4.4 Licence conditions
A waste management licence, once granted, will be subject to a considerable number of conditions. For a useful checklist of the types of conditions to be expected, see Appendix A to Waste Management Paper No 4, which lists a variety of specific matters under each of the following headings:

— general considerations (including the working plan, waste types and quantities, and financial provision);

— site infrastructure (including site security, access and plant design, and capacity);

— site preparation (including soil preparation, bunding, and containment systems);

— waste reception (including checking and inspection of loads, and handling); and

— site operations (including sequence of filling, and storage capacity).

Reference should also be made to the Waste Management Licensing Regulations 1994 and in particular to paragraph 6 of Schedule 4 to those regulations. Paragraph 6 states that where a permit granted by a competent pollution control authority deals with the disposal of waste (as a waste management licence does), that authority shall ensure that the permit covers the following matters:

— types and quantities of waste;

— the technical requirements;

— the security precautions to be taken;

— the disposal site; and

— the treatment method.

It is clear from the Scottish case of *Guthrie* v *Scottish Environment Protection Agency* 1997 GWD 6-244 that the first of these matters (and presumably the rest) must be dealt with on the face of the licence itself. It will not be sufficient for the types and quantities of waste permitted to be disposed of to be inferred from a number of unascertainable, variable factors. In *Guthrie*, a waste management licence which did not expressly specify the quantities of waste the disposal of which was permitted was quashed.

7.4.5 Licence surrender

Once granted, a waste management licence may not be surrendered unless and until SEPA accepts its surrender. When an application for surrender is received by SEPA it must consider, in terms of section 39(5) of EPA, whether it is likely or unlikely that the condition of the land, so far as that condition is the result of the use of the land for the treatment, keeping or disposal of waste (whether or not in pursuance of the licence), will cause pollution of the environment or harm to human health. If, in terms of section 39(6), SEPA is satisfied that the condition of the land is unlikely to cause pollution of the environment or harm to human health it must accept the surrender of the licence; if it is not so satisfied, it must refuse to accept the surrender. If surrender is accepted, SEPA will issue a 'certificate of completion' (section 39(9)). Section 39(7) provides that SEPA must, even if it is minded to accept the surrender of the licence, refer the surrender proposal to the relevant planning authority and consider any representations which they may make to SEPA. Under section 39(10) an application to surrender the waste management licence is deemed rejected if SEPA has not responded to the request for surrender within three months of the date of receipt of the surrender application, but there is provision for this three-month period to be extended by agreement between SEPA and the applicant.

For detailed guidance on the criteria for acceptance of surrender of waste management licences, reference should be made to Waste Management Paper No 26A, Landfill Completion, and also to Waste

Management Paper No 4. The period of post-closure monitoring and aftercare which is required before surrender of a waste management licence is likely to be accepted by SEPA will vary depending upon the types of waste which may have been deposited. The period will be considerably longer for biodegradable waste than for inert waste and could, in some circumstances, be as much as thirty years or more. The surrender provisions of EPA represent a very significant change from the ability to surrender a licence at will which was contained in the predecessor legislation, COPA. It is this potentially lengthy monitoring and aftercare period which is likely to be of concern to SEPA in considering adequate financial provision in respect of an application for a waste management licence (see paragraph 7.4.3.3).

7.4.6 Transferability of licences
Under section 40 of EPA, a waste management licence is transferable upon a joint application being made to SEPA by the licence holder and the proposed transferee and provided that SEPA is satisfied that the proposed transferee is a fit and proper person. Payment of a fee to SEPA is also required.

7.4.7 Appeals
Section 43 makes provision for appeals to the Secretary of State from decisions with respect to waste management licences. An appeal is competent in respect of any of the following matters:

— an application for a licence or for a modification of the conditions of a licence is rejected;

— a licence is granted subject to conditions (ie, the appeal is against specified conditions);

— the conditions of a licence are modified;

— a licence is suspended;

— a licence is revoked under section 38 or 42;

— an application to surrender a licence is rejected; or

— an application for the transfer of a licence is rejected.

For modification, suspension or revocation of waste management licences, see paragraph 7.8.2.

Notice of appeal must be lodged within six months of the occurrence of the event or decision appealed against. Any appeal will be conducted in writing, unless either party requests, or the Secretary of State decides, that it should be conducted in the form of a hearing. In circumstances where a licence has been modified or revoked and an appeal is made, the modification or revocation is generally not effective unless and until the appeal is dismissed or withdrawn. This does not apply in the case of an appeal against the suspension of a licence (see section 43(4) and (5) respectively). There is, however, provision for SEPA to give notice that a particular modification or revocation must take effect for the purpose of preventing or minimising pollution of the environment or harm to human health, notwithstanding any appeal (section 43(6)). For the detail of the appeal procedure, reference should be made to regulations 6–9 of the Waste Management Licensing Regulations 1994. For appeals in respect of commercial confidentiality, see paragraph 7.5.

7.5 PUBLIC REGISTERS OF WASTE MANAGEMENT LICENCES

Section 64 of EPA makes provision for the maintenance of public registers in relation to waste management licensing which must contain, *inter alia*, the following particulars:

— current or recently current licences granted ('current' means 'in force' and 'recently current' refers to the period of twelve months beginning with the date upon which the licence ceases to be in force);

— current or recently current applications for licences;

— applications for modification of licences;

— notices effecting the modification of licences;

— notices effecting the revocation or suspension of licences;

— appeals against decisions of SEPA;

— certificates of completion (issued under section 39(9) at the time of acceptance of surrender);

— convictions of licence holders under Part II of EPA (whether the conviction relates to the licence in question or not).

Regulation 10 of the Waste Management Licensing Regulations 1994 expands upon the publicity requirements by *inter alia* requiring that the register shall contain 'full particulars' of licence applications, including all supporting documents submitted with the licence application. Regulation 10 also requires the registers to contain particulars of any application for the transfer of a licence under section 40 of EPA.

Sections 65 and 66 of EPA provide that information otherwise required to be included in the public registers must be excluded if the Secretary of State determines that the inclusion of the information would be contrary to the interests of national security or if SEPA determines (upon request by any party providing it) that the information is commercially confidential. Commercial confidentiality is defined in terms of section 66(11) as being information which, if it were contained in the register 'would prejudice to an unreasonable degree the commercial interests' of any individual or person. Any confidentiality exclusion accepted by SEPA will lapse after four years, but the person who furnished such information may apply, in terms of section 66(8), for a further period of exclusion. If SEPA determines that information is not commercially confidential, its decision may be appealed to the Secretary of State within twenty-one days of that determination (see EPA, section 66(5) and the Waste Management Licensing Regulations 1994, regulation 7).

It would appear, from the approach taken to similar commercial confidentiality exclusion provisions in the context of IPC, that regulatory

137

authorities are likely to take a strong line against the exclusion of information on this ground. In particular, based on confidentiality appeals by PowerGen and National Power, it appears that importance will be attached to the question of how relevant the information (in respect of which commercial confidentiality is sought) is to the determination of any application or to any of the conditions likely to be imposed in the consent. The more relevant it is, the more likely it is that the public will be prejudiced by virtue of its exclusion and that commercial confidentiality will not be accepted.

7.6 SPECIAL WASTE

It has long been acknowledged that certain wastes are particularly dangerous or difficult to treat and that special provision requires to be made for them. Section 62(1) of EPA provides that if the Secretary of State considers that 'controlled waste' of any kind is or may be so dangerous or difficult to treat, keep or dispose of, that special provision is required for dealing with it, he shall make provision by regulations for the treatment, keeping or the disposal of waste of that kind, ie, 'special waste'. Section 75(9) defines special waste as controlled waste as respects which regulations are in force under section 62 of EPA.

Until 1st September 1996, special waste was regulated by the Control of Pollution (Special Waste) Regulations 1980 (SI 1980/1709) made under COPA. These have now been repealed and replaced by the Special Waste Regulations 1996 (made under section 62 of EPA) which came into force on 1st September 1996. They are designed not only to update the 1980 Regulations, but also to implement the EC Hazardous Waste Directive and Council Decision 94/904/EC, which established a European list of hazardous wastes.

It must be remembered that 'special waste' is a sub-set of 'controlled waste' which in turn is not coextensive with 'waste' as defined in section 75(2) (see, generally, paragraph 7.2). In addition to the Special Waste Regulations 1996, reference should also be made to the Scottish Office Agriculture Environment and Fisheries Department Circular 13/96, which provides a detailed commentary on the regulations. The principal regulations were amended prior to coming into force by the Special Waste (Amendment) Regulations 1996 (SI 1996/2019), the purpose of which was to clarify and simplify the definition of 'special waste' by substituting a new regulation 2 in the principal regulations. Scottish Office Circular 26/96 explains these amending regulations.

The essential feature of the new regulations, as of their predecessor, is to impose much stricter rules in respect of the movement of waste which is 'special waste'. As discussed earlier, section 34 of EPA (the duty of care as respects waste) requires a written description of waste to accompany that waste on any transfer. The Special Waste Regulations 1996 require much more detailed consignment notes to be utilised and, in most cases, movements of special waste must be pre-notified to SEPA. Consignment notes must carry codes assigned by SEPA which will enable each consignment to be uniquely identified. A fee is payable to SEPA in respect of most consignments of special waste. It is an offence to move special waste without a consignment note containing the unique identifying code. Additionally, the mixing of special waste with non-special waste is not permitted except where it is authorised by a waste management licence, or an IPC authorisation or a licensing exemption. In practice, only a limited number of landfill sites are authorised to accept special waste.

Controlled waste is special waste if it meets the definition of special waste set out in regulations 2 and 3 of the Special Waste Regulations 1996, as amended. There is one exception to this which is that household waste (as defined in section 75(5) of EPA and the Controlled Waste Regulations 1992) is not special waste. However, there are three exceptions to this exception, namely asbestos, waste from a laboratory and waste from a hospital (other than waste from a self-contained part of a hospital which is used wholly for the purposes of living accommodation).

Additionally, radioactive waste, which is not a controlled waste, is to be treated as a special waste if it falls within the bullet-point categories listed below (see regulation 3).

In summary, regulation 2 provides that controlled waste is special waste if

— it is a waste which is on the EU hazardous waste list (eg, ammonia) and displays any of fourteen particular hazardous properties (contained in a list of such properties (eg, 'irritant'));

— it is a waste which is not on the EU hazardous waste list but displays any of six specified hazardous properties (contained in the list of such properties); or

— it is a waste prescription-only medicine.

Part I of Schedule 2 to the regulations reproduces the EU hazardous waste list. As far as the hazardous properties list is concerned, this is set out in Part II of Schedule 2. In certain cases, however, looking at the hazardous properties alone will be insufficient and it is further necessary to consider whether these hazardous properties are manifest at or above specified thresholds, for which reference should be made to Part III of Schedule 2. Part IV of Schedule 2 (as inserted by the amending regulations) contains rules for the interpretation of Schedule 2.

The Scottish Office Circular 13/96 contains detailed guidance, and helpful 'decision trees', in respect of assessing whether or not particular controlled waste is special waste. It should be read alongside Circular 26/96 which explains the amending regulations.

The net effect of the new regulations is that most items which were special waste prior to 1st September 1996 will remain so, but that a number of additional items have become special waste by virtue of the implementation of the EC Hazardous Waste Directive. Additionally, the criteria for determining whether or not an item is special waste have become considerably more complex.

7.7 CIVIL REMEDIES
7.7.1 General
The civil remedies described in Chapter 2 are available in respect of

damage caused by waste notwithstanding Part II of EPA. On the applicability of the 'contaminated land' provisions of Part IIA of EPA, see paragraph 6.3.3.

7.7.2 Civil liability in respect of offences committed under EPA

Where damage is caused by waste which has been deposited in or on land, so as to commit an offence under section 33(1) (controlled waste) or section 63(2) (waste other than controlled waste) of EPA, section 73(6) imposes civil liability on any person who deposited it or knowingly caused or knowingly permitted it to be deposited. The three statutory defences available in the case of a section 33 prosecution (for which see paragraph 7.10.1) are available for cases brought under section 73(6).

If either offence referred to in section 73(6) has been committed and a successful prosecution brought, this provision may be useful. If not, it would be necessary to prove the commission of an offence to the criminal standard (beyond reasonable doubt) before proving civil liability on the balance of probability.

7.8 CRIMINAL REMEDIES AND OTHER SANCTIONS
7.8.1 Introduction

The wide range of controls contained in EPA is demonstrated particularly in relation to criminal sanctions and in the system of waste regulation. As mentioned in the introduction to this chapter, EPA has

— introduced a new, more stringent, system of waste licensing under the control (now) of SEPA;

— automatically converted waste disposal licences, issued under COPA, into waste management licences, governed by EPA; and

— extended the scope of waste offences generally.

7.8.2 Waste licensing under EPA

Section 33 of EPA provides that a person shall not

— deposit controlled waste, or knowingly cause or knowingly permit controlled waste to be deposited, in or on land unless:

  — a waste management licence authorising the deposit is in force; and

  — the deposit is in accordance with the licence;

— treat, keep or dispose of controlled waste, or knowingly cause or knowingly permit controlled waste to be treated, kept or disposed of in or on any land except under and in accordance with the terms of a waste management licence; or

— (as an overriding provision) treat, keep or dispose of controlled waste in a manner likely to cause pollution of the environment or harm to human health.

Failure to observe these requirements is a criminal offence. For a Scottish case on contravention of a licence condition, see *Normand* v *Patersons of Greenoakhill Ltd* 1997 GWD 1-48. Significant fines will be imposed where circumstances merit. In an English case on contravention of section 33, fines totalling £30,000 were imposed in respect of the deposit of 3,000 tonnes of special waste on an unlicensed site (see *Surrey County Council* v *Alan Greenwood & Co (Transport)* [1997] 258 ENDS Report 47).

Section 35 of EPA, which provides that SEPA may grant a waste management licence on such terms and conditions as appear to SEPA to be appropriate, is discussed at paragraph 7.4.2.

Section 37 obliges SEPA to modify the conditions of a waste management licence to the extent which SEPA considers is required for the purpose of ensuring that the activities authorised by the licence do not

— cause pollution of the environment;

— cause harm to human health; or

— become detrimental to the amenities of the locality affected by the activities.

In terms of section 38(1) of EPA, SEPA may revoke a licence (wholly or partially) where it appears that the continuation of the activities authorised by the licence would cause the pollution, harm or detriment referred to above and that such pollution, harm or detriment cannot be avoided by modification of the licence.

Section 38(7) provides that SEPA may suspend a licence (wholly or partially) if the activities to which the licence relates have resulted in, or are about to cause, serious pollution of the environment or serious harm to human health and that the continuation of these activities will continue, or cause, such serious pollution or serious harm.

A licence may also be revoked under section 38(1) where it appears that the holder of the licence has ceased to be a 'fit and proper person' to hold a licence by reason of his having been convicted of a relevant offence (see paragraph 7.4.3.1).

A further ground for suspension of a licence under section 38(7) is that the holder of a licence has ceased to be a fit and proper person due to the management of the activities authorised by the licence having ceased to be in the hands of a technically competent person (see paragraph 7.4.3.2).

Where there was an existing waste disposal licence when Part II of EPA came into force, that licence by virtue of section 77 of EPA automatically became a waste management licence under EPA and therefore subject to the increased powers of SEPA under EPA.

In relation to waste which is not controlled waste, section 63(2) provides that an unauthorised deposit of such waste which, if it were controlled waste, would be special waste, is to be treated as though it were the deposit without licence of special waste and, where applicable, subject to the same penalty.

Finally, in terms of section 34(7), breach of the duty of care as respects waste is also a criminal offence.

7.8.3 Waste offences under EPA

At paragraph 7.8.2 we referred to criminal offences imposed by sections 33 and 63(2) of EPA.

The criminal sanctions for offences under these sections are a maximum fine of £20,000 or six months' imprisonment (or both) on summary conviction and an unlimited fine or two years' imprisonment (or both) on conviction on indictment. Where the offence relates to special waste the maximum period of imprisonment on indictment is increased to five years.

The sanction for an offence in terms of section 34(7) of EPA is a fine not exceeding the statutory maximum on summary conviction and, on conviction or indictment, a fine.

7.8.4 Surrender of waste management licences

As discussed at paragraph 7.4.5, a waste management licence cannot be surrendered automatically.

7.8.5 Criminal liability of directors and other officers

By section 157 of EPA, where any offence under EPA is committed by a body corporate, and that offence is proved to have been committed with the consent or connivance of, or to have been attributable to any neglect on the part of, any director, manager, secretary or other similar officer of the body corporate, he as well as the body corporate is guilty of the offence and liable to be penalised accordingly.

The section extends similar provisions to the members (ie, in most cases the shareholders) of a body corporate which commits an offence where the affairs of the body corporate are managed by those members (eg, by a parent company).

7.9 STATUTORY CLEAN-UP POWERS OF SEPA

Section 59 of EPA provides that if any controlled waste is deposited in or on land in contravention of section 33(1) of EPA, SEPA can take action against the occupier. Section 33(1) relates to

— an unauthorised deposit of controlled waste;

— the treatment, keeping and disposal of controlled waste in or on any land except under and in accordance with a waste management licence; and

— (as an overriding provision) the treatment, keeping and disposal of controlled waste in a manner likely to cause pollution of the environment or harm to human health.

In the event of contravention of section 33(1), SEPA is empowered by section 59 to require the occupier by means of a notice served on him

— to remove the controlled waste; or

— to take steps to eliminate or reduce the consequence of the deposit of the waste.

There is an innocent occupier defence under section 59 of EPA. If the occupier can satisfy the court that he neither deposited nor knowingly caused nor knowingly permitted the deposit of the controlled waste the sheriff is obliged to quash the notice requiring removal of the waste. The occupier has a period of twenty-one days from service of the notice in which to raise this defence before the sheriff.

Failing compliance, SEPA may do what the person was required to do in the notice and recover any expenses reasonably incurred from the occupier.

If a person is served with a notice under section 59 of EPA and fails without reasonable excuse to comply with it he may be liable to a fine on summary conviction not exceeding level 5, and to a further fine of an amount equal to one-tenth of level 5 for each day on which the offence continues after conviction.

However, in cases where (1) it is necessary that the waste be forthwith removed or other steps be taken to eliminate or reduce the consequences of the deposit (or both) in order to remove or prevent pollution of land, water or air or harm to human health or (2) there is no occupier of the land, or (3) the occupier neither made nor knowingly permitted the deposit, EPA empowers SEPA to take immediate action to clean up a site, without any requirement to serve notice. It can exercise these powers in cases where it appears to it that waste has been deposited in or on land in contravention of section 33(1). Clean-up costs necessarily incurred in such an exercise may be recovered from

— in case (1) above, the occupier of the land unless he proves that he neither made nor knowingly caused nor knowingly permitted the deposit of waste; or

— in cases (2) and (3) above, the person who deposited or knowingly caused or knowingly permitted the deposit of any of the waste.

It should be noted that the powers of clean-up under section 59 of EPA simply relate to the removal of specific deposits of waste, and there is no additional provision for general decontamination.

7.10 SCOPE OF LIABILITY

Under Part II of EPA, the scope of the offences and civil liability provisions is broad.

7.10.1 Under the central provision, section 33, criminal liability attaches to any person, which will include a polluter, owner or occupier, anyone who treats, keeps or disposes of waste and may extend to waste brokers and carriers if they, for example, knowingly caused or knowingly permit the deposit, treatment or keeping of waste without a waste management licence.

There are three statutory defences available. It is a defence for a person to prove

— that he took all reasonable precautions and exercised all due diligence to avoid the commission of the offence; or

— that he acted under instructions from his employer and neither knew nor had reason to suppose that the acts done by him constituted a contravention of section 33(1); or

143

— that the acts alleged to constitute the contravention were done in an emergency in order to avoid danger to the public and that, as soon as reasonably practicable after they were done, particulars of them were furnished to SEPA.

7.10.2 An unauthorised deposit of waste which is not controlled waste but which, if it were, would be special waste, is treated as if it were a deposit of special waste and liability attaches accordingly (section 63(2)).

7.10.3 Furthermore, any person, which will include a polluter or owner or occupier or person who treats, keeps or disposes of waste may also be subject to civil liability under section 73(6) of EPA if he commits an offence under section 33(1) (controlled waste) or section 63(2) (waste other than controlled waste). Such a person will not be liable if he can establish that the damage was due wholly to the fault of the person who suffered it or was suffered by a person who voluntarily accepted the risk of the damage being caused.

Civil liability may also be modified by reason of contributory negligence of the person who suffered damage. In addition, any liability among a polluter, owner and occupier may be joint and several.

7.10.4 Under section 59 of EPA (the trigger for which is the deposit of controlled waste in or on land in contravention of section 33(1) of EPA) SEPA may serve a notice on the occupier requiring the removal of the waste or the taking of steps to eliminate or reduce the consequences of the deposit. If the occupier fails to comply with such a requirement criminal liability may attach to him, unless he can show that he neither deposited nor knowingly caused nor knowingly permitted the deposit.

Where SEPA acts without serving notice, either because it is necessary that the waste be forthwith removed or other steps be taken to eliminate or reduce the consequences of the deposit (or both) in order to remove or prevent pollution of land, water or air or harm to human health, or because there is no occupier of the land, or because the occupier neither made nor knowingly permitted the deposit, it may recover its costs from the occupier, or from any person who knowingly caused or knowingly permitted the deposit of any of the waste.

Chapter 8

WATER

8.1 INTRODUCTION

The objective of protecting and maintaining water quality is achieved primarily through laws relating to the supply of water, sewerage and drainage, and water pollution. Since 1st April 1996, water, sewerage and drainage responsibilities have passed to the West of Scotland, East of Scotland and North of Scotland Water Authorities. SEPA deals with water pollution matters.

This chapter deals primarily with water pollution. To place this in context, the chapter begins with a summary of the statutory framework for water supply, sewerage and drainage, and water pollution, and an outline of measures relating to water quality objectives.

8.1.1 Water supply

Under the Water (Scotland) Act 1980, as amended

— the water authority have a duty to provide a supply of wholesome water for domestic purposes to every part of their limits of supply, but are not required to do anything which is not practicable at reasonable cost;

— the authority have a more limited duty to supply water for non-domestic use. In particular, there is no 'wholesome' requirement.

8.1.2 Sewerage and drainage

The Sewerage (Scotland) Act 1968, as amended, provides that

— the sewerage authority must provide public sewers for effectually draining their area of domestic sewage, surface water and trade effluent, and treatment works for dealing with the contents of those sewers;

— the authority are not required to provide sewers for connection to premises where this is not practicable at reasonable cost;

— owners and occupiers have the right to connect drains and private sewers to the public system to carry away domestic sewage and surface water. Consent must be obtained from the authority to discharge trade effluent;

— it is an offence to allow to pass into the sewerage system anything which itself or in combination with other matter with which it is

145

liable to come into contact in the system, is likely to damage the system, sewers or works, or impede the flow of its contents, or make treatment or disposal of sewage more difficult or which is prejudicial to health.

8.1.3 Water pollution
Under COPA, as amended

— consent is obtained from SEPA for the discharge of effluent into controlled waters. COPA also specifies various water pollution offences. The provisions of COPA are discussed at paragraph 8.4.

8.2 WATER QUALITY OBJECTIVES
COPA permits the Secretary of State to specify water quality objectives for the purpose of maintaining and improving water quality. Once objectives have been specified, the Secretary of State and SEPA have a duty to exercise their relevant statutory powers to ensure, so far as practicable, that these objectives are achieved at all times (COPA, sections 30C, D).

These statutory provisions have been used to comply with the UK's obligations under EU legislation. For example, the following list is of European legislation that has been implemented in the UK, partly by the regulations referred to, for the purpose specified.

— Dangerous Substances Discharged into the Aquatic Environment Directive (76/464/EEC) (and 'daughter' directives)
Surface Waters (Dangerous Substances) (Classification) (Scotland) Regulations 1990 (SI 1990/126)

Elimination of pollution of waters by some substances and reduction of pollution by others.

— Bathing Water Directive (76/160/EEC)
Bathing Water (Classification) (Scotland) Regulations 1991 (SI 1991/1609)

Measures to be taken to ensure that the quality of bathing waters conforms to prescribed values.

— Surface Water for Drinking Directive (75/440/EEC)
Surface Waters (Classification) (Scotland) Regulations 1990 (SI 1990/121)

Treatment of specified categories of water.

— Quality of Water for Human Consumption Directive (80/778/EEC)
Water Supply (Water Quality) (Scotland) Regulations 1990 (SI 1990/119, as amended by SI 1991/1333)
Private Water Supply (Scotland) Regulations 1992 (SI 1992/575)

Quality standards for drinking water and private water supplies.

— Pollution by Nitrates from Agriculture Directive (91/676/EEC)
COPA, section 31B

Designation of waters which are or may be affected by pollution by nitrates, and the areas of land draining into such waters which contribute to such pollution. The order designating a nitrate-sensitive area may impose requirements, prohibitions or restrictions on specified activities on agricultural land, and COPA provides for management agreements to be entered into. The catchment of a public supply borehole at Balmalcolm in Fife has been designated by the Secretary of State as a nitrate-sensitive area.

— Urban Waste Water Treatment Directive (91/271/EEC)
Urban Waste Water Treatment (Scotland) Regulations 1994 (SI 1994/2842)

Sewerage authorities to meet standards on the collection, treatment and discharge of waste water from urban areas, as well as certain industrial users producing discharges directly into receiving waters and not via treatment plants. SEPA must ensure that discharges comply with these requirements.

There are a large number of EU directives which deal with water pollution and water policy matters. The European Commission published a communication on water policy in 1996 (COM (96) 59), in which it was announced that all EU water directives were to be reviewed, the aim being to simplify and recast European legislation in this area, in particular so that water quality will be covered by only five or six directives. This communication has resulted in a Commission proposal of 26th February 1997 for a Water Framework Directive. The directive will seek to establish a common framework and structure for dealing with all aspects of water resource management, covering fresh water, seawater, surface and underground waters based on river basin management, rather than administrative or geographical boundaries, and involving limit values to control individual emissions and quality standards to limit the cumulative impact (within a river basin) of such emissions. It is possible that the directive will be adopted by the end of 1997. It is likely to result in the repeal and replacement of a number of directives, including the Surface Water for Drinking Directive, referred to above, the Groundwater Directive (80/68/EEC), the Fish Water Directive (78/659/EEC) and the Shellfish Water Directive (79/923/EEC). It appears that the other directives referred to above will be complemented, rather than directly affected, by the proposal.

8.3 ROLE OF SEPA
Under section 34 of EA SEPA has a duty to

— promote the cleanliness of rivers, other inland waters and groundwaters, and the tidal waters of Scotland ('cleanliness' is not defined);

— conserve so far as practicable the water resources of Scotland;

— promote the conservation and enhancement of the natural beauty and amenity of inland and coastal waters and of land associated with such waters; and

— promote the conservation of flora and fauna which are dependent on an aquatic environment.

These general duties will be fulfilled by SEPA exercising its water pollution powers under COPA (see paragraph 8.4), which the 1995 Act requires to be exercised for the purpose of preventing or minimising, or remedying or mitigating the effects of pollution of the environment.

Under sections 21, 24, 25 and 33 of EA SEPA's statutory role is to

— ensure that specified water quality objectives are achieved;

— determine applications for consent to discharge effluent and keep consents under review;

— monitor pollution in controlled waters;

— enforce water pollution controls;

— carry out preventive or remedial anti-pollution works and operations;

— be consulted by any person proposing to carry out drainage works, other than excepted works as are specified by the Secretary of State, as to precautions to be taken to prevent pollution to controlled waters;

— control water abstraction for irrigation purposes under the limited powers conferred by the Natural Heritage (Scotland) Act 1991;

— make byelaws prohibiting or regulating the keeping or use on controlled waters of vessels which are provided with sanitary appliances; arrange for the collection and disposal of waste from vessels which needs collection as a result of such byelaws; and for the provision of facilities for the washing-out of prescribed appliances from vessels;

— assess, as far as it considers appropriate, the risk of flooding in any area.

8.4 WATER POLLUTION

The principal statute dealing with water pollution is Part II of COPA, as amended, particularly by the Water Act 1989 and EA.

Under COPA, consent from SEPA is required for

— the discharge of effluent into controlled waters (section 34);

— removal of a deposit from any part of the bottom, channel or bed of any inland waters which has accumulated by reason of any dam, weir or sluice holding back the waters, by causing the deposit to be carried away in suspension in the waters (section 49); or

— cutting or uprooting any substantial amount of vegetation in any inland waters, or so near to any such waters that it falls into it, and allowing it to remain in the waters (section 49).

8.4.1 Definition of controlled waters

The water pollution provisions in COPA apply to 'controlled waters', which is defined under the headings of relevant territorial waters, coastal waters, inland waters and groundwaters (section 30A):

— 'relevant territorial waters' – three miles seaward from the baseline of the territorial sea adjacent to Scotland;

— 'coastal waters' – any waters landward from those baselines as far as the limit of:

— the highest tide; or

— the fresh-water limit of any river or watercourse, including an underground river or watercourse and an artificial river or watercourse, but not a public sewer or a sewer or drain which drains into a public sewer ('relevant river or watercourse'), together with the waters of any enclosed dock which adjoins waters within that area. The fresh-water limit of a river or watercourse is shown on a map, which must be deposited with SEPA by the Secretary of State and available for public inspection free of charge at all reasonable times;

'watercourse' (section 56) – all rivers, streams, ditches, drains, cuts, culverts, dykes, sluices, sewers and passages through which water flows, other than water mains and other pipes used to supply water to premises. This includes water which overflows from a watercourse on to fields (*R v Dovermoss Ltd* [1995] 241 ENDS Report 42). Where the river or watercourse (or loch or pond, below) is for the time being dry, this includes reference to the bottom, channel or bed;

— 'inland waters' – the waters of any relevant loch or pond, including any reservoir, or of so much of any relevant river or watercourse as is above the fresh-water limit.

'relevant loch or pond' – any loch or pond, whether natural or artificial or above or below ground, which discharges into a relevant river or watercourse (above) or into another loch or pond which is itself a relevant loch or pond, and other lochs and ponds which may be specified by order of the Secretary of State, such as the Controlled Waters (Lochs and Ponds) (Scotland) Order 1990 (SI 1990/120);

— 'ground waters' – any waters contained in underground strata, or in a well, borehole or similar work sunk into such strata, including any associated adit or passage, or any excavation into such strata where the level of water in the excavation depends wholly or mainly on water entering it from the strata. This does not include water contained in a sewer, pipe, reservoir, tank or other undergound works constructed in any such strata.

8.4.2 Discharge consents

Application for consent to discharge effluent or other matter into controlled waters is made to SEPA (section 34). The application must include such information as SEPA may reasonably require. It is an offence to make knowingly or recklessly a statement which is false in a material particular.

On receipt of the application, SEPA must publish notice in the prescribed form in two successive weeks in a newspaper circulating in the area in which the discharges are proposed, and in the area in the vicinity of any controlled waters which SEPA considers likely to be affected by the discharges (section 36). A notice must also be published in the Edinburgh Gazette. The publication costs can be recovered from the applicant. Copies of the application must be sent to the appropriate local authority and water authority. Where the application relates to coastal waters, relevant territorial waters, or waters outside the seaward limits of relevant territorial waters, a copy must be sent to the Secretary of State.

These publicity requirements do not apply if (section 36)

— following an application by the applicant the Secretary of State issues an exemption certificate on the grounds of national security or unreasonable prejudice to commercial interests of any person; or

— SEPA proposes to grant consent for a discharge which it considers will have no appreciable effect on the receiving water (any requirement to send a copy of the application to the Secretary of State will still apply).

In determining the application, SEPA must

— take into account written representations submitted by any person within six weeks of the publication of the notice in the Edinburgh Gazette (section 36);

— ensure that the requirements of the Urban Waste Water Treatment (Scotland) Regulations 1994 (SI 1994/2842) are satisfied;

— ensure that water quality objectives specified by the Secretary of State are achieved (see paragraph 8.2);

— exercise its general duties, including promoting the cleanliness of rivers, other inland waters and groundwaters, and tidal waters (see paragraph 8.3).

If SEPA proposes to give consent, it must notify any person/body which submitted written representations of the right to submit a request within twenty-one days to the Secretary of State seeking call-in of the application for his determination. The consent cannot be issued until the expiry of this twenty-one-day period, or, if such a request is submitted, until the Secretary of State gives notice to SEPA that he declines to comply with the request (section 36).

SEPA may grant the consent unconditionally or subject to conditions or refuse it, but must not withhold the consent unreasonably (section 34). Any consent granted by SEPA may be subject to such reasonable conditions as SEPA thinks fit. These conditions may regulate matters such as:

— the places at which the discharges may be made and the design and construction of any outlets for the discharges;

— the nature, origin, composition, temperature, volume and rate of the discharges and the period during which the discharges may be made;

— the provision of facilities for taking samples of the matter discharged, and the keeping of records in relation to the discharges and in particular of readings of meters and other apparatus;

— the making of returns and the giving of other information to SEPA; and

— the steps to be taken for minimising the polluting effects of the discharges, including treating any substance likely to affect the description of matter discharged.

There is a right of appeal to the Secretary of State on the grounds that SEPA unreasonably withheld its consent, or has given its consent subject to unreasonable conditions (section 39, discussed at paragraph 8.4.5). If an application for discharge consent has not been determined by SEPA within four months, or such longer period as agreed in writing between SEPA and the applicant, the applicant may treat the application as having been refused (section 34). In calculating the four-month period, any period in which SEPA is prohibited from granting consent must be ignored.

Discharge consents are not personal to the applicant and accordingly permit any person to carry out the discharges described in the consent (section 36(7)).

If SEPA is of the opinion that the holder of a consent is contravening, or is likely to contravene, any condition of the consent, it can serve an enforcement notice requiring specified steps to be taken to remedy the contravention within a specified period (section 49A, introduced by EA). There is a right of appeal to the Secretary of State against an enforcement notice, but submission of an appeal does not suspend the operation of the notice. In determining the appeal, the Secretary of State may quash or affirm the notice, with or without modifications (section 49B).

Failure to comply with an enforcement notice is an offence, with liability following summary conviction to imprisonment for up to three months and/or a fine not exceeding £20,000, and following conviction on indictment to imprisonment for up to two years and/or an unlimited fine. If SEPA is of the opinion that prosecution would afford an ineffectual remedy, it may take civil court proceedings to secure compliance with the enforcement notice (section 49A).

SEPA may periodically review any consent. Following such a review, it can serve a notice on the person making the discharge revoking the consent, if it is reasonable to do so, or modify the conditions attached to the consent (section 37). There is a right of appeal to the Secretary of State (see paragraph 8.4.5). There are restrictions on revoking or varying a consent within four years of its grant or previous variation, although, in certain circumstances (such as a direction from the Secretary of State to SEPA to secure compliance with an EU or international treaty obligation – see section 37(2)(a) and (b)) these limits will not apply. In very limited circumstances SEPA is liable to pay compensation to any person who sustains any loss or damage as a result of the notice (section 38).

8.4.3 Remedial or preventive works
SEPA will have power to serve a works notice where it appears to it that any poisonous, noxious or polluting matter or any solid waste matter is

likely to enter, or to be or to have been present in, any controlled waters (section 46A, introduced by EA) (not yet commenced). The notice requires specified operations to be carried out within a specified time

— to prevent the matter from entering the controlled waters;

— for its removal or disposal;

— remedying or mitigating any pollution caused by its presence in the waters;

— restoring the waters to their state immediately before the matter became present in the waters, so far as it is reasonably practicable to do so, including any flora and fauna dependent on the aquatic environment of the waters.

The works notice is served on any person who caused or knowingly permitted the matter in question to be present in any controlled waters or at the place from which it is likely in the opinion of SEPA to enter such waters. Before serving the notice, SEPA must reasonably endeavour to consult that person concerning the operations which are to be specified in the notice, and every owner and occupier of land or water affected (for owners and occupiers, see section 46B). However, the notice is not to be regarded as invalid or invalidly served by reason only of any failure to consult prior to its service. A works notice can require a person to carry out operations notwithstanding that he is not entitled to carry out those operations (section 46B). This is intended to apply to situations where the landowner's consent would otherwise be required – provision is also made for regulations to be made to prescribe levels of compensation for landowners in respect of the grant of the necessary access rights.

SEPA can recover from the person on whom the works notice is served the costs or expenses reasonably incurred in carrying out investigations to establish the source of the matter and the identity of the causer or knowing permitter, unless the notice is quashed or withdrawn (section 46A).

The recipient of the works notice has a right of appeal to the Secretary of State within twenty-one days of the date of service. The Secretary of State must quash the notice if he is satisfied that there is a material defect in it, and otherwise may confirm the notice, with or without modification, or quash it (section 46C).

Failure to comply with a works notice is an offence, with liability on summary conviction to imprisonment for up to three months and/or a maximum fine of £20,000, and on conviction on indictment to imprisonment for up to two years and/or an unlimited fine. If the recipient of the notice fails to comply with any of its requirements, SEPA may carry out the required work and recover the costs or expenses from that person. In addition, if SEPA is of the opinion that prosecution would afford an ineffectual remedy, it may take civil court proceedings to secure compliance with the notice (section 46D).

SEPA also has the power to take direct action by carrying out remedial or preventive operations where it appears to it that any poisonous, noxious or polluting matter or any solid waste matter is likely to enter, or is or was present in, any controlled waters (section 46). However, following the introduction of the power to serve a works notice, the power to take direct action can only be exercised if SEPA considers it necessary that the operations be carried out forthwith, or, after reasonable inquiry, it appears to SEPA that no person can be found on whom to serve a works notice. SEPA can recover the cost of the operations and investigations from any persons who caused or knowingly permitted the matter in question to be present at the place from which it was likely in the opinion of SEPA to enter the controlled waters or to be present in those waters, unless the person satisfies the court that the costs were incurred unnecessarily.

If it appears to SEPA that a person has without its consent caused or permitted matter to be discharged in contravention of COPA and that a similar contravention is likely, SEPA may issue a discharge consent for future discharges (section 34). Prior to issuing the consent, SEPA must comply with the publicity requirements applicable to applications (see paragraph 8.4.2).

8.4.4 Prohibition/restriction of discharges

SEPA has power to give notice to a person prohibiting him from making or continuing a discharge, or imposing conditions on the discharge (other than discharges from a vessel) (section 30G, introduced by EA). The notice will take effect on the expiry of a specified period which must be at least three months from the date of service of the notice, except in cases where SEPA is satisfied that there is an emergency which requires the prohibition to come into force earlier. If an application for discharge consent is made prior to expiry of the specified period, the notice will not take effect until the result of the application becomes 'final', ie, following the grant or withdrawal of the application or of any appeal, or the expiry of the period for submission of an appeal if no appeal is lodged.

To prevent poisonous, noxious or polluting matter from entering any controlled waters, the Secretary of State has power, exercisable by making regulations, to designate areas within which prescribed activities cannot be carried on without the consent of SEPA, which consent cannot be unreasonably withheld. Prior to making the appropriate regulations, a copy of the proposed regulations and a notice explaining the objection procedure must be published in the Edinburgh Gazette and a local newspaper (section 31).

The Secretary of State also has the power to make regulations requiring a person having custody or control of any poisonous, noxious or polluting matter to carry out prescribed works and take precautions to prevent the matter from entering controlled waters, and prohibiting a person from having custody or control of such matter unless the works or precautions have been carried out (section 31A; eg, the Control of Pollution (Silage, Slurry and Agricultural Fuel Oil) (Scotland) Regulations 1991 (SI 1991/346)).

SEPA may by byelaws make such provisions as it considers appropriate for prohibiting or regulating the washing or cleaning, in any controlled waters, of things of a kind specified in the byelaws (section 31).

8.4.5 Appeals to the Secretary of State

There are rights of appeal to the Secretary of State on the grounds that (section 39)

— SEPA has unreasonably withheld its consent, or has given its consent subject to unreasonable conditions, in relation to an application for discharge consent (section 34), or for carrying on a prescribed activity within an area designated by the Secretary of State (section 31);

— a notice revoking or varying a consent (section 37) contains terms which are unreasonable;

— the period specified in the decision letter issuing the discharge consent, or in the notice varying the consent, during which no notice revoking or varying the consent can be served (section 38), is unreasonable.

There are also rights of appeal to the Secretary of State against enforcement and works notices (see paragraphs 8.4.2 and 8.4.3) and against the unreasonable withholding of consent by SEPA to the removal of a deposit from the bed of inland waters or for cutting or uprooting of vegetation in or near inland waters (section 49).

The procedure for appeals is specified by the Control of Pollution (Consents for Discharges) (Secretary of State Functions) Regulations 1984 (SI 1984/865), as amended (these regulations were revoked in England and Wales but still apply in Scotland). The notice of appeal must be submitted within three months of the notification of SEPA's decision, or of its deemed refusal of consent under section 34(2), or of the service of the notice in terms of section 37. Where the appeal relates to an application for consent under section 34 in respect of which a third party lodged representations, that party must be notified by SEPA that there is a right to lodge further representations within twenty-one days. The Secretary of State must take account of any further representations made by these parties (section 39). The Secretary of State may require the appellant or SEPA to submit a further written statement. If the Secretary of State is satisfied that he is sufficiently informed to reach a decision, he may determine the appeal after giving fourteen days' notice of his intention to the appellant and SEPA. However, if within that fourteen days either the appellant or SEPA request the Secretary of State not to determine the question without further investigation, he must arrange for a public local inquiry or other hearing to be held. The Secretary of State may delegate determination of the appeal to an appointed person (EA, section 114).

Subject to the exceptions noted below, the decision, conditions, or period challenged are treated as reasonable until the contrary is determined (section 39(5)).

There are only two instances where submission of an appeal suspends the decision or notice challenged.

— Appeal against a notice revoking or varying a consent (section 37) – the notice does not take effect while the appeal is pending, unless the notice includes a statement that in the opinion of SEPA this is necessary for the purpose of preventing or, where that is not practicable, minimising the entry into controlled waters of any poisonous, noxious or polluting matter or any solid waste matter, or harm to human health (section 39(5A), (5B)). However, the holder (the person who has the consent) or former holder of the consent may apply to the Secretary of State for a determination that SEPA acted unreasonably in requiring the notice to take effect. Following such a determination, the notice has no effect while the appeal is pending, and the holder or former holder of the consent is entitled to compensation from SEPA in respect of any loss suffered by him in consequence of that requirement (section 39(5C)).

— Appeal against the reasonableness of conditions attached to a consent to carry on a prescribed activity within an area designated by the Secretary of State (section 31) – the consent is treated as unconditional pending determination of the appeal (section 39(5)).

At any stage in the appeal proceedings, the Secretary of State may refer any question of law which arises for the decision of the Court of Session by stating a special case. In addition, the Court of Session may require the Secretary of State to state a special case (section 39(6)).

In determining the appeal, if the Secretary of State determines that consent was unreasonably withheld or that the conditions or terms or periods in question are unreasonable, he must give such direction to SEPA as he thinks fit (section 39(4)).

8.4.6 Pollution offences
The following water pollution offences are contained in COPA:

— causing or knowingly permitting pollution of controlled waters (section 30F, discussed below);

— failure to comply with an enforcement or works notice (discussed at paragraphs 8.4.2 and 8.4.3);

— removal of a deposit from the bed of inland waters, or cutting or uprooting vegetation in certain circumstances without consent from SEPA (see paragraph 8.4).

Unlike English law, failure to comply with the terms and conditions of a discharge consent is not an offence unless and until that failure gives rise to a discharge. However, it should be noted that an enforcement notice may be served by SEPA in respect of such failure to comply and that breach of such a notice is an offence.

The penalty for contravening section 30F, or failing to comply with a works or enforcement notice, is imprisonment for up to three months and/or a maximum fine of £20,000 on summary conviction, and on indictment to imprisonment for up to two years and/or an unlimited fine. The penalty for unauthorised removal of a deposit from inland waters or cutting or uprooting vegetation is a maximum fine of level 4 on the standard scale (currently £2,500).

Other statutory offences include:

— the Water (Scotland) Act 1980, section 75, as amended – pollution, either by act or neglect, of any water in a spring, well or adit, used for human consumption or domestic purposes or for manufacture of food or drink for human consumption;

— the Health and Safety At Work etc Act 1974, sections 3(1), 33(1)(a) – failure of employer to discharge the duty to conduct his undertaking in such a way, so far as is reasonably practicable, that persons not in his employment who may be affected thereby are not thereby exposed to risks to their health or safety (*HM Advocate* v *Kettle Produce Ltd* 1996 GWD 3-159);

— EPA waste offences (see paragraph 7.8).

In 1995 there were thirty-five successful prosecutions in Scotland for water pollution offences, with an average fine of £2,715 ([1996] 253 ENDS Report 10). Appendix 4 outlines the water pollution prosecutions in Scotland reported in legal journals.

In terms of COPA (section 30F), it is an offence to cause or knowingly permit

(a) any poisonous, noxious or polluting matter or any solid waste matter to enter any controlled waters. Although the Act does not define 'polluting matter', this term is thought to focus on the nature of the material being discharged and not its actual effect on the quality of the receiving water. Discolouration of the water may be sufficient (*National Rivers Authority* v *Egger UK Ltd* Newcastle upon Tyne Crown Court, 15th–17th June 1992, unreported). No actual harm has to be shown (*R* v *Dovermoss Ltd* [1995] 241 ENDS Report 42);

(b) any matter, other than trade or sewage effluent, to enter controlled waters by being discharged from a sewer or drain in contravention of a prohibition imposed by SEPA, or which contains a prescribed substance or a prescribed concentration of such a substance, or derives from a prescribed process or from a process involving the use of prescribed substances or the use of such substances in quantities which exceed the prescribed limits (previously, only any discharge without consent from a sewer or drain into controlled waters of matter other than trade or sewage effluent was an offence; EA introduced the additional criteria at section 30G(2));

(c) any trade or sewage effluent to be discharged

— into controlled waters, or from land in Scotland, through a pipe, into the sea outside the seaward limits of controlled waters;

— from a building or from any plant on to or into any land, or into any waters of a loch or pond which are not inland waters, in contravention of a prohibition imposed by SEPA, or which contains a prescribed substance or a prescribed concentration of such a substance, or derives from a prescribed process or from a process involving the use of prescribed substances or the use of such substances in quantities which exceed the prescribed limits (previously, only any such discharge of trade or sewerage effluent without consent was an offence; EA introduced the additional criteria at section 30G(2));

A sewerage authority or other person in which a sewerage system or works is vested (pursuant, for example, to a Private Finance Initiative scheme) is deemed to have caused any discharge of sewage effluent from its sewer or works if it was bound, either unconditionally or subject to conditions which were observed, to receive into the sewer or works matter included in the discharge (section 30H(1)). In such circumstances, the person making the initial discharge into the sewer or works does not commit an offence (below). The authority or other person does not commit an offence if it was not bound to receive the matter in the sewer or works, or if the conditions under which it was bound to receive it were not observed (below);

(d) any matter whatever to enter any inland waters so as to tend (either directly or in combination with other matter which he or another person causes or permits to enter those waters) to impede the proper flow of the waters in a manner leading, or likely to lead, to a substantial aggravation of pollution due to other causes, or the consequences of such pollution.

No offence is committed if

(a) the discharge is made under and in accordance with, or as result of, any act or omission under and in accordance with a consent under section 34 of COPA issued by SEPA, an IPC authorisation (see Chapter 9), a licence granted under Part II of the Food and Environment Protection Act 1985, section 33 of the Water (Scotland) Act 1980 relating to temporary discharges by water authorities in connection with the construction of works, any provision of a local act or statutory order which expressly confers power to discharge effluent into water, or any prescribed enactment. A waste management or disposal licence (see Chapter 7) provides a defence to some but not all these offences (see, generally, section 30I);

(b) the entry is caused or permitted, or the discharge is made, in an emergency in order to avoid danger to life or health, provided that the person takes all steps that are reasonably practicable in the circumstances for minimising the extent of the entry or discharge and of its polluting effects, and particulars of the entry or discharge are furnished to SEPA as soon as reasonably practicable after the entry occurs (section 30J(1));

(c) trade or sewage effluent is discharged from a vessel (section 30J(2));

(d) water from an abandoned mine or an abandoned part of a mine is permitted to enter controlled waters, except for the owner or former operator if it was abandoned after 31st December 1999 (causing pollution in this manner is an offence) (section 30J(3)–(6) – see paragraph 8.4.8);

(e) the solid refuse of a mine or quarry is deposited on any land so that it falls or is carried into inland waters, if the refuse is deposited with the consent of SEPA, no other site for the deposit is reasonably practicable, and all reasonably practicable steps were taken to prevent the refuse from entering those inland waters. This defence does not apply to the entry of any poisonous, noxious or polluting matter into any controlled waters (section 30J(7));

(f) a roads authority cause or permit a discharge to be made from a drain kept open by virtue of section 31 of the Roads (Scotland) Act 1984, unless the discharge is made in contravention of a prohibition imposed by SEPA under section 30G (section 30J(8));

(g) there is a discharge from a sewer or works vested in a sewerage authority, or other person in whom a sewerage system or works is vested, contravening conditions of a consent, if the contravention is attributable to a discharge which another person caused or permitted to be made into the sewer or works, and the authority either were not bound to receive the discharge or the conditions under which they were bound to receive it were not observed, and the authority could not reasonably have been expected to prevent the discharge into the sewer or works (eg, *National Rivers Authority* v *Yorkshire Water Services Ltd* [1995] 1 AC 444) (section 30H(2), (3));

(h) a person causes or permits a discharge to be made into a sewer or works vested in a sewerage authority, or other person, and that discharge had to be received by the authority or that person either unconditionally, or subject to conditions which were observed (section 30H(2), (3)).

It must be noted that there is no due diligence defence – 'took all reasonable precautions and exercised all due diligence to avoid commission of the offence' – in contrast to the waste management licensing régime.

In a prosecution for allowing diesel oil to enter controlled waters, it was not a defence that the Secretary of State had failed to deposit a map showing the fresh-water limit, as an offence was committed whether it was coastal or inland waters which were polluted (*MacKenzie* v *Tractor Shovels Tawse Ltd* 1992 SCCR 71).

The concept of causing or knowingly permitting pollution has been the subject of much judicial and other discussion. In *Lockhart* v *National Coal Board* 1981 SLT 161, following the decision of the House of Lords in *Alphacell Ltd* v *Woodward* [1972] AC 824; [1972] 2 All ER 475, it was held that pollution is 'caused' where

— the accused carried out some active operation or chain of operations the natural consequence of which is that polluted matter entered the water;

— knowledge and foreseeability are not matters which require to be proved;

— a commonsense meaning must be given to 'causing';

— neither negligence nor *mens rea* (intention) need be established;

— consideration has to be given to such things as natural forces, the act of a third party or an act of God, if the evidence justifies the bringing of such matters into consideration.

In essence, the accused causes pollution where he creates the latent danger of pollution by establishing an operation which could lead to water pollution, even where the risk is addressed by the provision of safeguards. However, the case-law is in a state of some confusion.

Thus a manufacturer 'caused' pollution where polluted water overflowed into a river from its premises as a result of pumps not operating properly without its knowledge and in the absence of negligence (*Alphacell Ltd* v *Woodward*). Similarly, but for the statutory defence (at section 30H(2), (3)), a water authority would be responsible for pollution discharged from their works, even where the pollution was caused by an illegal discharge into the sewer by a third party, because they set up a system for gathering effluent into their sewers and thence into their sewage works for treatment, with an arrangement deliberately intended to carry the resulting treated effluent into controlled waters (*National Rivers Authority* v *Yorkshire Water Services Ltd*). A company caused pollution which resulted from a latent defect in a pipe which had been installed before its purchase of the premises (*R* v *CPC (UK) Ltd, The Times*, 4th August 1994; [1995] Env LR 131).

However, this principle does not necessarily mean that a landlord causes pollution where it provides a drainage system which is used by a tenant to discharge effluent contrary to the terms of the lease (*National Rivers Authority* v *Welsh Development Agency* [1993] Env LR 407).

The offence of causing pollution can be committed by more than one person acting in a joint enterprise, or by separate acts of those persons (*Attorney-General's Reference (No 1 of 1994)* [1995] 1 WLR 599). Thus both a water authority and the third party who made the initial discharge into the sewer can be held to have caused the pollution.

A person can be guilty of causing pollution by failing to maintain properly a system or running it in an unmaintained state (*Attorney-General's Reference (No 1 of 1994)*). It is not a defence that the accused was not in a legal position to do anything after its lease had expired (*Lockhart* v *National Coal Board*). 'Mere tacit standing by and looking on' is not sufficient to amount to causing pollution (*Price* v *Cromack* [1975] 1 WLR 988). Thus a failure to act promptly to discover the source of raw sewage polluting controlled waters and clear the blockage did not amount to causing pollution (*Wychavon District Council* v *National Rivers Authority* [1993] 2 All ER 440, but see the comments on this decision in *National Rivers Authority* v *Yorkshire Water Services Ltd*).

Where vandals caused the escape of oil, the company storing the oil was found not guilty of causing the resultant pollution (*National Rivers Authority* v *Wright Engineering Co Ltd* [1994] 4 All ER 281). This case may be contrasted with *Empress Car Co (Abertillery) Ltd* v *National Rivers Authority* [1997] Env LR 227 where persons unknown opened a tap, resulting in an oil spillage – the company was held to have caused the pollution. Pollution from a spillage in the course of a delivery of oil by an independent supplier was not caused by the company receiving the delivery (*Welsh Water Authority* v *Williams Motors (Cwmdu) Ltd, The Times,* 5th December 1988). It seems clear from these cases that an act of a third party will not necessarily interrupt the chain of causation.

A company will be criminally liable for causing pollution which resulted from the acts or omissions of its employees acting within the course and scope of their employment, regardless of whether they could be said to be exercising the controlling mind and will of the company (*National Rivers Authority* v *Alfred McAlpine Homes East Ltd* [1994] 4 All ER 286).

The offence of 'knowingly permitting' pollution involves a failure to prevent pollution accompanied by actual or constructive knowledge of that pollution (*Alphacell Ltd* v *Woodward*). A conviction for knowingly permitting pollution was quashed where there was evidence that the appellants knew of the initial spillage, but no finding that they could have prevented the escape of fuel oil into the brook sooner than they did, nor that there was an escape during any period when they could have prevented but failed to prevent it. In particular, there was nothing to show any realisation on their part that the contents of the drainage system would probably find their way into the brook before the system was due to be cleaned the following day (*Schulmans Incorporated Ltd* v *National Rivers Authority* [1992] Env LR D1).

8.4.7 Public information/registers

Under section 41 of COPA and the Control of Pollution (Registers) (Scotland) Regulations 1993 (SI 1993/1155, as amended), SEPA is required to maintain a register, open at all reasonable hours for inspection by the public free of charge, and to provide facilities for members of the public to obtain copies of entries on the payment of reasonable charges.

The register must be indexed to enable information relating to a particular discharge or a particular place to be located. Generally information must be entered in the register within twenty-eight days. The register must contain particulars of

— notices of water quality objectives;

— applications for consents;

— consents granted and the conditions to which they are subject;

— samples of effluent and water and information produced by analyses of the samples and the steps taken in consequence of that information;

— enforcement notices;

— directions given by the Secretary of State;

— convictions;

— information obtained or furnished in pursuance of conditions attached to consents;

— works notices, appeals against works notices, and convictions relating to works notices;

— other prescribed matters relating to the quality of water.

Information is excluded from the register if in the opinion of the Secretary of State its inclusion would be contrary to the interests of national security. If a person gives notice to the Secretary of State that information may fall within this description, and notifies SEPA that this notice has been given, the information shall not be included in the register until the Secretary of State has determined that it should be included (section 42A).

Information which is determined to be commercially confidential by SEPA, or by the Secretary of State on appeal, cannot be included in the register without the consent of the individual or the person carrying on the business to which the information relates, or unless the information is subject to a direction to SEPA by the Secretary of State requiring the information to be included in the register notwithstanding its commercial confidentiality. The information is initially excluded for four years, but an application for further extension can be made to SEPA on the grounds that the information remains commercially confidential (section 42B).

Information is commercially confidential in relation to any individual or person, if its being contained in the register would prejudice to an unreasonable degree the commercial interests of that individual or person (section 42B(11)).

The issue of commercial confidentiality can arise in two ways.

(1) A person furnishing the information to SEPA for a discharge consent application, or in compliance either with a condition attached to a consent, or a section 93 notice (that is, a notice from SEPA requiring information to be provided to it for the discharge of its functions in terms of COPA), can apply to have the information excluded from the register on the ground that it is commercially confidential (as regards himself or another person). If SEPA fails to determine the application within fourteen days the information is deemed to be commercially confidential (section 42B(2), (3)).

(2) If SEPA obtains in any other manner under or by virtue of any statutory provision information which might be commercially confidential, SEPA must give notice to the person to whom or to whose business it relates notice that the information is required to be included in the register, and give him a reasonable opportunity of objecting to its inclusion on the grounds of commercial confidentiality. If an objection is made, SEPA must take into account the representations justifying the objection and determine whether the information is commercially confidential (section 42B(4)).

If SEPA determines that the information is not commercially confidential, the information cannot be entered in the register until twenty-one days after the date of notification of this determination to the person concerned. If that person appeals to the Secretary of State during that period, the information cannot be entered on the register until the appeal is determined or withdrawn (section 42B(5)).

8.4.8 Water pollution from abandoned mines
8.4.8.1 Introduction
A particularly serious source of water pollution in Scotland is the discharge of bright orange, highly acidic ferruginous water from abandoned mines which is highly damaging to aquatic life. SEPA's State of the Environment Report 1996 indicates that 167 such discharges in Scotland adversely affect up to 180 km of rivers (p 59). SEPA expects the problem to increase in the more recently abandoned coalfields as the water table rebounds to its natural level on the cessation of pumping operations and as a result of the increase in opencast mining.

8.4.8.2 Removal of the defence of permitting water pollution from abandoned mines
Although it is an offence under COPA and its predecessor statutes for a person to cause water pollution from an abandoned mine (section 30F; *Lockhart* v *National Coal Board* 1981 SCCR 9; 1981 SLT 161), COPA provides a defence for a person permitting water pollution from an abandoned mine (section 30J(3)). An exemption is also applicable in the case of a civil action by SEPA for the costs of preventive or remedial anti-pollution works undertaken by virtue of section 46(3)(b) of COPA, which enables SEPA to recover its costs from a person causing the pollution but not from a person permitting the pollution from an abandoned mine. Works notices which SEPA may serve on persons to require them to carry out anti-pollution works (section 46A) likewise may not be served on a person permitting water pollution from an abandoned mine (section 46A(8)). The existence of these defences and exemptions has been the target of considerable criticism because there seems to be little justification for this exceptional treatment of pollution from a particular source. A further criticism has been that the defences and exemptions have made the task of dealing with the problem of water pollution from abandoned mines more difficult, especially as it has proved to be very difficult to establish that a person has caused such water pollution (*R* v *British Coal Corporation* [1993] 227 ENDS Report 44).

The government was finally persuaded of the need to withdraw these various defences and exemptions in relation to permitting water pollution from an abandoned mine; this was done by means of amendments to COPA introduced by EA, but prospectively as from 31st December 1999 (COPA, sections 30J(4), 46(3A), 46A(9)). The delay seems largely to have been motivated by the privatisation of the coal industry and the desire not to impose any new liabilities which might have disturbed that process. The delayed withdrawal of the defence has resulted in criticism, not least because the coal supply contracts between the major mining companies and the electricity generators expire in 1998 (DTI, The Energy Report: Markets in Transition (HMSO, 1994), paragraph 4.24) and it is possible that many of the remaining deep mines in the UK will be closed at that time, prior to the withdrawal of the defences and exemptions.

8.4.8.3 Duty to notify SEPA of abandonment
However, EA has inserted a new Part IA into COPA which may assist in dealing with water pollution from abandoned mines. First, section

30Y of COPA contains a definition of abandonment in relation to a mine, while section 30Z imposes a new duty on mine operators to give SEPA six months' written notice of any proposed abandonment.

Abandonment is not exhaustively defined but includes a variety of physical indicators, as below, which make it clear that partial abandonment is encompassed within the definition:

— the discontinuation of any or all of the operations for the removal of water from the mine;

— the cessation of working of any relevant seam, vein or vein-system;

— the cessation of any shaft or outlet of the mine;

— in the case of a mine where activities other than mining activities are carried on (whether or not mining activities are also carried on in the mine):

  — the discontinuance of some or all of those other activities in the mine; and

  — any substantial change in the operations for the removal of water from the mine.

It is clearly possible for there to be several abandonments at a single colliery, in relation to each of which SEPA must be notified. Failure to notify SEPA is an offence (section 30Z(3)). There are defences available where the abandonment happens in an emergency in order to avoid danger to life or health and notice is given as soon as reasonably practicable after the incident (section 30Z(4)) and where the operator of the mine is an insolvency practitioner and he gives notice to SEPA as soon as reasonably practicable (section 30Z(5)). The notice must contain such information as is prescribed in regulations (section 30Z(2)) and must also be published in a newspaper circulating in the locality where the mine is situated (section 30Z(6)). Where SEPA receives such notification or otherwise learns of an abandonment and it considers that as a result of the abandonment land is or is likely to become contaminated, it must inform the local authority in whose area the land is situated (section 30Z(7)). The local authority's contaminated land functions will then come into play, although they cannot be used in relation to permitting water pollution from an abandoned mine until after 31st December 1999.

Finally, there may be some scope for use of contract law in dealing with this source of water pollution. In April 1995 an agreement was entered into between Forth River Purification Board (FRPB), the Coal Authority and the British Coal Corporation in relation to the Frances and Michael Collieries in Fife. This agreement required a specified monitoring and pumping programme to be carried out by British Coal and, from the termination of their interest in the collieries, by the Coal Authority, and for FRPB to be notified of any cessation of pumping. Since pumping has ceased at both collieries and British Coal's interest has reverted to the Coal Authority, should there be a default in its monitoring obligations and assuming that those obligations are sufficiently precise, SEPA, which has inherited this agreement from FRPB, could, if necessary, seek to enforce those obligations in the courts by way of contractual remedies.

Chapter 9

INTEGRATED POLLUTION CONTROL AND AIR POLLUTION CONTROL

9.1 INTRODUCTION

Prior to the coming into force of Part I of EPA, major emissions to different environmental media (air, land or water) were dealt with separately, often by different agencies. The solution implemented by Part I of EPA is IPC, with releases to all media considered as a whole by a single enforcing agency (SEPA) in order to minimise the total environmental impact.

IPC operates through the requirement for an authorisation to be obtained from SEPA for the release of prescribed substances and for the carrying on of prescribed processes. Authorisations are granted by SEPA subject to conditions to ensure that the best available technique not entailing excessive cost is used. Where the process is likely to involve the release of substances into more than one environmental medium, SEPA must also ensure that the best practicable environmental option is used.

Part I of EPA also regulates emissions to air through APC. The systems of IPC and APC are separate but largely identical. The Clean Air Act 1993 also contains controls on emissions to air, and air quality is regulated by EA. The statutory nuisance powers outlined in Chapter 10 are also relevant.

The practical operation of IPC and APC is assisted by non-statutory guidance. EA transferred responsibility to SEPA for IPC and APC from HMIPI and local authorities respectively.

The British system of IPC was the model for that contained in the Integrated Pollution Prevention and Control Directive (96/61/EC) which will introduce an integrated approach to pollution control throughout the EU, and require employment of the best available techniques of pollution prevention. Implementation of the directive, which is to be achieved by 14th October 1999, is likely to bring more processes in the UK within IPC (see, further, paragraph 9.4).

9.2 INTEGRATED POLLUTION CONTROL
9.2.1 Objectives

The purpose of IPC is to prevent or minimise pollution of the environment due to the release of substances into any environmental medium. Section 1 of EPA defines the key terms as follows:

— 'pollution of the environment' means pollution of the environment due to the release (into any environmental medium) from any process of substances which are capable of causing harm to man or any other living organisms supported by the environment;

— 'environment' consists of all, or any, of the following media, namely the air, water and land; the medium of air includes the air within buildings and the air within other natural or man-made structures above or below ground;

— 'harm' is defined as harm to the health of living organisms or other interference with the ecological systems of which they form part, and, in the case of man, includes offence caused to any of his senses or harm to his property; and 'harmless' has a corresponding meaning.

The underlying objectives of IPC are (section 7):

— ensuring that BATNEEC (the best available techniques not entailing excessive cost) are used to prevent the release of any prescribed substances, or, where that is not practicable by such means, to reduce the release to a minimum and render it harmless, and render harmless any other substances which might cause harm.

In relation to a process, BATNEEC not only refers to technical means and technology, but also to the number, qualifications, training and supervision of persons employed in the process, and the design, construction, lay-out and maintenance of the buildings in which it is carried on;

— where the process is likely to involve the release of substances into more than one environmental medium, ensuring that BPEO (the best practicable environmental option) available in respect of those substances is used to minimise pollution to the environment as a whole;

— compliance with any directions by the Secretary of State given for the implementation of obligations under EU treaties or international law relating to environmental protection;

— compliance with any limits or requirements and achievement of any quality standards or objectives prescribed by the Secretary of State; and

— compliance with any relevant requirements specified by or under a plan made by the Secretary of State with regard to emission limits and quality objectives;

— for prescribed processes involving disposal or recovery of waste the following objectives also apply (Waste Management Licensing Regulations 1994 (SI 1994/1056), Schedule 4, paragraphs 4, 8): ensuring that waste is recovered or disposed of without endangering human health and without using processes or methods which could harm the environment and in particular without

— risk to water, air, soil, plants or animals; or

— causing nuisance through noise or odours; or

— adversely affecting the countryside or places of special interest.

(Where planning permission has been granted after 30th April 1994, SEPA is not obliged to take account of the prevention of detriment to the amenities of the locality, presumably because this issue was taken into consideration by the planning authority when they granted the permission.)

In deciding the conditions to be attached to an authorisation to fulfil these objectives, SEPA must have regard to the guidance issued by the Secretary of State as to the techniques and environmental options that are appropriate for any description of prescribed process.

9.2.2 Authorisation

Authorisation is required from SEPA for the release of prescribed substances and for carrying on prescribed processes. It is an offence to carry on a prescribed process without an authorisation, or fail to comply with its conditions (sections 6, 23).

An authorisation must not be granted unless SEPA considers that the applicant will be able to carry on the process so as to comply with the conditions which would be included in the authorisation (section 6). For attempts by the English courts to determine what considerations are relevant for this purpose, see *R* v *Secretary of State for the Environment and N C Compton t/a R J Compton and Sons*, ex parte *West Wiltshire District Council* [1996] Env LR 312 and *R* v *Secretary of State for the Environment*, ex parte *Torridge District Council* [1997] EGCS 61. There is no equivalent to the 'fit and proper person' requirement in relation to waste management licences (see paragraph 7.4.3).

IPC authorisations are granted subject to such conditions as SEPA considers appropriate to achieve the objectives outlined above, having regard to any guidance issued by the Secretary of State as to the techniques and environmental options that are appropriate for any description of prescribed process. No conditions can be imposed for the sole purpose of securing the health of persons at work, or for regulating the final disposal by deposit in or on land of controlled waste (section 7(1), (9)).

In the absence of a specific condition, there is an implied condition attached to every authorisation that BATNEEC will be used (section 7(4)).

Possible conditions include those imposing limits on the amount or composition of any substance produced by or utilised in the process in any period, and requiring advance notification of any proposed change in the manner of carrying on the process.

The conditions of each authorisation should be reviewed by SEPA at least every four years (section 6(6)), and in accordance with the principle of BATNEEC can be varied to take account of improvements in attainable standards.

In addition to an IPC authorisation, planning permission may also be required. Chapter 5 discusses the issues which arise in these circumstances.

Where there is a proposal to make a change in a prescribed process which is capable of altering the substances released from the process or of affecting the amount or any other characteristic of any substance so released, it is possible to obtain a prior determination from SEPA (section 11):

— whether the proposed change would involve a breach of any condition or other provision of the authorisation, and, if so, whether SEPA would consider varying the condition/provision so that the change may be made;

— if it would not involve a breach, whether SEPA would be likely to vary the condition/provision as a result of the change; and

— whether the change would involve a substantial change in the manner in which the process is being carried on. If a substantial change would be involved, the holder is required to advertise the variation application, and SEPA must give notice of it to prescribed persons. In making its decision, SEPA must consider any representations received.

9.2.3 Prescribed processes and substances
The processes and substances for which authorisation is required are prescribed by the Environmental Protection (Prescribed Processes and Substances) Regulations 1991 (SI 1991/472), as amended by SI 1991/836, SI 1992/614, SI 1993/1749, SI 1993/2405, SI 1994/1271, SI 1994/1329, SI 1995/3247 and SI 1996/2678. The requirement for authorisations was progressively phased in over the period from 1st April 1992 to 31st August 1996 (see Schedule 3 (Part III) to the regulations).

Schedule 1 to the 1991 Regulations divides processes into six categories.

(1) Fuel production processes, combustion processes (including power generation).

(2) Metal production and processing.

(3) Mineral industries.

(4) Chemical industry.

(5) Waste disposal and recycling.

(6) Other industries.

Within each of these categories, there is a further subdivision into main categories of process. Under these main categories, actual processes are listed as Part A or B. However, in determining whether a process falls within Part A or B, regard must be had to the interpretation rules in Schedule 2, and the exceptions specified in regulation 4. Part A processes are subject to IPC, while Part B processes are regulated under APC.

Schedule 2 states that the description of a process includes any other process carried on at the same location by the same person as part of that process. In *HM Inspectorate of Pollution* v *Safety Kleen UK Ltd* [1994] 236 ENDS Report 41 it was held that the authorised process included keeping a tanker load of product from the process on the same site, and leakage from the tanker therefore amounted to a breach of the authorisation conditions.

Schedules 4, 5 and 6 to the 1991 Regulations prescribe substances the release of which to air, water and land respectively requires authorisation.

9.2.4 Application procedure

The procedures for obtaining an IPC authorisation are specified in the Environmental Protection (Applications, Appeals and Registers) Regulations 1991 (SI 1991/507), as amended by SI 1991/836, SI 1994/1271, SI 1996/667, SI 1996/979 and SI 1996/2678.

Application is made in writing to SEPA, accompanied by payment of the prescribed fee. The application must include the following information:

— the name, telephone number and address of the applicant;

— the address of the premises where the prescribed process will be carried on, and a map or plan showing the location of the premises;

— a description of the prescribed process;

— a list of prescribed substances, and any other substances which might cause harm if released into any environmental medium, which will be used in connection with, or which will result from, the carrying on of the process;

— a description of the techniques to be used for preventing the release of such substances into any environmental medium, for reducing the release to a minimum and for rendering harmless any such substances which are released;

— details of any proposed release of such substances into any environmental medium and an assessment of the environmental consequences;

— proposals for monitoring any release of such substances, the environmental consequences of any such release and the use of techniques to prevent or reduce the release to a minimum and for rendering harmless any such substances which are released;

— how the applicant proposes to comply with the implied conditions of BATNEEC and BPEO (see paragraph 9.2.1).

The applicant can request that information included in the application be excluded from the public register on grounds of its commercial confidentiality (see paragraph 9.2.10). There is also provision for the Secretary of State to direct that information be excluded from the public register where its inclusion would be contrary to the interests of national security.

The applicant is required to publish an advertisement in one or more newspapers circulating in the locality of the premises in which the pre-scribed process will be carried on. The advertisement must contain specified information, giving brief details of the application and where it may be inspected, and explaining that any person may make represen-tations in writing to SEPA within twenty-eight days beginning with the date of the advertisement. In contrast to planning applications, there is no system of neighbour notification.

Prior to determining the application, SEPA is required to consult the Secretary of State and relevant statutory bodies, such as the local auth-ority in whose area the process will be carried on, the Health and Safety Executive, the water authority and Scottish Natural Heritage. The nature and circumstances of the prescribed process determine which bodies are consulted.

Any representations received and comments from statutory consultees are taken into account by SEPA in the determination of the application. SEPA can either grant the authorisation subject to conditions (see para-graph 9.2.2) or refuse it. The applicant has a right of appeal against a refusal or against the conditions attached to the authorisation (see para-graph 9.2.7). There is also a right of appeal against a deemed refusal, where SEPA fails to determine the application within four months (with some exceptions), or such extended period as may be agreed by SEPA with the applicant.

9.2.5 Transfer, variation and revocation

An IPC authorisation can be transferred to a person who proposes to carry on the prescribed process in the holder's place, and will continue to apply on the same terms and conditions. The transferee must notify SEPA in writing of the transfer within twenty-one days of the date of transfer (section 9). In the absence of any provision for SEPA to con-sider whether the transferee will be able to comply with the conditions attached to the authorisation, SEPA's powers are limited to revocation or the service of an enforcement or prohibition notice (see paragraph 9.2.6).

SEPA may at any time vary an authorisation by serving a variation notice on the holder (section 10). In particular, it must vary an authori-sation if it appears to SEPA that different conditions should be imposed to secure compliance with the objectives set out in section 7 (see para-graph 9.2.2). Where the action to be taken in consequence of the variation will involve a substantial change in the manner in which the process is being carried on, the holder is required to advertise the action, and SEPA must give notice of it to statutory consultees. In making its decision, SEPA must consider any representations received. Following amendment of section 10 by EA, a further notice can be served amend-ing the variation notice. There is a right of appeal to the Secretary of State against a variation notice or a notice amending the same (see para-graph 9.2.7).

The holder of an authorisation may at any time apply to SEPA for variation of the conditions or other provisions of the authorisation. It is also possible to apply to SEPA for a prior determination of whether variation of the authorisation is required, and, if so, whether SEPA would grant the variation (see paragraph 9.2.2). The application procedure is prescribed in the Environmental Protection (Applications, Appeals and Registers) Regulations 1991. There is a right of appeal to the Secretary of State against a refusal of a variation application (see paragraph 9.2.7).

SEPA may at any time revoke an authorisation by notice in writing to the person holding the authorisation, but the revocation may not take effect until at least twenty-eight days from the date of service of the notice (section 12). In particular, an authorisation may be revoked where SEPA has reason to believe that the authorised prescribed process has never been carried on, or not for a period of twelve months. There is a right of appeal to the Secretary of State against revocation of an authorisation (see paragraph 9.2.7).

9.2.6 Enforcement and prohibition notices

SEPA may serve an enforcement notice if it is of the opinion that the person carrying on a prescribed process is contravening any condition of the authorisation, or is likely to contravene any such condition (section 13). The notice must specify the steps which must be taken to remedy the contravention or the matters making it likely that the contravention will arise, and the period within which these steps must be taken. There is a right of appeal to the Secretary of State against an enforcement notice (see paragraph 9.2.7).

A prohibition notice must be served by SEPA where it is of the opinion that continuing to carry on a prescribed process, or carrying it on in a particular manner, involves an imminent risk of serious pollution of the environment (section 14). A prohibition notice can be served even if no condition of the authorisation is being contravened, and may relate to any aspects of the process, whether regulated by the conditions of the authorisation or not. The notice must specify the steps to be taken to remove the risk and the period within which these must be taken; and directs that the authorisation shall cease to have effect to authorise the carrying on of the process, either wholly or to the extent specified, until the notice is withdrawn. Where the notice applies to part of the process, it may impose conditions to be observed in carrying on the part which is authorised to be carried on. SEPA must withdraw the notice once it is satisfied that the steps required by the notice have been taken. There is a right of appeal to the Secretary of State against a prohibition notice (see paragraph 9.2.7).

It is an offence to fail to comply with or contravene any requirement or prohibition imposed by an enforcement notice or prohibition notice, with liability on summary conviction to a fine not exceeding £20,000 and/or imprisonment for up to three months, and on conviction on indictment to an unlimited fine and/or imprisonment for up to two years (section 23).

In addition, if SEPA is of the opinion that prosecution would afford an ineffectual remedy, it may take civil proceedings in any court of competent jurisdiction for the purpose of securing compliance with the notice (section 24). The court's refusal to grant an injunction (interdict in Scotland) in *Tameside Metropolitan Borough Council* v *Smith Brothers*

(Hyde) Ltd [1995] 250 ENDS Report 42; [1996] Env LR D4 indicates that it will be difficult to show that prosecution will be ineffectual, particularly as the court also has power to order remediation following conviction (see paragraph 9.2.8).

9.2.7 Appeals to the Secretary of State

There is a right of appeal to the Secretary of State against the following decisions and notices (sections 15, 22):

— a refusal of authorisation, including a deemed refusal;

— grant of authorisation subject to conditions;

— refusal of a variation application;

— revocation of an authorisation;

— a variation notice;

— an enforcement notice;

— a prohibition notice;

— a determination that information is not commercially confidential.

The effect of an appeal against revocation is to prevent the revocation from taking effect pending determination or withdrawal of the appeal. In contrast, the operation of a variation, enforcement or prohibition notice is not suspended by the submission of an appeal. An appeal against a determination that information is not commercially confidential suspends the effect of that determination pending the outcome of the appeal.

The procedure for appeals is laid down in the Environmental Protection (Applications, Appeals and Registers) Regulations 1991 (see paragraph 9.2.4). Notice of appeal must be lodged within

— six months of the date of the decision on the application for authorisation or variation;

— six months from the end of the period of four months (with some exceptions) from the date of receipt by SEPA of the application for authorisation, if SEPA fails to determine the application within the four-month period, or within any longer period agreed by SEPA with the applicant (this is known as a deemed refusal appeal);

— the period before the date the revocation takes effect;

— two months from the date of the variation notice, or enforcement notice, or prohibition notice;

— twenty-one days from the date of notice of the determination that information is not commercially confidential.

The notice of appeal and supporting documents are submitted to the Secretary of State. A copy must be sent by the appellant to SEPA. If the appeal relates to an application, SEPA must in turn send notification of the appeal to any person who submitted representations and all statutory consultees. In relation to a revocation, variation notice, enforcement notice or prohibition notice, notification must be sent to any person who appears to SEPA likely to have a particular interest in the subject matter of the appeal. This notification explains that representations previously submitted will be sent by SEPA to the Secretary of State and will be considered in determining the appeal, and that further representations may be made to the Secretary of State within twenty-one days of the date of the notice.

The appeal can be determined on the basis of written submissions or a hearing or local inquiry. Either party is entitled as of right to a hearing, but the Secretary of State decides whether this will take the form of a hearing or a local inquiry. The appellant should indicate the choice of procedure in the notice of appeal. The written submissions procedure involves an exchange of written representations within the following timetable, which can be modified by the Secretary of State in individual cases. SEPA must submit any written representations to the Secretary of State within twenty-eight days of receiving the notice of appeal and supporting documents. The appellant has seventeen days to respond to these representations. Each party should send to the other a copy of the representations submitted to the Secretary of State. Any representations submitted by a third party will be copied by the Secretary of State to the appellant and SEPA, who must submit any response within fourteen days.

Where a hearing or inquiry is held, this will be chaired by a reporter appointed by the Secretary of State. The procedure adopted is at the reporter's discretion. The persons entitled to participate in the hearing or inquiry are the appellant, SEPA, and any statutory consultees. Other persons may be heard at the discretion of the reporter, who should not unreasonably withhold permission. Written notice of the date, time and place of the hearing or inquiry is given to the appellant, SEPA, statutory consultees, and any persons notified of the appeal who have made written representations to the Secretary of State. A notice giving this information will also be placed in a local newspaper, unless the appeal relates to a commercial confidentiality determination.

Following the hearing or inquiry, the reporter submits a written report of his conclusions and recommendations to the Secretary of State. In making his determination the Secretary of State is not bound to follow those recommendations. Notice of the decision by the Secretary of State on the appeal, together with a copy of the report where there has been a hearing or inquiry, is sent to the appellant, SEPA, and statutory consultees. Any other person who submitted representations or appeared at the hearing or inquiry is entitled to receive notice of the decision, but not a copy of the report.

Section 114 of EA permits the Secretary of State to delegate determination of certain appeals, including IPC appeals, to reporters. Where the reporter has been delegated power to determine the appeal, notice of his decision and a copy of the report is issued.

In determining the appeal, the Secretary of State or the reporter may

— affirm the decision appealed against;

— in an appeal against a refusal to grant an authorisation or a variation, direct SEPA to grant the authorisation or variation subject to conditions;

— quash all or any of the conditions challenged, and specify the conditions to be attached to the authorisation;

— quash the revocation, and give directions as to the conditions to be attached to the authorisation;

— quash or affirm the variation, enforcement or prohibition notice, with such modifications as he thinks fit.

Judicial review, of course, is available, provided that the appropriate criteria are satisfied (see paragraph 2.10), against an appeal decision of the Secretary of State or a reporter (see the cases referred to at paragraph 9.2.2).

9.2.8 Offences and remediation

IPC offences fall into two categories (section 23). The following offences carry liability on summary conviction to a fine not exceeding £20,000 and/or imprisonment for up to three months, and on conviction on indictment to an unlimited fine and/or imprisonment for up to two years:

— carrying on a prescribed process without an authorisation, or in breach of its conditions;

— failure to comply with or contravention of any requirement or prohibition imposed by an enforcement notice or a prohibition notice (SEPA also has power to take civil proceedings – see paragraph 9.2.6);

— failure to comply with an order made by the court requiring remedial steps to be taken (see below).

In a prosecution alleging failure to comply with a condition requiring the use of BATNEEC, the accused has the onus of proving that there was no better alternative technique not entailing excessive cost than was in fact used to satisfy the condition.

The following further offences carry liability on summary conviction to a fine not exceeding the statutory maximum (currently £5,000) and on conviction on indictment to an unlimited fine and/or imprisonment for up to two years:

— failure by the person to whom the authorisation is transferred to give notice of the transfer;

— failure without reasonable excuse to comply with a notice served by SEPA requiring information to be furnished;

— knowingly or recklessly making a statement which is false or misleading in a material particular, where the statement is made in purported compliance with a statutory requirement to furnish information, or for the purpose of obtaining the grant or variation of an authorisation to himself or any other person;

173

— intentionally making a false entry in any record required to be kept by virtue of a condition attached to an authorisation;

— with intent to deceive, forging or using a document issued or authorised in relation to a condition attached to an authorisation or required for any purpose associated therewith or making or possessing a document so closely resembling any such document as to be likely to deceive.

Following conviction for the offence of carrying on a prescribed process without an authorisation, or other than in accordance with its conditions, or for failure to comply with or contravention of any requirement or prohibition imposed by an enforcement notice or a prohibition notice, the court may, in addition to or instead of imposing any punishment, order the offender to take specified steps within a specified time to remedy any matters which relate to the offence and appear to the court to be matters which it is in his power to remedy (section 26). Failure to comply with such an order is an offence (above).

Where remediable harm is caused by commission of the offence of carrying on a prescribed process without an authorisation, or other than in accordance with its conditions, or for failure to comply with or contravention of any requirement or prohibition imposed by an enforcement notice or a prohibition notice, SEPA may arrange for any reasonable steps to be taken towards remedying the harm, and may recover the cost from any person convicted of that offence (section 27). This power can only be exercised with the written approval of the Secretary of State. Where any of the steps are to be taken on or will affect land in the occupation of any person other than the person on whose land the prescribed process is being carried on, the permission of that person is also required.

The first prosecution for breach of an IPC authorisation resulted in fines of £7,000 and £500 (*HM Inspectorate of Pollution* v *National Power* [1994] 229 ENDS Report 45). In contrast, the two prosecutions thus far in Scotland have resulted in admonishment and a fine of £250 respectively (*Adam* v *Scottish Hydro-Electric plc; Hamilton* v *Scottish Power plc* [1995] 247 ENDS Report 43).

9.2.9 Powers of SEPA
SEPA's general powers of entry, examination, investigation and seizure apply (see paragraph 1.5). SEPA also has a specific power to serve notice on any person requiring information to be furnished which SEPA reasonably considers it needs to discharge its IPC functions (section 19).

9.2.10 Public information
SEPA is required to maintain a register available at all reasonable times for inspection by the public free of charge, and to provide facilities for members of the public to obtain copies of entries on payment of reasonable charges (section 20).

The register must contain details of applications, authorisations, appeals, variation, enforcement and prohibition notices, revocations, convictions, and information obtained or furnished in pursuance of the conditions of authorisations. The Environmental Protection (Application, Appeals and Registers) Regulations 1991 require the register to contain details of other matters relating to the carrying on of prescribed processes or any pollution of the environment caused thereby, including any monitoring information obtained by SEPA as a result of its own monitoring or supplied to it by virtue of an authorisation condition, and any report published by SEPA relating to an assessment of the environmental consequences of the carrying on of a prescribed process in the locality of premises where the prescribed process is carried on under an authorisation.

Where information is excluded from the register on the grounds of national security or commercial confidentiality, the register must contain a statement indicating the existence of information of that description.

The Secretary of State has power to direct that information be excluded where its inclusion in the register would be contrary to the interests of national security (section 21). He also has power to direct that the public interest requires information to be included which would otherwise be commercially confidential (section 22).

Information which is determined to be commercially confidential by SEPA or the Secretary of State on appeal cannot be included in the register without the consent of the appropriate person. Information is commercially confidential, in relation to any individual or person, if its being contained in the register would prejudice to an unreasonable degree the commercial interests of that individual or person (section 22(11)). The information is initially excluded for four years, but an application for further exclusion can be made to SEPA on the grounds that the information remains commercially confidential (section 22(8)).

The issue of commercial confidentiality can arise in two ways.

(1) The person furnishing the information can request that it be excluded from the register on the grounds that it is commercially confidential, as regards himself or another person. SEPA has fourteen days to determine whether the information is commercially confidential (section 22(2),(3)).

(2) If SEPA obtains information which might be commercially confidential, it must give notice to the person to whom or to whose business the information relates, and provide a reasonable opportunity for that person to object to the inclusion of the information on the ground that it is commercially confidential. Following receipt of representations, SEPA must determine whether the information is commercially confidential (section 22(4)).

If SEPA determines that the information is not commercially confidential, the information cannot be entered in the register until twenty-one days after the date of notification of this determination to the applicant (section 22(5)). This provides an opportunity for an appeal to be submitted to the Secretary of State (above).

9.3 AIR POLLUTION CONTROL
9.3.1 EPA

Part I of EPA also regulates emissions to air through APC. The purpose of APC is to prevent or minimise pollution of the environment due to the release of substances into the air. APC was formerly operated by district and islands councils (and thus was known as local authority air pollution control or LAAPC), but is now the responsibility of SEPA. IPC/APC has progressively replaced the air pollution controls under the Alkali, etc, Works Regulation Act 1906.

APC applies to Part B processes and substances specified in the Environmental Protection (Prescribed Processes and Substances) Regulations 1991 (see paragraph 9.2.3). It was introduced in Scotland over the period from 1st April 1992 to 31st March 1993 (see Schedule 3 (Part IV) to the 1991 Regulations).

The framework and powers relating to APC are largely the same as the IPC régime outlined above. The main difference is that the implied condition of BPEO does not apply. There is a separate set of guidance notes for Part B processes.

9.3.2 The Clean Air Act 1993

The Clean Air Act 1993 (which consolidates a number of earlier legislative provisions) controls emissions of dark smoke from chimneys and industrial or trade premises (Part I), smoke, grit, dust and fumes in the context of furnaces (Part II), smoke control areas (Part III), and regulation of the lead content of motor fuel and the sulphur content of engine and furnace oil (Part IV). Processes controlled under Part 1 of EPA are excluded from Parts I to III of the 1993 Act by virtue of section 41.

9.3.3 Air quality standards

Sections 80–91 of EA (not yet in force) contain new provisions relating to air quality. The Secretary of State is required to prepare a national air quality strategy, which must be taken into account by SEPA when exercising its pollution control powers. In particular, IPC and APC are part of the means whereby the strategy is to be achieved. Local authorities must review current and likely future air quality within their areas, and designate air quality management areas. The Secretary of State is given wide powers to make regulations implementing the national air quality strategy, and generally relating to the assessment or management of air quality.

EU directives require the UK to maintain air quality standards. The Air Quality Standards Regulations 1989 (SI 1989/317) and the Ozone Monitoring and Information Regulations (SI 1994/440) implement directives setting limits for sulphur dioxide, nitrogen dioxide, lead and ozone. In terms of the regulations the Secretary of State is required to ensure that levels are measured and reduced to below the prescribed limits. Other directives impose limits on large combustion plants, municipal and hazardous waste incinerators, road vehicles, ozone depleting compounds such as CFCs, and volatile organic compounds.

The Air Quality Assessment and Management Directive (96/62/EC) will lead to 'daughter' directives on up to thirteen air pollutants, will require assessments of air quality in certain areas, and will require remedial plans to be drawn up in areas of poor air quality.

9.3.4 Statutory nuisance

Air pollution is also subject to control under the statutory nuisance régime contained in Part III of EPA (see Chapter 10).

9.4 Integrated pollution prevention and control (IPPC)

As mentioned in paragraph 9.1, the EU has now enacted the Integrated Pollution Prevention and Control Directive, the model for which was the IPC régime contained in Part I of EPA. Member states must implement the directive by 14th October 1999.

As the title of the directive suggests, there is an emphasis not only on control of pollution but also on prevention of pollution, although it should by no means be thought that the system of IPC is not also concerned with prevention – the twin concepts of BATNEEC and BPEO are both intended to ensure prevention as well as control. Additionally, at Annex I the directive contains a list of activities which are subject to its provisions. That list is more extensive than the list of processes which are presently subject to IPC. The directive focuses upon 'installations' where the activities set out in Annex I are carried out, which in turn suggests a greater concentration on particular types of business rather than on particular prescribed processes or substances.

Article 1 states that the purpose of the directive is to achieve integrated prevention and control of pollution arising from the Annex I activities and further that the directive lays down measures designed to prevent or, where that is not practicable, to reduce emissions in the air, water and land from these activities. The standard to be used to achieve these aims is that of 'best available techniques', defined in article 2. The definition explains that the word 'available' means techniques which have been developed on a scale which allows implementation in the relevant industrial sector under economically and technically viable conditions, taking into consideration the costs and advantages. In this respect, the standard of 'best available techniques' does have regard to what may be described as 'excessive costs', and is therefore very similar to BATNEEC.

Article 3 of the directive, which sets out the general principles, stresses, much more explicitly than the IPC régime, the concepts of prevention, waste avoidance and energy efficiency. In particular, installations must be operated in such a way that

— all the appropriate preventive measures are taken against pollution, in particular through application of the best available techniques;

— no significant pollution is caused;

— waste production is avoided, and where waste is produced, it is recovered or, if that is not technically and economically possible, it is disposed of so as to avoid or reduce any impact on the environment;

— energy is used efficiently;

— measures are taken to prevent accidents and limit their consequences; and

— measures are taken upon the closure of an installation to avoid pollution risk and to return the site to a satisfactory state.

The system, like IPC, is authorisation (permit)-based – see article 6. New installations will be subject to the terms of the directive with effect from 14th October 1999, ie, the date on which the directive must be implemented by member states (article 4). Existing installations must be brought into full compliance over an eight-year period starting from the date upon which the directive is brought into effect, ie, by 14th October 2007 (article 5).

Permits must be reviewed periodically – no time period is specified, in contrast to the IPC régime, where authorisations must be reconsidered every four years (article 13). However, it is provided that in any event permits must be reviewed (ie, not periodically) in certain events, such as where the pollution caused by the installation is of such significance that the existing emission limit values need to be revised or new values need to be included, or substantial changes in best available techniques make it possible to reduce emissions significantly without imposing excessive costs.

The list of activities referred to in article 1 and contained in Annex I is, as previously mentioned, broader than that which is relevant for the purposes of IPC. In particular, certain agricultural enterprises, including specified installations for the intensive rearing of poultry or pigs, and slaughterhouses, are covered (see Annex I, paragraph 6), as are landfills receiving more than 10 tonnes a day of waste or with a total capacity exceeding 25,000 tonnes, under exclusion of inert waste landfills (see Annex I, paragraph 5.4) and also a number of activities which are presently only subject to APC. The effect of these and other inclusions will be substantially to increase the number of installations which will be subject to IPC in Scotland – it is estimated that the number will more than double from its present level of about 200.

The consultation exercise to be carried out with a view to implementing the directive in the UK commenced in July 1997. It appears likely that the directive will be implemented by making adjustments to the scope and possibly also the content of the present IPC régime – given the origin and background of the directive, the necessary foundations are already in place in this jurisdiction.

Chapter 10

STATUTORY NUISANCE AND NOISE

10.1 INTRODUCTION

Property law has long recognised the concept of nuisance (for a further discussion, see paragraph 2.2). Broadly this amounts to infringement of a person's right to the use and enjoyment of his land by another person's conduct which falls short of physical intrusion on to that land. A nuisance may consist of physical damage to property, injury to health, or interference with physical comfort. For example, the noise caused by the construction of the grandstand for the Edinburgh Military Tattoo was held to be a nuisance to an occupier of a neighbouring flat (see paragraph 2.2.5). A person whose rights are infringed by a nuisance may seek a court order preventing it from continuing or reoccurring.

Specified categories of nuisances referred to as statutory nuisances can be the subject of action by councils or aggrieved individuals. Where a statutory nuisance is identified, the council for the area must serve an abatement notice. If this notice is not complied with, an offence is committed, and the council may carry out the work required to abate the nuisance and recover its expenses. A person aggrieved by the existence of a statutory nuisance may seek an order from the sheriff court requiring abatement of the nuisance.

From 1st April 1996 statutory nuisances have been regulated by Part III of EPA, as amended by the Noise and Statutory Nuisance Act 1993 and EA. This replaces the former provisions in the Public Health (Scotland) Act 1897 and COPA.

Noise is one of the forms of environmental pollution which are dealt with under the statutory nuisance provisions. Further noise controls are provided by Part III of COPA and other statutes.

10.2 STATUTORY NUISANCE
10.2.1 Enforcing agencies

All councils in Scotland have a duty to inspect their area from time to time to detect any statutory nuisances. Where a complaint of a statutory nuisance is made to them by a person living within their area, the council must take such steps as are reasonably practicable to investigate the complaint (EPA, section 79(1)). Powers of entry are conferred for the purpose of ascertaining whether or not a statutory nuisance exists, and taking any action, or executing any work, authorised or required by Part III of EPA (Schedule 3, paragraph 2). There are also powers to enter or open a vehicle, machinery or equipment, or remove it from the road to a secure place (Schedule 3, paragraph 2A). There is protection from personal liability for anything done in good faith for the purpose of executing Part III. The general powers of entry contained in section 108 of EA do not apply in respect of statutory nuisances.

For the purposes of the statutory nuisance provisions, the area for which the council are responsible includes the territorial sea lying seawards from any part of the seashore within their area (section 79(11)), and any vessels thereon other than a vessel powered by steam-reciprocating machinery.

Where the statutory nuisance appears to be wholly or partly caused by some act or default committed or taking place outside the council's area, the council may act as if the act or default were wholly within their area. The jurisdiction of the relevant sheriff court will remain unaffected (section 81(2)).

Where a port local authority or joint port local authority have been constituted, the functions in relation to statutory nuisances apply to that authority (section 79(8)), with the exception of the nuisances specified at section 79(1)(g) and (ga).

10.2.2 The list of statutory nuisances

Section 79(1) of EPA identifies the following as statutory nuisances:

(a) premises in such a state as to be prejudicial to health or a nuisance (discussed below);

(b) smoke, including soot, ash, grit and gritty particles emitted in smoke, emitted from premises so as to be prejudicial to health or a nuisance.
Exceptions: premises occupied on behalf of the Crown for naval, military or air force purposes or for the purposes of the Ministry of Defence or a visiting force (as defined in the Visiting Forces Act 1952); smoke emitted from a chimney of a private dwelling within a smoke control area; dark smoke emitted from a chimney of a building or a chimney serving the furnace of a boiler or industrial plant attached to a building or for the time being fixed to or installed on any land; smoke emitted from a railway locomotive steam engine; other dark smoke emitted from industrial or trade premises;

(c) fumes or gases emitted from private dwellings so as to be prejudicial to health or a nuisance;

(d) dust, steam, smell or other effluvia arising on industrial, trade or business premises and being prejudicial to health or a nuisance.
Exception: steam emitted from a railway locomotive engine;

(e) any accumulation or deposit which is prejudicial to health or a nuisance;

(f) any animal kept in such a place or manner as to be prejudicial to health or a nuisance;

(g) noise (including vibration) emitted from premises so as to be prejudicial to health or a nuisance.

Exceptions: premises occupied on behalf of the Crown for naval, military or air force purposes or for the purposes of the Ministry of Defence or a visiting force; and noise caused by aircraft other than model aircraft;

(ga) noise (including vibration) that is prejudicial to health or a nuisance and is emitted from or caused by a vehicle, machinery or equipment (including a musical instrument) in a road.
Exceptions: noise made by traffic; by any naval, military or air force of the Crown, or by a visiting force; or by a political demonstration or a demonstration supporting or opposing a cause or campaign;

(h) any other matter declared by any enactment to be a statutory nuisance.

References to 'premises' include land and any vessel other than a vessel powered by steam-reciprocating machinery.

Apart from the specific exceptions noted above, in terms of section 79(1A) (which is not yet commenced), no matter shall constitute a statutory nuisance to the extent that it consists of, or is caused by, any land being in a 'contaminated state'. This will prevent the use of statutory nuisance powers to remove a deposit of asbestos in similar circumstances to *Clydebank District Council* v *Monaville Estates Ltd* 1982 SLT (Sh Ct) 2. Land is in a 'contaminated state' where it is in such a condition, by reason of substances in, on or under the land, that harm is being caused or there is a possibility of harm being caused, or pollution of controlled waters is being, or is likely to be caused, as these terms are as defined by section 78A. As the powers conferred by Part IIA of EPA in relation to contaminated land refer to 'significant harm' and 'a significant possibility of such harm being caused', this exclusion of the statutory nuisance powers goes well beyond the extent of the Part IIA powers (which are examined in Chapter 6).

The various categories of statutory nuisance are all restricted to instances which are prejudicial to health or a nuisance. '[P]rejudicial to health' is defined as injurious, or likely to cause injury, to health.

EPA provides no definition of 'nuisance'. In Scotland, the word is given the meaning which it has at common law (*Meri Mate Ltd* v *City of Dundee District Council* (Sh Ct) 1994 SCLR 960 (Notes)). It therefore appears that a statutory nuisance only exists where there is a common law nuisance which falls within one of the categories of statutory nuisance. This may place limits on the usefulness of statutory nuisance for environmental, as opposed to public health, purposes, particularly as it has been declared in a judgment relating to statutory nuisance (*Perth County Council* v *Moncrieff* 1957 SLT (Sh Ct) 33) that

> 'An essential element of nuisance is that it is an act of one party which materially infringes the natural rights of others or of another. There cannot be a nuisance in the abstract; there must be both an author and a sufferer.'

The scope of nuisance at common law in Scotland is narrower than in English law (Stair Memorial Encyclopaedia, Volume 14, paragraphs 2018–2025). It is unclear what effect, if any, this has on the corresponding laws of statutory nuisance, but it cannot be assumed that decisions of the English courts on statutory nuisance will be followed by the Scottish courts.

At common law nuisance refers to the invasion of either an interest in the use and enjoyment of property (such as the interest of an owner or occupier), or an interest of a member of the public in the use and enjoyment of public places such as roads or navigable rivers (Stair Memorial Encyclopaedia, Volume 14, paragraph 2002). This may consist of physical damage to property, injury to health, or interference with personal comfort.

The following principles should be applied in identifying a nuisance (*Watt* v *Jamieson* 1954 SC 56 at p 58).

— A balance has to be held between the freedom of a proprietor to use his property as he pleases and the duty of a proprietor not to inflict material loss or inconvenience on adjoining proprietors or adjoining property.

— In every case the answer depends on considerations of fact and of degree.

— It is not always necessary to aver that the type of use complained of was in itself non-natural, unreasonable and unusual.

— The proper approach is from the standpoint of the victim.

— It must be accepted that a certain amount of inconvenience, annoyance, disturbance and even damage must be accepted depending upon the locality – for example, where the pursuer stays in a city tenement.

  Thus the character of the locality may be relevant in assessing whether a nuisance exists. Following a grant of planning permission for dockyard use, it was held that the character of the area had changed, and the allegations of nuisance were assessed on the basis that the area was a dockyard rather than a residential area (*Gillingham Borough Council* v *Medway (Chatham) Dock Co Ltd* [1992] JPL 458; [1992] 1 PLR 113). The mere fact of the existence of a planning permission is not, however, conclusive.

— The critical question is whether what the victim was exposed to was more than reasonably tolerable when due weight has been given to all the surrounding circumstances of the offensive conduct and its effects.

  A one-off event may not involve noise nuisance such as to inconvenience beyond a reasonable level of tolerance (*Cumnock and Doon Valley District Council* v *Dance Energy Associates Ltd* 1992 GWD 25-1441).

— If that test is satisfied, the law does not accept as a defence that the nature of the user complained of was usual, familiar and normal.

In addition, an activity authorised by a grant of planning permission can still be a nuisance (*Wheeler* v *J J Saunders Ltd* [1995] JPL 619; [1995] 1 PLR 55; (1995) 48 SPEL 35).

The difficulties of applying these principles are illustrated in the following judicial statement (*Wivenhoe Port* v *Colchester Borough Council* [1985] JPL 175 at p 178):

> '[A] nuisance to be a statutory nuisance had to be one interfering materially with the personal comfort of the residents, in the sense that it materially affected their wellbeing although it might not be prejudicial to their health. Thus, dust falling on motor cars might cause inconvenience to their owners; it might even diminish the value of their motor car; but this would not be a statutory nuisance. In the same way, dust falling on gardens or trees, or on stock held in shop would not be a statutory nuisance. But dust in eyes or hair, even if not shown to be prejudicial to health, would be so as an interference with personal comfort.'

The category 'premises in such a state as to be prejudicial to health or a nuisance' has been the subject of several court decisions.

— Offensive odours caused by keeping cats in a dwelling house were held not to be a nuisance (*City of Glasgow District Council* v *Carroll* 1991 SLT (Sh Ct) 46).

— Condensation in homes amounted to a nuisance (*Renfrew District Council* v *McGourlick* 1987 SLT 538), but not a leaking roof and worm-eaten floor (*Perth County Council* v *Moncrieff*).

— Noise and vibration from road and rail traffic rendered premises in such a state as to be prejudicial to health or a nuisance due to lack of sound insulation. The question was not whether the noise itself was a statutory nuisance but whether the premises are in such a state as to be prejudicial to health; that may be the case for a variety of external factors, such as weather, noise, or the incursion of sewage (*Southwark London Borough Council* v *Ince* (1989) 21 HLR 504).

— '[P]remises' means the premises which are affected by the nuisance, not the premises causing the nuisance. The 'premises' were the flat with rising damp and not the outside wall which caused the rising damp, irrespective of whether the owner of those premises is responsible for causing the statutory nuisance (*Pollway Nominees* v *Havering London Borough Council* (1989) 21 HLR 462).

10.2.3 Abatement notices

Where the council are satisfied that a statutory nuisance exists, or is likely to occur or recur, they must serve an abatement notice (section 80(1)). If a statutory nuisance has been identified, service of an abatement notice is mandatory, and not a matter for the council's discretion (*R* v *Carrick District Council*, ex parte *Shelley* [1996] Env LR 273).

The consent of the Secretary of State is required before an abatement notice can be served in relation to certain categories of statutory nuisance if proceedings might be instituted under Part I of EPA (IPC and APC; see Chapter 9), the Alkali, etc, Works Regulation Act 1906 or the Health and Safety at Work etc Act 1974, section 5 (section 79(10)).

The notice requires the abatement of the nuisance within a specified time or prohibits or restricts its occurrence or recurrence, and can require the execution of works and the taking of other steps as may be necessary for these purposes (section 80(1)). Where an abatement notice prohibits the nuisance recurring, this operates as an indefinite restriction (*R v Birmingham Justices*, ex parte *Guppy* (1988) 86 LGR 264).

An abatement notice will only be invalid if its requirements are so imprecise as to be void for uncertainty or are manifestly impracticable (*Strathclyde Regional Council v Tudhope* 1983 SLT 22). However, the notice should give sufficient details of the alleged nuisance to give the recipient fair notice of the nature of the complaint (*Meri Mate Ltd v City of Dundee District Council*). The notice must also include reference to the right of appeal, and intimate the time-limit for the submission of such an appeal (Schedule 3, paragraph 6).

The abatement notice is served (section 80(2)) on:

— the 'person responsible' for the nuisance;

— the owner of the premises where the nuisance arises from any defect of a structural character;

— the owner or occupier of the premises where the person responsible for the nuisance cannot be found or the nuisance has not yet occurred.

The 'person responsible' for the nuisance is the person to whose act, default or sufferance the nuisance is attributable (section 79(7)). In relation to a vehicle, this includes the registered owner and the driver. In relation to machinery or equipment, this includes the operator. Where asbestos had been deposited on land prior to the land being sold, the owner was held to be the author of the nuisance caused by the deposit, and it was irrelevant that the notice did not state that the true authors could not be found (*Clydebank District Council v Monaville Estates Ltd*). Where more than one person is responsible for a statutory nuisance, the abatement notice procedure will apply to each of them whether or not what any one of them is responsible for would by itself amount to a nuisance (section 81(1)).

Where the statutory nuisance consists of noise emitted from or caused by a vehicle, machinery or equipment in a road, and more than one person is responsible for the nuisance, the abatement notice can be served on any one of those persons (section 81(1A)). Where this category of statutory nuisance has not yet occurred, or arises from noise emitted from or caused by an unattended vehicle or unattended machinery or equipment, there is a procedure for serving the abatement notice by fixing the notice to the vehicle, machinery or equipment (section 80A).

10.2.4 Appeals
The person served with the abatement notice has twenty-one days from the date of service to appeal against the notice to the sheriff court (section 80(3)). If no appeal is lodged against the notice, the terms of the notice cannot be challenged in any subsequent prosecution (*Stagecoach Ltd v McPhail* 1988 SCCR 289; the position in England appears to be the opposite, see *Sterling Homes (Midlands) Ltd v Birmingham City Council* [1996] Env LR D8).

The appeal is by way of summary application (Schedule 3, paragraph

1A). The procedure for these appeals is prescribed by the Statutory Nuisance (Appeals) (Scotland) Regulations 1996 (SI 1996/1076). These state that the following grounds of appeal are competent:

— that the abatement notice is not justified by section 80, presumably because a statutory nuisance does not exist, or is not likely to occur or recur. On an appeal, the relevant time to assess the nuisance is as the date of the hearing and not the date of the notice (*Meri Mate Ltd v City of Dundee District Council; Johnsons News of London v Ealing London Borough Council, The Times*, 26th July 1989);

— that there has been some informality, defect or error in, or in connection with, the abatement notice, or in, or in connection with, any copy of the notice served under section 80A(3) (certain notices in respect of vehicles, machinery or equipment). However, the court is directed to dismiss the appeal if it is satisfied that the informality, defect or error was not a material one;

— that the authority have refused unreasonably to accept compliance with alternative requirements, or that the requirements of the notice are otherwise unreasonable in character or extent, or are unnecessary;

— that the time(s) specified within which the requirements of the notice are to be complied with is not reasonably sufficient for the purpose;

— where the defence of best practical means would be available in a prosecution (below), that best practical means were used to prevent the nuisance, or to counteract its effects;

— in relation to noise nuisance, that the level of noise did not exceed a level specified in certain forms of notices or consents issued by the council (this also operates as a defence to prosecution, see below);

— in relation to noise emitted from or caused by a vehicle, machinery or equipment in a road, that the requirements of the abatement notice are more onerous than the requirements in force in relation to that noise by virtue of a condition attached to a consent given under the Noise and Statutory Nuisance Act 1993, Schedule 2, paragraph 1 (loudspeakers in roads);

— that the notice should have been served on some other person, being the person responsible for the nuisance, or for the vehicle, machinery or equipment; or, in the case of a nuisance arising from any defect of a structural character, the owner of the premises; or, in the case where the person responsible for the nuisance cannot be found or the nuisance has not yet occurred, the owner or occupier of the premises;

— that rather than serving the notice on the appellant, it would have been lawful and equitable for the notice to have been served on the occupier of the premises, where the appellant is the owner, or on the owner, where the appellant is the occupier;

— that in addition to serving the notice on the appellant, it would have been lawful and equitable for the notice to have been served on the person also responsible for the nuisance, or a person who is also owner of the premises, or a person who is also the occupier, or a person who is also the person responsible for the vehicle, machinery or equipment.

Where the appellant contends that the notice should have been served on another person, either in substitution for or in addition to service on the appellant, the appellant must serve a copy of the notice of appeal on that person. He may also serve a copy of the notice of appeal on any other person having an interest in the premises, vehicle, machinery or equipment in question.

The court may quash the notice, or vary its terms in favour of the appellant in such manner as it thinks fit, or dismiss the appeal. A notice varied by the court is final and has effect as if it had been varied by the council.

The court may also make such order as it thinks fit in relation to the person by whom any work is to be executed and the contribution to be made by any person towards the cost of the work, or as to the proportions in which any expenses which may become recoverable by the council (such as the expenses of work undertaken to abate the nuisance, see below) are to be borne by the appellant and any other person. In exercising these powers, the court is directed to have regard to the terms and conditions of any relevant tenancy and to the nature of the works required, and must be satisfied before it imposes any requirement on a person other than the appellant that that person has received a copy of the notice of appeal.

Submission of an appeal does not necessarily suspend the operation of the notice pending determination or abandonment of the appeal. The notice is only suspended if

— compliance would involve any person in expenditure on the carrying out of works before the hearing of the appeal, or, in the use of noise nuisances only, the noise to which the notice relates is noise necessarily caused in the course of the performance of some duty imposed by law on the appellant; and

— the nuisance to which the notice relates is (1) not injurious to health, or (2) not likely to be of a limited duration such that suspension of the notice would render it of no practical effect, or if (3) the expenditure which would be incurred by any person in the carrying out of works in compliance with the abatement notice before any appeal has been decided would be disproportionate to the public benefit to be expected in that period from such compliance (if any of these criteria do apply (ie, if the nuisance is injurious to health, etc) the abatement notice is required to include a statement that the notice shall have effect notwithstanding any appeal).

10.2.5 Offences and penalties

It is an offence for the person on whom the abatement notice is served, without reasonable excuse, to contravene or fail to comply with any requirement or prohibition imposed by the notice. On summary conviction there is liability to a fine not exceeding level 5 on the standard scale (currently £5,000) together with a further fine of one-tenth of that level for each day on which the offence continues after the conviction. If the offence is committed on industrial, trade or business premises, the maximum fine on summary conviction is increased to £20,000 (section 80(4)–(6)).

10.2.6 Defences

It is a defence to prosecution to prove that the best practicable means were used to prevent the nuisance, or to counteract its effects (section 80(7)). This defence is not available in relation to some of the categories of statutory nuisance, and only applies to others in restricted circumstances (see section 80(8)).

'Best practicable means' is to be interpreted as follows (section 79(9)):

— 'practicable' means reasonably practicable having regard among other things to local conditions and circumstances, to the current state of technical knowledge and to the financial implications;

— the means to be employed include the design, installation, maintenance and manner and periods of operation of plant and machinery, and the design, construction and maintenance of buildings and structures;

— the test is to apply only insofar as compatible with any duty imposed by law;

— the test is to apply only insofar as compatible with safety and safe working conditions, and with the exigencies of any emergency or unforeseeable circumstances;

— where a code of practice under section 71 of COPA (noise minimisation) is applicable, regard shall also be had to guidance given in it.

Where the statutory nuisance involved falls within either of the categories directed at noise, it is a defence (see section 80(9)) to prove that

— the alleged offence was covered by a notice served under section 60 or a consent given under section 61 or 65 of COPA (maximum or agreed levels of noise); or

— the level of noise emitted from the premises did not contravene a notice served in relation to the premises under section 66 of COPA, or in the absence of such a notice, did not exceed the level fixed under section 67.

10.2.7 Remedies on failure to comply with abatement notices

If the abatement notice is not complied with, the council may abate the nuisance and do whatever may be necessary in execution of the notice, whether or not the offence has been prosecuted. Any expenses reasonably incurred may be recovered from the person by whose act or default the nuisance was caused and, if that person is the owner of the premises, from any person who is for the time being the owner thereof. The sher-

POLLUTION CONTROL: THE LAW IN SCOTLAND

iff may apportion the expenses between the persons by whose acts or defaults the nuisance is caused in a fair and reasonable manner (section 81(3), (4)). The provisions of section 81A making the expenses a charge on premises do not apply to Scotland.

If the council consider that prosecution would afford an inadequate remedy, they may take civil court proceedings for the purpose of securing the abatement, prohibition or restriction of the nuisance, notwithstanding that the council have suffered no damage from the nuisance (section 81(5)). The requirements of section 81(5) cannot be sidestepped by the use of any more general power of a council to institute civil proceedings (*Vale of White Horse District Council* v *Allen* [1997] Env LR 212).

In relation to statutory nuisance consisting of noise emitted from premises, it should be noted that the provisions of the Noise Act 1996 permitting seizure and removal of equipment do not extend to Scotland.

10.2.8 Summary proceedings by person aggrieved by statutory nuisances

It is competent for any person aggrieved by the existence of a statutory nuisance to make a summary application to the sheriff court (section 82). There is no requirement that the person first give notice of the alleged statutory nuisance and allow a reasonable opportunity for it to be abated (*Sandwell Metropolitan Borough Council* v *Bujok* [1990] 3 All ER 385). Unlike the abatement notice provisions, a section 82 application can only be made where a statutory nuisance exists (ie, not where it is likely to occur).

The term 'person aggrieved' is not defined by the Act, but it seems likely that the person making the summary application would require to demonstrate a link between himself and the alleged nuisance, such as a prejudicial effect on his health as a result of the alleged nuisance or an interference with use or enjoyment of property. This provision has been used by occupants of substandard premises to force their landlord to carry out repairs (see paragraph 10.2.2). However, an environmental pressure group might not have sufficient interest to raise proceedings under section 82.

Written notice must be given of the intention to make the summary application, specifying the matter complained of. Not less than twenty-one days' notice must be given, or not less than three days in relation to noise nuisance (section 82(6), (7)). Notice must be given (section 82(4)) to

— the person responsible for the nuisance; or

— where the nuisance arises from any defect of a structural character, the owner of the premises; or

— where the person responsible for the nuisance cannot be found, the owner or occupier of the premises; or

— in relation to a nuisance caused by noise emitted from or caused by an unattended vehicle or unattended machinery or equipment, the person responsible for the vehicle, machinery or equipment.

Where more than one person is responsible, proceedings may be brought against each of them whether or not what any one of them is responsible for would by itself amount to a nuisance (section 82(5)).

If the sheriff is satisfied that the alleged nuisance exists, or that although abated it is likely to recur on the same premises or road, section 82(2) requires an order to be made

— requiring the defender to abate the nuisance within a specified time and to execute any works necessary for that purpose; and/or

— prohibiting a recurrence of the nuisance and requiring the defender within a specified time to execute any works necessary to prevent the recurrence.

The power to order that works be carried out is not limited to works of repair and may extend to improvements to premises (*Birmingham District Council* v *Kelly* (1985) 17 HLR 573). Where the defender is served notice of the proceedings as the person responsible for the nuisance, an order prohibiting recurrence cannot be made where the defender is not the person responsible for the nuisance recurring (*Carr* v *Hackney London Borough Council, The Times,* 9th March 1995).

If the sheriff is satisfied that the alleged nuisance exists and is of the opinion that it renders the premises unfit for human habitation, the order may also prohibit the use of the premises for such habitation until works are carried out to render it fit for that purpose to the satisfaction of the sheriff (section 82(3)).

If neither the person responsible for the nuisance nor the owner or occupier of the premises, nor the person responsible for the vehicle, machinery or equipment, can be found, the sheriff may direct the council to carry out the required steps, but only after giving the council an opportunity to be heard (section 82(13)). A similar power exists (section 82(11)) after a person has been convicted for contravening an order made by the sheriff under section 82.

The sheriff court is not given the power conferred on the magistrates' court in England and Wales to impose a fine at the same time as ordering a nuisance to be abated. In consequence, there is no requirement for proof beyond reasonable doubt as the proceedings do not have a criminal element.

If it is proved that the alleged nuisance existed at the date of the summary application, then, whether or not at the date of the hearing it still exists or is likely to recur, the sheriff must order the defender to pay to the person bringing the proceedings such amount as the sheriff considers reasonably sufficient to compensate him for any expenses properly incurred by him in the proceedings (section 82(12)). Where there is more than one defender, the sheriff may order payment in such proportions as appears fair and reasonable.

It is an offence without reasonable excuse (section 82(8)) to contravene any requirement or prohibition imposed by an order made by the sheriff under section 82. On summary conviction there is liability to a maximum fine of level 5 on the standard scale together with a further fine of one-tenth of that level for each day on which the offence continues after the conviction.

The best practicable means defence applies (or not) to prosecutions in the same circumstances as are outlined above (see paragraph 10.2.6). It does not apply in the case of a nuisance which is such as to render the premises unfit for human habitation.

10.3 NOISE

The main statutory provisions relating to noise are found in the statutory nuisance provisions in EPA (see paragraph 10.2) and the noise provisions in Part III of COPA. With the exception of provisions relating to loudspeakers and audible intruder alarms, the Noise and Statutory Nuisance Act 1993 amends EPA and COPA provisions. Other relevant statutory provisions include

— the Civic Government (Scotland) Act 1982, which makes it an offence in certain circumstances to play an instrument, sing or play a radio;

— the Criminal Justice and Public Order Act 1994, which provides the police with powers in relation to open-air raves;

— the Land Compensation (Scotland) Act 1973, which confers a right to compensation for depreciation in value of property caused by noise or vibration from the use of public works.

The Noise Act 1996, which provides a summary procedure for dealing with noise emitted from dwellings, does not apply to Scotland.

It should also be noted that noise levels can be regulated by planning conditions and agreements.

10.3.1 Statutory nuisance (EPA)

The categories of statutory nuisance (see paragraph 10.2.2) include noise and/or vibration which is

— emitted from premises so as to be prejudicial to health or a nuisance; or

— prejudicial to health or a nuisance and is emitted from or caused by a vehicle, machinery or equipment (including a musical instrument) in a road.

The exceptions are (in relation to both categories) noise made by naval, military or air forces, and in relation to the first category, noise caused by aircraft other than model aircraft, and for the second category, noise made by traffic or by a political demonstration or a demonstration supporting or opposing a cause or campaign (EPA, section 79(1)).

For example, a nuisance may occur due to noise caused by the loading and unloading of vehicles within premises (*Greenline Carriers (Tayside)* v *City of Dundee District Council* 1991 SLT 673).

In addition to these categories, noise can also result in the occurrence of other statutory nuisances. For example, noise and vibration from road and rail traffic rendered premises in such a state as to be prejudicial to health or a nuisance due to lack of sound insulation (*Southwark London Borough Council* v *Ince*).

The disadvantage of these provisions is that once a statutory nuisance has been identified, the council must serve an abatement notice on the person responsible and allow a period for compliance with that notice before they can take further action.

10.3.2 Noise from construction sites (COPA)

To control noise and vibration from construction sites councils have the power to impose requirements either during or in advance of work (COPA, section 60). Any person intending to carry out construction work is also given the right to apply to the council for a prior consent (section 61).

These provisions apply to the following works:

— the erection, construction, alteration, repair or maintenance of buildings, structures or roads;

— breaking up, opening or boring under any road or adjacent land in connection with the construction, inspection, maintenance or removal of works;

— demolition or dredging work;

— the construction, structural alteration, maintenance or repair of any railway line or siding or any dock, harbour, inland navigation, tunnel, bridge, viaduct, waterworks, reservoir, pipeline, aqueduct, sewer, sewage works or gas-holder.

In exercising their power to serve a notice, the council must have regard to

— any code of practice (see paragraph 10.3.6);

— the need to ensure that the best practicable means (defined by section 72) are employed to minimise noise;

— the desirability in the interests of the recipient(s) of the notice of specifying other methods or plant or machinery which would be substantially as effective in minimising noise as other options and more acceptable to them;

— the need to protect any persons in the locality in which the premises in question are situated from the effects of noise.

The notice imposes requirements as to the way in which the works are to be carried out, and can include

— the plant or machinery which is or is not to be used;

— the hours during which the works may be carried out;

— the levels of noise and/or vibration which may be emitted from the premises in question or at any specified point on those premises or which may be so emitted during specified hours; and

— provision for any change of circumstances.

The notice may specify the time within which it is to be complied with, and require the execution of works and the taking of other steps as may be necessary for the purposes of the notice or as may be specified in the notice. The notice will be valid unless it is so imprecise as to be void for uncertainty or manifestly impracticable (*Strathclyde Regional Council* v *Tudhope*).

The notice is served on the person who appears to be carrying out, or going to carry out, the works. If they think fit, the council can also serve the notice on other persons who appear to be responsible for, or to have control over, the carrying out of the works.

A person served with the notice may appeal to the sheriff court within twenty-one days from the date of service. A notice restricting audible works to 8 am to 7 pm (1 pm on Saturdays) and prohibiting such works on a Sunday in a residential area was upheld on appeal (*Adam (Scotland) Ltd* v *Bearsden and Milngavie District Council* 1996 SLT (Sh Ct) 21).

The procedure for appealing against a section 60 notice, including the grounds of appeal, the powers of the court, and the circumstances in which the effect of the notice is suspended pending determination of the appeal, is prescribed by the Control of Noise (Appeals) (Scotland) Regulations 1983 (SI 1983/1455).

It is an offence for any person on whom the notice is served without reasonable excuse to contravene or fail to comply with its requirements. On summary conviction there is liability to a fine not exceeding level 5 (currently £5,000) on the standard scale, together with a further fine not exceeding £50 for each day on which the offence continues after conviction. It may also be possible for the council to obtain an interdict to prevent infringement of the notice (*City of London Corporation* v *Bovis Construction Ltd* [1992] 3 All ER 697).

The reason for seeking a prior consent from the council is that it provides a defence to any prosecution under section 60 (section 61(8)). It also provides a ground of appeal against an abatement notice and a defence to any prosecution for failure to comply with such a notice (paragraph 10.2.6). However, the consent does not provide a defence to a summary application by an aggrieved person (see paragraph 10.2.8).

The application for consent must contain particulars of

— the works, and the method by which they are to be carried out; and

— the steps proposed to be taken to minimise noise and vibration resulting from the works.

The application cannot be made in advance of any application for a building warrant which may be required for the works.

The council have twenty-eight days to determine the application. They must have regard to the same considerations which apply to the decision to serve a notice under section 60. If they consider that the application contains sufficient information and that, if the works are carried out in accordance with the application, they would not serve a section 60 notice, a consent must be issued. The consent can be issued subject to conditions, including limitations on the duration of the consent, and limitations or qualifications allowing for any change of circumstances.

It is an offence

— knowingly to carry out works, or permit works to be carried out, in contravention of any conditions attached to a section 61 consent;

— for the applicant for consent to fail to take all reasonable steps to bring the consent to the notice of any other person who is carrying out the works.

The penalties applicable to a contravention of a section 60 notice apply (above).

There is a right of appeal to the sheriff court if the council fail to give a consent within twenty-eight days, or if any condition is attached to the consent or it is limited or qualified in any way. The appeal must be lodged within twenty-one days of the decision or the expiry of the twenty-eight-day period. The grounds of appeal and powers of the court are specified in the Control of Noise (Appeals) (Scotland) Regulations 1983.

10.3.3 Loudspeakers

Unless the council have granted a consent under Schedule 2 to the Noise and Statutory Nuisance Act 1993, it is an offence to operate or permit the operation of a loudspeaker in a road between 9 pm and 8 am; and at any other time for the purpose of advertising any entertainment, trade or business (COPA, section 62). On summary conviction there is liability to a fine not exceeding level 5 (currently £5,000) on the standard scale, together with a further fine not exceeding £50 for each day on which the offence continues after conviction.

There is an exception made in relation to loudspeakers operated by ice-cream vans between 12 noon and 7 pm, but only if the loudspeaker is operated so as not to give reasonable cause for annoyance to persons in the vicinity. It is unclear whether the effect of section 7(6)(a) of the 1993 Act is to disapply in Scotland the exceptions listed in section 62(2) of COPA, which include loudspeakers used by the emergency services and public utilities.

The council cannot give consent to the operation of a loudspeaker in connection with any election or for the purpose of advertising any entertainment, trade or business.

10.3.4 Noise abatement zones and orders, noise level registers, noise reduction notices (COPA)

Every council have a duty to inspect their area from time to time to decide how to exercise their powers concerning noise abatement zones (COPA, section 57). Such zones enable the council to record existing noise levels which cannot then be exceeded without their written consent. It is competent for the zone to apply only to specified classes of premises. Within the zone the council also have power to require reduction of noise levels, and can specify acceptable noise limits for new or altered premises.

A noise abatement zone is designated by a noise abatement order made by the council (section 63). Before making such an order the council must follow the procedural requirements specified in Schedule 1, including service of notice on every owner, lessee and occupier of premises to which the order will relate and an advertisement for two successive weeks in a local newspaper, indicating the general effect of the proposed order and specifying the period within which any objections can be submitted. The council must consider any objections before making the order, but there is no requirement to hold a public local inquiry.

Following designation of a noise abatement zone, the council must measure the level of noise emanating from premises within the zone to which the noise abatement order relates (section 64). It is for the council to determine where these measurements are to be made. The methods of taking these measurements are specified in the Noise Levels (Measurement and Registers) (Scotland) Regulations 1982 (SI 1982/600). The measurements must be recorded in the noise level register kept by the council, which must be open to public inspection free of charge at all reasonable hours. A copy of the record must be served on the owner and occupier of the premises to which the measurement relates. Any person receiving a copy of the record may appeal to the Secretary of State against the record within twenty-eight days of its service. The procedure for appeals is specified by the Control of Noise (Appeals) (Scotland) Regulations 1983. The validity or accuracy of any entry in the noise level register cannot be questioned in any other proceedings under Part III of COPA.

The noise level recorded in the register cannot be exceeded without the written consent of the council (section 65). In granting consent, the council can impose conditions specifying the permitted increase in noise level, and the period(s) for or during which the level may be increased. There is a right of appeal to the Secretary of State against the council's decision. Where the council have failed to determine the application for consent within two months, they are deemed to have refused consent. Any appeal must be lodged within three months of the date of the decision or deemed refusal. The procedure for appeals is specified by the 1983 Regulations.

The person to whose act, default or sufferance the noise is attributable commits an offence if the noise exceeds the recorded level without consent, or contravenes a condition attached to a consent. On summary conviction there is liability to a fine not exceeding level 5 (currently £5,000) on the standard scale, together with a further fine of up to £50 for each day on which the offence continues after conviction. Following conviction, if satisfied that the offence is likely to continue or recur, the sheriff may make an order requiring the execution of any works necessary to prevent this, and/or direct the council to carry out such works. If the works are carried out by the council they can recover the cost from the person convicted of the offence (section 69). If the council raise a court action to recover these costs, that person cannot raise any question which he could have raised on an appeal against the notice.

A section 65 consent provides a defence to an abatement notice, but not to a summary application by a person aggrieved by a statutory nuisance (above).

The council may serve a noise reduction notice where (section 66)

— the level of noise emanating from premises to which a noise abatement order applies is not acceptable having regard to the purposes for which the order was made; and

— a reduction in that level is practicable at reasonable cost and would afford a public benefit.

It is irrelevant that a section 65 consent authorises a higher level of noise than that specified in the notice.

The notice is served on the person by whose act, default or sufferance the noise is attributable, and requires him to

— reduce the level of noise to a specified level;

— prevent any subsequent increase in the noise level without the council's consent; and

— take specified steps to achieve these purposes.

The notice must specify a period of at least six months within which the noise level must be reduced and the specified steps taken. Any person served with a notice may submit an appeal to the sheriff court within three months of the date of service. The grounds of appeal, the powers of the court and the circumstances in which the notice is suspended pending determination of the appeal, are specified by the 1983 Regulations.

A person who without reasonable excuse contravenes a noise reduction notice commits an offence, with liability on summary conviction to a fine not exceeding level 5 (currently £5,000) on the standard scale, together with a further fine of up to £50 for each day on which the offence continues after conviction. Where the noise is caused in the course of a trade or business, it is a defence to prove that the best practicable means (defined by section 72) had been used for preventing or counteracting the effect of the noise.

If the works specified in the notice are not carried out within the specified period, the council may carry out the works and recover the cost from the person to whom the notice relates (section 69). If the council raise a court action to recover these costs, that person cannot raise any question which he could have raised on an appeal against the notice.

It is a defence to an abatement notice to prove that the level of noise did not contravene a section 66 notice. This defence is not applicable in relation to a summary application by a person aggrieved by a statutory nuisance (above).

The acceptable level of noise from new or altered premises which will be subject to a noise abatement order can be determined by the council either on their own initiative or following an application by the owner, occupier or a person negotiating to acquire an interest in the premises (section 67). The level of noise fixed by the council must be recorded in the noise level register. The council must give notice of their intended decision to the applicant, or to the owner or occupier where the determination has been made without any application. The recipient of the notice may appeal to the Secretary of State within three months of the date of notification. A right of appeal also arises where the council have failed to determine an application within two months. The appeal procedure is specified by the 1983 Regulations.

If no acceptable level of noise has been set for new or altered premises which become subject to a noise abatement order following their construction or alteration, the council can serve a noise reduction notice if the level of noise emanating from the premises is unacceptable. The provisions relating to such an order are as described above, although there is no requirement that the reduction in the noise level be practicable at reasonable cost and afford a public benefit. The minimum period which can be specified for compliance is reduced from six to three months, and there is no best practicable means defence.

It is a defence to an abatement notice to prove that the level of noise did not contravene a level set under section 67. This defence is not applicable in relation to a summary application by a person aggrieved by a statutory nuisance (above).

10.3.5 Noise from plant or machinery (COPA)
The Secretary of State has power to make regulations requiring noise reduction devices or arrangements to be used in connection with any plant or machinery, and for limiting the level of noise which may be caused by any plant or machinery used on construction sites or in factories (COPA, section 68).

10.3.6 Codes of practice
To give guidance on appropriate methods for minimising noise, the Secretary of State may prepare and approve and issue codes of practice, or approve such codes as may be issued by other persons or bodies (COPA, section 71). One example is the Control of Noise (Codes of Practice for Construction and Open Sites) (Scotland) Order 1985 (SI 1985/145), to which any council proposing to issue a section 60 notice (see paragraph 10.3.2) must have regard.

10.3.7 Audible intruder alarms
Section 9 of the Noise and Statutory Nuisance Act 1993 gives councils the power to introduce requirements relating to audible intruder alarms within their area. This section has yet to be brought into force.

These provisions would require any person installing such an alarm on or in any premises to comply with prescribed requirements and to notify the council within forty-eight hours of the installation. In addition the occupier must ensure that the police are notified in writing of the names, addresses and telephone numbers of the current key-holders, and the council informed of the address of the police station to which this notification has been sent.

Once in force, section 9 will also empower a duly authorised council officer to enter premises, but not by force, to turn off an alarm which has been operating audibly for more than one hour and is such as to give persons living or working in the vicinity reasonable cause for annoyance. A warrant can be obtained to authorise entry to premises where access cannot be obtained other than by force.

Chapter 11

RADIOACTIVE SUBSTANCES

11.1 INTRODUCTION

The harmful effects of radioactive substances, which may be described as those which emit ionising radiation, are well known. This chapter considers principally the controls over the keeping and use of radioactive substances and mobile radioactive apparatus as well as the accumulation and disposal of radioactive waste under the Radioactive Substances Act 1993 (RSA), which consolidated earlier legislation – in particular, the Radioactive Substances Act 1960. There is also a brief account of the controls over the operation of nuclear reactors and related facilities under the Nuclear Installations Act 1965 and the transport of radioactive materials.

Current policy on radioactive waste management in the UK is set out in the White Paper, Review of Radioactive Waste Management Policy: Final Conclusions (Cm 2919, 1995). It should also be noted that the efficacy of the present system of controls over radioactive waste in Scotland has recently been thrown into doubt by revelations of contamination resulting from an explosion in a shaft used for the disposal of intermediate radioactive waste in 1977 at the UK Atomic Energy Authority nuclear facility at Dounreay, albeit when that plant enjoyed Crown immunity from enforcement action (see, eg, [1995] 245 ENDS Report 22). Concerns have also been voiced regarding the role of the body then responsible for administering radioactive waste controls, Her Majesty's Industrial Pollution Inspectorate (HMIPI), in relation to the incident in question.

11.2 ADMINISTRATION OF THE RADIOACTIVE SUBSTANCES CONTROLS

From 1st April 1996, SEPA took over the administration of radioactive substances regulation under RSA. Formerly HMIPI was responsible for the administration of these controls. Nuclear installations controls under the Nuclear Installations Act 1965 are administered by the Nuclear Installations Inspectorate (NII), part of the Health and Safety Executive.

11.3 RELATIONSHIP OF THE RADIOACTIVE SUBSTANCES ACT 1993 TO OTHER STATUTORY CONTROLS

A potential overlap exists between RSA and a variety of other environmental legislation. RSA deals with this by providing that other statutory controls (specified in Schedule 3 to RSA) continue to apply to radioactive substances but, insofar as they do apply, no account must be taken of any radioactivity possessed by the substance or article or premises in question. In relation to Scotland, RSA applies this approach in the case of the Sewerage (Scotland) Act 1968; the Clean Air Act 1993; the statutory nuisance controls in Part III of EPA; the hazardous substances consent provisions of the Planning (Hazardous Substances) (Scotland) Act 1997; and the water pollution provisions of COPA and the Water (Scotland) Act 1980.

Parts I, II and IIA of EPA contain provisions governing their relationship with the controls in RSA. Where activities comprising a process prescribed for control under Part I of EPA are regulated both by an IPC or LAPC authorisation and a registration or authorisation under RSA, if different obligations are imposed as respects the same material, section 28(2) of EPA provides that it is RSA conditions which apply and the IPC or LAPC conditions are not binding. Furthermore, section 78 of EPA provides that radioactive waste is not a controlled waste for the purposes of Part II of EPA, which regulates controlled waste although the Secretary of State has the power to extend Part II to cover radioactive waste. Section 78YC of Part IIA of EPA provides that Part IIA's contaminated land régime does not apply to harm or pollution so far as it is attributable to any radioactivity possessed by any substance unless regulations provide otherwise. However, it should be noted that the contaminated land provisions of Part IIA are applicable to the non-radioactive properties of such substances.

11.4 DEFINITIONS
RSA defines the key terms as follows:

— 'nuclear site' is defined by section 47(1) as (a) any site in respect of which a nuclear site licence under the Nuclear Installations Act 1965 is in force, or (b) any site where the responsibility of the licensee has yet to cease although the site licence has been revoked or surrendered. The principal nuclear sites are those used for the production or use of atomic energy, ie, nuclear power stations;

— 'radioactive material' is defined by section 1 as anything which, not being waste, is either any such substance or an article made wholly or partly from or incorporating such a substance. Such a substance is either

— one which contains an element specified in Schedule 1 (below) in such a proportion that the number of becquerels of that element contained in the substance, divided by the number of grams which the substance weighs, is a number greater than that specified in the appropriate column of that Schedule:

or

— one which possesses radioactivity which is wholly or partly due to a process of nuclear fission or other process of subjecting a substance to bombardment by neutrons or to ionising radiations, not being a process occurring in the course of nature, or in consequence of the disposal of radioactive waste, or by ways of contamination in the course of the application of a process to some other substance;

Schedule 1

Element	Becquerels per Gram $(BQ\ G^{-1})$		
	Solid	Liquid	Gas or Vapour
1. Actinium	0.37	7.40×10^{-2}	2.59×10^{-6}
2. Lead	0.74	3.70×10^{-3}	1.11×10^{-4}
3. Polonium	0.37	2.59×10^{-2}	2.22×10^{-4}
4. Protoactinium	0.37	3.33×10^{-2}	1.11×10^{-6}
5. Radium	0.37	3.70×10^{-4}	3.70×10^{-5}
6. Radon	—	—	3.70×10^{-2}
7. Thorium	2.59	3.70×10^{-2}	2.22×10^{-5}
8. Uranium	11.1	0.74	7.40×10^{-5}

(The becquerel (BQ) (formerly the curie) is the standard measure of radiation. The radio-activity of a substance is expressed in becquerels per unit of weight (normally per gram) of the substance in question.

— 'radioactive waste' is defined by section 2 as waste which consists wholly or partly of (a) a substance or article which, if it were not waste, would be radioactive material, or (b) a substance or article which has been contaminated in the course of the production, keeping or use of radioactive material, or by contact with or proximity to other waste falling within (a) or (b);

— 'waste' is defined by section 47(1) as including any substance which constitutes scrap material or an effluent or other unwanted surplus arising from the application of any process, and also includes any substance or article which requires to be disposed of as being broken, worn out, contaminated or otherwise spoilt. It should be noted that this definition of waste is identical to the definition of waste in Part II of EPA prior to its amendment to reflect the new EC definition of waste (see paragraph 7.2) and that the new definition of waste has not been applied to radioactive waste;

— 'mobile radioactive apparatus' is defined by section 3 as any apparatus, equipment, appliance or other thing which is radioactive material and is constructed or adapted for being transported from place to place or is portable and designed or intended to be used for releasing radioactive material into the environment or introducing it into organisms.

11.5 CONTROLS OVER KEEPING AND USE OF RADIOACTIVE MATERIAL AND MOBILE RADIOACTIVE SUBSTANCES

11.5.1 Scope of controls over keeping and use of radioactive material

Section 6 prohibits any person, on any premises used for the purposes of an undertaking carried on by him, from keeping or using, or causing or permitting to be kept or used, radioactive material of any description, unless he has a certificate of registration for those premises and in respect of the keeping or use of radioactive material of that description or unless he is exempt from registration. It should be noted that this prohibition only applies where the person knows or has reasonable grounds for believing that the material is radioactive material. Contravention of section 6 is an offence (section 32; for penalties, see paragraph 11.12).

Section 8 provides that a person is exempt from the requirement for registration where

— the radioactive material in question consists of mobile radioactive apparatus which is covered by a registration or an exemption under separate provision of RSA (see paragraph 11.5.4);

— the person is a licensee of a site where a nuclear site licence is in force or where at any time after such a licence has been revoked or surrendered but before his period of responsibility as licensee has ceased (this exemption may be subject to specific limitations or conditions)(see also paragraph 11.16);

— the radioactive material consists of clocks and watches (although premises where clocks or watches are manufactured or repaired by processes involving the use of luminous material are not exempt); or

— the Secretary of State has exercised his power to grant an exemption by order under RSA and formerly under the Radioactive Substances Act 1960. Such exemptions may be subject to such limitations or conditions specified in the order as apply. Numerous exemption orders have been made (eg, the Radioactive Substances (Exhibitions) Exemption (Scotland) Order 1962 (SI 1962/2766); the Radioactive Substances (Schools etc) Exemption (Scotland) Order 1963 (SI 1963/1878); and the Radioactive Substances (Substances of Low Activity) Exemption Order 1986 (SI 1986/1002), as amended).

It is an offence to contravene any limitations or conditions laid down in any exemptions (section 32; for penalties, see paragraph 11.12).

11.5.2 Application for registration for keeping etc radioactive material

The procedures governing registration are laid down in section 7 of RSA. Applications are made to SEPA on a form available from SEPA and must be accompanied by the prescribed fee. The application must include the following information:

— the premises to which the application relates;

— the undertaking for the purposes of which those premises are used;

— the description(s) of radioactive material proposed to be kept or used on the premises and the maximum quantity of radioactive material of each such description likely to be kept or used on the premises at any one time; and

— the manner, if any, in which radioactive material is proposed to be used on the premises.

The application form also requires the provision of considerable additional information including:

— the applicant's name, address (the address of the registered office if the applicant is a limited company) and telephone number;

— the local authority area in which the premises are situated;

— the name, business address and telephone number of the person responsible for the safekeeping of radioactive substances; and

— the radioactive waste (if any) arising from use of the materials.

When an application is made, SEPA must send a copy of the application to each local authority in whose area the premises in question are situated (section 7(3)) unless, by virtue of section 25, the Secretary of State has directed that knowledge of some or all of the information contained in the application should be restricted on grounds of national security.

11.5.3 Determination of the application for keeping etc radioactive material

SEPA can either register the applicant or refuse the application (section 7(4)). If the application relates to two or more descriptions of radioactive material, SEPA may register the applicant in respect of such one or more of those descriptions (ibid).

In any case where the application is granted, SEPA may register the applicant subject to such limitations or conditions as it thinks fit (section 7(6)). These may include conditions in respect of any part of the premises including requirements involving structural or other alterations or in respect of any apparatus, equipment or appliance to be used on any part of the premises for the purposes of any use of radioactive material from which radioactive waste is likely to arise. In exercising the foregoing power SEPA must have regard exclusively to the amount and character of the radioactive waste likely to arise from the keeping or use of radioactive material on the premises in question (section 7(7)).

SEPA may also impose conditions requiring the furnishing of information as to the removal of radioactive material from those premises to any other premises, or conditions prohibiting the sale of radioactive material from those premises unless it bears a label or other mark indicating that it is radioactive material (section 7(6)).

Failure to comply with any limitation or condition imposed is an offence (section 32; for penalties, see paragraph 11.12). For example, in *Crowe* v *Omec Engineering Ltd* 1997 GWD 7-283 a company which was registered under section 7 of RSA sold and vacated a mine, leaving behind a radioactive source on site. Omec's failure to notify SEPA of its vacation of the site constituted a breach of one of the conditions in its certificate of registration and led to a fine of £500 being imposed.

Section 7(8) provides that on registering a person, SEPA must furnish that person with a certificate containing all material particulars of the registration and must also send a copy of the certificate to each local authority in whose area the premises are situated unless, by virtue of section 25, the Secretary of State has directed that knowledge of some or all of the information contained in the application should be restricted on grounds of national security.

11.5.4 SCOPE OF CONTROLS OVER MOBILE RADIOACTIVE APPARATUS

Section 9(1) prohibits a person keeping, using, lending or letting on hire, mobile radioactive apparatus or causing or permitting the same, unless the person is registered or exempt from registration in respect of the apparatus concerned. Contravention of section 9 is an offence (section 32; for penalties, see paragraph 11.12).

However, the application of this prohibition is subject to the requirement that it only applies to activities involving the use of apparatus for testing, measuring or otherwise investigating any of the characteristics of substances or articles or releasing quantities of radioactive material into the environment or introducing such material into organisms (section 9(2)).

The Secretary of State is empowered by section 11(1) to exempt by order classes of persons and descriptions of mobile radioactive apparatus from registration. These exemptions may be subject to conditions. Two orders are currently in force in Scotland: the Radioactive Substances (Electronic Valves) Exemption (Scotland) Order 1967 (SI 1967/1803); and the Radioactive Substances (Testing Instruments) Exemption Order 1985 (SI 1985/1049).

It is an offence to contravene any limitations or conditions laid down in any exemptions (section 32; for penalties, see paragraph 11.12).

11.5.5 Application for registration of person using etc mobile radioactive apparatus

Section 10 provides that an application for registration must be made to SEPA on a form available from SEPA and be accompanied by the appropriate fee. The application must specify

— the apparatus to which the application relates;

— the manner in which it is proposed to use the apparatus; and

any other information prescribed by regulations. To date no regulations have been made prescribing further information to be supplied although the application form also requires the provision of considerable additional information, including

— the applicant's name, address (the address of the registered office if the applicant is a limited company) and telephone number;

— the premises where the apparatus is normally to be kept when not in use elsewhere;

— the local authority area where the apparatus may be used;

— the name, business address and telephone number of the person responsible for the safekeeping of radioactive substances;

— the activity for which the apparatus is to be used;

— the radioactive sources to be used;

— whether the apparatus is to be lent or let on hire;

— the way in which materials will be stored; and

— the manner of disposal of superfluous radionuclides.

Interestingly the application form does not fully comply with the requirements of the statute as it does not actually ask the applicant either to specify the apparatus to which the application relates, or to specify the manner in which the apparatus is to be used (although this may be apparent from the question relating to the activity for which it is to be used).

On receipt of an application section 10(3) provides that SEPA must send a copy of the application to each local authority in whose area it appears to it that the apparatus will be kept or will be used for releasing radioactive material into the environment unless, by virtue of section 25, the Secretary of State has directed that knowledge of some or all of the information contained in the application should be restricted on grounds of national security.

11.5.6 Determination of the application for using etc mobile radioactive apparatus

SEPA may register the applicant either unconditionally or subject to limitations or conditions or may refuse to register the applicant (section 10(2)). It is an offence to contravene any limitation or condition subject to which the registration has effect (section 32; for penalties, see paragraph 11.12).

On registering a person, SEPA must furnish that person with a certificate containing all material particulars of the registration and must also send a copy of the certificate to each local authority in whose area the apparatus will be kept or used unless, by virtue of section 25, the Secretary of State has directed that knowledge of some or all of the information contained in the application should be restricted on grounds of national security (section 10(5)).

11.6 PROVISIONS COMMON TO REGISTRATIONS FOR THE KEEPING ETC OF RADIOACTIVE MATERIAL AND MOBILE RADIOACTIVE APPARATUS

11.6.1 Cancellation and variation of registration

SEPA may at any time cancel the registration (section 12(1)). SEPA may also at any time vary the registration by attaching limitations or conditions to an unconditional registration or where the registration is subject to conditions or limitations by revoking or varying existing conditions or limitations or by attaching further conditions or limitations to the registration (ibid).

Where SEPA cancels or varies a registration, notice must be sent to the person to whom the registration relates and to the appropriate local authorities (section 12(2)).

11.6.2 Appeal rights in relation to registrations

The applicant has a right of appeal against a refusal to register him or against the conditions or limitations imposed in a registration (section 26). Where SEPA fails to determine an application within four months, or such extended period as may be agreed with the applicant, this is deemed to be a refusal to register and the applicant may appeal. There is also a right of appeal against cancellation or revocation of a registration (on appeals generally, see also paragraph 11.9).

11.6.3 Transfer of registrations

There are no provisions in RSA governing the transfer of registrations.

Since registration is personal to the applicant, if radioactive material or apparatus is transferred to another person, the registered person must remain in control until the transferee becomes registered.

11.7 CONTROLS OVER DISPOSAL OR ACCUMULATION OF RADIOACTIVE WASTE

RSA controls the disposal or accumulation of radioactive waste by making it an offence for a person to dispose of or accumulate radioactive waste unless an authorisation is granted by SEPA or there is an applicable exemption (for penalties, see paragraph 11.12).

11.7.1 Scope of disposal controls

The disposal of waste in RSA is defined by section 47(1) in fairly comprehensive terms to include its removal, deposit, destruction, discharge into the air, water or into a sewer or otherwise or its burial underground or otherwise.

An authorisation is required for the disposal of radioactive waste if a person knows or has reasonable grounds for believing that the material in question is radioactive waste and it

— is disposed on or from any premises used by a person for the purpose of carrying on an undertaking;

— arises from any mobile radioactive apparatus; or

— is received by a person in the course of carrying on an undertaking for the purpose of disposal (although no authorisation will be required in these circumstances where if the waste concerned falls within the provisions of an authorisation granted in relation to one of the first two cases above and the disposal complies with the terms of that authorisation)(section 13).

Contravention of these provisions is an offence (section 32; for penalties, see paragraph 11.12).

11.7.2 Scope of accumulation controls

RSA also prohibits the accumulation of radioactive waste with a view to its subsequent disposal by any person without an authorisation if he knows or has reasonable grounds for believing that it is radioactive waste (section 14(1)). However, there are some exceptions to this

— where a disposal authorisation has been granted and requires or permits the accumulation of radioactive waste with a view to its subsequent disposal, no accumulation authorisation is required (section 14(2)); or

— where the accumulation occurs on a site covered by a nuclear site licence since that licence will deal with accumulation (section 14(3)).

There is a presumption that where any substance arises from the production, keeping or use of radioactive material on any premises and is accumulated in a part of the premises appropriated for that purpose and is retained there for more than three months, it is radioactive waste and it is being accumulated on the premises with a view to its subsequent disposal (section 14(4)).

There are certain other exemptions from the requirement to obtain a disposal or accumulation authorisation (section 15). These include

— an exemption from the need for an authorisation in the case of radioactive waste arising from clocks or watches (except where it arises on premises on which clocks or watches are manufactured or repaired by processes involving the use of luminous material); and

— exemptions granted absolutely or subject to limitations or conditions by order by the Secretary of State (see paragraph 11.5.1 for some examples).

It is an offence to contravene any limitation or condition subject to which an exemption has effect (section 32; for penalties, see paragraph 11.12).

11.7.3 Application for authorisation

An application for authorisation must be made to SEPA on a form available from SEPA and must be accompanied by the appropriate fee (section 16). Although RSA stipulates that certain information must be included in an application for a registration it does not do so at all in the case of an application for an authorisation. The reason for this discrepancy is unclear. However, the forms available from SEPA require the following information:

— the applicant's name, address (the address of the registered office if the applicant is a company) and telephone number;

— the premises to which the application relates and whether any part of the premises is a nuclear site;

— the local authority in whose area the premises are situated;

— details of the undertaking for which the premises are used;

— details of the radioactive waste for disposal or accumulation;

— whether solid radioactive waste is to be disposed of, the details of such waste and of its proposed disposal;

— whether radioactive waste is to be disposed of to the atmosphere, the details of such waste and of its proposed disposal;

— whether radioactive waste is to be disposed of by incineration, details of such waste and its proposed disposal;

— proposals for accumulation of radioactive waste; and

— a list of documents accompanying the application.

SEPA must send a copy of the application to each local authority in whose area radioactive waste is to be accumulated or disposed of unless, by virtue of section 25, the Secretary of State has directed that knowledge of some or all of the information contained in the application should be restricted on grounds of national security (section 16(6)).

11.7.4 Determination of an application for authorisation

Before granting an authorisation in respect of the disposal of radioactive waste on or from premises situated on a nuclear site SEPA must consult such local authorities, relevant water bodies (ie, a district salmon fishery board or a water authority) or other public or local authorities as appear proper to it (section 16(5)).

Euratom Directive 80/836/EURATOM provides by article 6 that

> 'the various types of activity resulting in an exposure to ionising radiation shall have been justified in advance by the advantages which they produce'.

RSA is designed to implement this directive and although it does not contain express language requiring the above advance justification, it has nevertheless been held that RSA must be construed in such a manner as to conform to the requirements of the directive and therefore that the grant of an authorisation must be justified in advance by the advantages which it produces (*R* v *Secretary of State for the Environment*, ex parte *Greenpeace Ltd* [1994] 4 All ER 352; [1994] Env LR 401). Hence any decision to grant an authorisation without advance justification is unlawful. In this case, although the ministers did not consider that they were required by law to justify the advantages of THORP at Sellafield, none the less they had in practice carried out the requisite justification exercise. The government's recent White Paper, Review of Radioactive Waste Management Policy: Final Conclusions, advocates a system of early application for authorisations in the light of the above decision of the English High Court. Directive 96/29/EURATOM which will replace Directive 80/836/EURATOM from 13th May 2000 clarifies the definition of advance justification.

If it appears to SEPA, when it is considering an application for a disposal authorisation, that the disposal is likely to involve the need for special precautions to be taken by a local authority, district salmon fishery board, water authority or other public or local authority, SEPA must consult with the appropriate body before granting the authorisation (section 18(1)). Where such special precautions are taken the public or local authority have the power to charge the person to whom the authorisation was granted and to recover the charges from that person (section 18(2)). The charges may be agreed between the two parties or, if agreement is not reached, SEPA may determine the charges.

An authorisation may be granted either in respect of radioactive waste generally or in respect of one or more particular descriptions of radioactive waste and this must be specified in the authorisation (section 16(8)). Also, an authorisation may be subject to such limitations and conditions as SEPA thinks fit (ibid). It is an offence to contravene any such limitation or condition (section 32; for penalties, see paragraph 11.12).

Where an authorisation for the disposal of radioactive waste requires or permits the waste in question to be removed to a disposal facility provided by a local authority, the local authority must accept any waste removed to that facility in accordance with the authorisation and must deal with it in the manner indicated in the authorisation (section 18(3)).

Where an authorisation is granted, SEPA must furnish the applicant with a certificate containing all material particulars of the authorisation and must, unless by virtue of section 25 the Secretary of State has directed that knowledge of some or all of the information contained in the application should be restricted on grounds of national security, also send a copy of the certificate to each local authority in whose area the radioactive waste is to be disposed of or accumulated and, in cases of authorisations granted for the disposal of radioactive waste on or from any nuclear site, to any other public or local authorities which were consulted (section 16(9)).

11.7.5 Revocation and variation of authorisations
SEPA may at any time revoke or vary an authorisation (section 17(1)). The power to vary an authorisation may take the form of attaching limitations or conditions to an unconditional authorisation or may involve revoking or varying existing limitations and conditions or attaching additional limitations or conditions (section 17(2)).

It has been held that the power to vary an authorisation was properly exercised in circumstances where the variation did not extend the description of radioactive waste already included within an existing authorisation and did not authorise disposal of new descriptions of radioactive waste even though the relevant waste would be emitted from a new plant rather than from existing operations (*R* v *HM Inspectorate of Pollution and Ministry of Agriculture Fisheries and Food*, ex parte *Greenpeace* [1994] Env LR 76).

Notice of the revocation or variation must be sent to the person to whom the authorisation was granted and the appropriate local authorities (section 17(3)).

11.7.6 Appeal rights in relation to authorisations
The applicant has a right of appeal against a refusal to grant an authorisation or against the conditions or limitations imposed in an authorisation (section 26). Where SEPA fails to determine the application within four months, or such extended period as may be agreed with the applicant, this is deemed to be a refusal to grant an authorisation and the applicant may appeal. There is also a right of appeal against revocation or variation of an authorisation (on appeals generally, see also paragraph 11.9).

11.7.7 Record keeping
A person with a registration or authorisation may be required by SEPA to keep records not only for the period of the registration or authorisation but also for a specified period thereafter (section 20). Where a registration has been cancelled or an authorisation revoked or the activities permitted by the registration or the authorisation have ceased, SEPA may require a person to produce the appropriate records (ibid).

11.8 ENFORCEMENT AND PROHIBITION NOTICES
Where SEPA is of the opinion that a person to whom a registration relates or to whom an authorisation was granted is failing to comply or is likely to fail to comply with any limitation or condition in the registration or authorisation, it may serve an enforcement notice on that person (section 21(1)). The notice must state that SEPA is of that opinion, specify the failure to comply or the matters making it likely that there will be a failure to comply and specify the remedial steps to be taken and the period within which such steps must be taken (section 21(2)). There is a

right of appeal to the Secretary of State against an enforcement notice (section 26; on appeals generally, see also paragraph 11.9).

Where a person is carrying on an activity or carrying on an activity in a particular way in pursuance of a registration or authorisation and SEPA is of the opinion that to continue to do so involves an imminent risk of serious pollution of the environment or harm to human health, it may serve a prohibition notice (section 22(1)). The notice must state SEPA's opinion, the matters giving rise to the risk, the steps that must be taken to remove the risk and the period within which those steps must be taken (section 22(3)). The notice must also direct that the registration or authorisation shall cease to have effect wholly or in part until the notice ceases to have effect (ibid). There is a right of appeal to the Secretary of State against a prohibition notice (section 26; on appeals generally, see also paragraph 11.9).

It is an offence to fail to comply with any requirement of an enforcement or prohibition notice (section 32(1)(d); for penalties, see paragraph 11.12).

In addition, if SEPA is of the opinion that prosecution would afford an ineffectual remedy, it may take proceedings in any court of competent jurisdiction to obtain an interdict for the purpose of securing compliance with the notice (section 32(3)). *Tameside Metropolitan Borough Council* v *Smith Brothers (Hyde) Ltd* [1996] Env LR D4 has provided some judicial guidance on the use of such proceedings in the context of IPC and LAPC (see paragraph 9.2.6). In that case the court held that before an injunction (the English equivalent of an interdict) would be granted (a) there had to be a serious case to answer involving breach of the notice; (b) the balance of convenience including employment factors had to be considered; (c) the sanctions concerned had to be out of date to the extent that they did not provide an effective remedy which was not the case with EPA; and (d) all the available remedies had to have been exhausted, including the power in EPA which enabled the court to order the convicted person to remedy the cause of the offence in addition or as alternative to imposing a criminal penalty. Although this decision indicates that it will be difficult to obtain an interdict in such a case under EPA, it may not be quite so difficult under RSA since it does not contain any equivalent provisions enabling the court to order the convicted person to remedy the cause of the offence. Furthermore, the court's view that the sanctions contained in the Act in question need to be out of date appears to be misconceived (see also paragraph 2.11.8).

11.9 APPEALS

Section 26 provides that there is a right of appeal to the Secretary of State against the following decisions and notices:

— a refusal of registration, including a deemed refusal;

— a refusal of authorisation, including a deemed refusal;

— attachment of conditions or limitations to a registration or authorisation;

— variation of a registration or authorisation, otherwise than by revocation of limitations or conditions subject to which it has effect;

— cancellation of a registration or revocation of an authorisation;

— an enforcement notice; and

— a prohibition notice.

The effect of an appeal against a cancellation or revocation of a registration or authorisation has the effect of suspending the cancellation or revocation pending determination of the appeal unless the Secretary of State otherwise directs. In other cases an appeal does not affect the validity of the decision or notice unless the Secretary of State otherwise directs.

The detailed procedure for appeals is set out in the Radioactive Substances (Appeals) Regulations 1990 (SI 1990/2504). The regulations provide that notice of appeal must be lodged within

— two months of the date on which the decision or notice was sent to the appellant or the date on which the application is deemed to be refused; or

— twenty-eight days in the case of appeals against the cancellation of a registration or the revocation of an authorisation.

The notice of appeal and supporting documents must be submitted to the Secretary of State. When the Secretary of State receives the notice and supporting documents he must send a copy thereof to SEPA. Where the appeal relates to a decision in respect of an application for authorisation on which SEPA consulted any local authority, relevant water body (ie, district salmon fishery board or water authority) or any other public or local authority, SEPA must notify the Secretary of State of the names of the consultees and the Secretary of State in turn must notify the consultees. They have twenty-one days from the date of service of that notice to make representations to the Secretary of State.

The appeal can be determined on the basis of written representations or in the form of a hearing. RSA provides that if either party to the appeal so requests, the appeal must be held in the form of a hearing which may be held (or held to any extent) in private if the person hearing the appeal so decides (section 27(3)). The appellant should indicate in the documents submitted to the Secretary of State his choice of appeal procedure.

Where the appeal is determined by written representations, SEPA must make any written representations which it wishes to make to the Secretary of State within twenty-eight days of receiving the notice of appeal and supporting documents. The appellant has a further seventeen days to respond to these representations. Each party should send to the other a copy of representations made to the Secretary of State. The Secretary of State must also send to the appellant and to SEPA copies of any representations made by the consultees. The appellant and SEPA must make any representations which they wish to make on the consultees' representations within fourteen days. The Secretary of State has the discretion to extend any of these time-limits in a particular case.

Where the appeal proceeds by way of hearing, the Secretary of State must give the appellant and SEPA at least twenty-eight days' written notice of the date, time and place of the hearing unless a shorter period is otherwise agreed. Where the hearing is to be held wholly or partly in public, the Secretary of State must publish the foregoing notice in at least one local newspaper and where the Secretary of State is advised that SEPA has consulted any authority, he must serve a copy of the notice on each authority consulted. The Secretary of State may also vary the date, time and place of the hearing although notice of such alterations must be given. The hearing will be conducted by a reporter appointed by the Secretary of State. The procedure adopted is at the reporter's discretion. The regulations make no express provision as to which parties may be heard at the hearing although it would appear that the appellant and any person required to be notified must be heard. Given that there are provisions for advertising hearings, it would appear that any other person may be entitled to be heard at the discretion of the reporter. This is confirmed by the guidance note on appeals which was issued by the Department of the Environment and the Welsh Office.

After the conclusion of the hearing the reporter must submit a written report to the Secretary of State including his conclusions and recommendations. In determining the appeal, the Secretary of State is not bound to follow these recommendations. The Secretary of State must notify the appellant of his determination and his reasons for it and, where the appeal proceeded by way of a hearing, he must also send the appellant a copy of the reporter's report. These documents must at the same time be copied by the Secretary of State to SEPA and to any consultee who was required to be notified of the appeal.

Section 114 of EA permits the Secretary of State to delegate determination of certain appeals, including appeals under RSA, to reporters. Where the reporter has delegated power to determine the appeal, notice of his decision and a copy of the report is issued.

In determining the appeal, the Secretary of State/reporter may

— affirm the decision appealed against;

— in an appeal against the refusal of an application for registration or authorisation, direct SEPA to grant the application subject to such conditions or limitations as he may direct;

— in an appeal against limitations or conditions attached to a registration or authorisation, quash those limitations or conditions in whole or in part and give directions to SEPA as to conditions or limitations to be attached to the registration or authorisation;

— in an appeal against a cancellation or revocation of a registration or authorisation, quash the decision and give directions to SEPA as to conditions or limitations to be attached to the registration or authorisation;

— cancel or affirm an enforcement or prohibition notice with such modifications as he thinks fit.

However, there is no appeal against a decision taken by SEPA in pursuance of a direction of the Secretary of State. It would, however, be open to an applicant aggrieved by such a decision to challenge it by way of judicial review in the Court of Session (see paragraph 2.10).

11.10 POWERS OF THE SECRETARY OF STATE

The Secretary of State has considerable reserve powers under RSA. He may, if he thinks fit, direct SEPA

— to refuse an application for registration or authorisation;

— to effect or grant a registration or authorisation and attach limitations or conditions as may be specified in the direction;

— to vary a registration or authorisation;

— to cancel or revoke (or not to cancel or revoke) a registration or authorisation; or

— to serve an enforcement or prohibition notice in relation to any registration or authorisation (section 23).

The Secretary of State may also require SEPA to refer applications for registration or authorisation to him for determination (section 24). Where an application is referred to the Secretary of State he may hold a local inquiry in relation to the application. The discretion conferred on the Secretary of State by this provision is wide. Provided that the Secretary of State applies his mind genuinely and rationally to the issue of whether or not to hold an inquiry, his decision cannot be impugned in the courts regardless of the scale of representations in favour of an inquiry or the extent of public anxiety (*R* v *Secretary of State for the Environment*, ex parte *Greenpeace Ltd*). In that case the court held that the Secretary of State had satisfied himself that he was in a position to take account of the representations made and to weigh the information received and he was accordingly entitled to decide not to order an inquiry to be held.

Furthermore, the Secretary of State also has reserve powers to provide facilities for the safe disposal or accumulation of radioactive waste or to arrange for their provision by other persons in circumstances where it appears to him that adequate facilities are not available (section 29). Before implementing any proposal to provide such facilities the Secretary of State must consult with the local authority in whose area the facilities would be sited and with any other public or local authorities as appear proper to him.

In addition and without prejudice to the above reserve powers, the Secretary of State may give a direction of a general or specific character to SEPA in relation to the carrying out of any of its functions including those under RSA by virtue of section 40 of EA.

11.11 POWERS OF ENTRY AND INSPECTION

The search and inspection powers of SEPA officers in relation to RSA, contained in sections 108–110 of EA, are discussed in Chapter 1.

11.12 PENALTIES

The failure to obtain a registration or an authorisation, the contravention of a condition or a limitation subject to which a person is registered or exempt from registration or subject to which an authorisation has effect and the contravention of an enforcement or prohibition notice are offences punishable, on summary conviction, by a maximum fine of £20,000 and/or up to six months' imprisonment and, on conviction on indictment, by an unlimited fine and/or up to five years' imprisonment or both (section 32).

The penalties for contravention of the duty to display certificates of registration or authorisation are, on summary conviction, a maximum fine of £5,000 and, on conviction on indictment, an unlimited fine (section 33(1); see paragraph 11.15.2). The pulling down or defacing of such a document is punishable on summary conviction only by a maximum fine of £500 (section 33(2)).

The penalties for contravention of the requirements to retain or produce records are, on summary conviction, a maximum fine of £5,000 and/or up to three months' imprisonment and, on conviction on indictment, an unlimited fine and/or up to two years' imprisonment (section 33(3); see paragraph 11.7.7).

Where there is a disclosure of trade secrets unless one of the defences apply, an offence is committed and is punishable, on summary conviction, with a maximum fine of £5,000 and/or up to three months' imprisonment and, on conviction on indictment, with an unlimited fine and/or up to two years' imprisonment (section 34; see paragraph 11.15.1).

The penalties for obstruction of SEPA inspectors when exercising their search and inspection powers are detailed in paragraph 1.5.4.

RSA also makes provision for personal liability of corporate officers in certain circumstances. Where an offence is committed by a body corporate and a director, a manager, a company secretary or other similar officer or any person purporting to act in such a capacity, may also be convicted if the offence is proved to have been committed with his consent or connivance or to have been attributable to his neglect (section 36(1)). Members of a body corporate may also be convicted in circumstances where they are managing the affairs of the body corporate (section 36(2)). This latter provision is designed to enable conviction of parent companies where appropriate. For a more detailed discussion of the liability of corporate officers and members, see paragraph 2.11.5.

The HMIPI report for 1st April 1988 to 31st March 1992 indicates that five prosecutions were taken during that period under the Radioactive Substances Act 1960 with fines ranging from £30,000 in the case of *Ryan Industrial Fuels Ltd* (1992) to £250 in the case of *Marconi Command & Control Systems Ltd* (1990). In a recent prosecution, *Crowe* v *Omec Engineering Ltd* 1997 GWD 7-283, a company which breached a condition of its certificate of registration by failing to notify SEPA that it had vacated a mine and left a radioactive source behind, was fined £500.

11.13 REMEDIATION

Under section 30 SEPA has the power (formerly exercised by the Secretary of State) to dispose of radioactive waste in circumstances where there is radioactive waste on any premises and SEPA is satisfied that the waste ought to be disposed of but by reason that the premises are unoccupied, or that the occupier is absent or is insolvent or for any other reason it is unlikely that the waste will lawfully be disposed of unless SEPA exercises its powers. SEPA may recover any expenses reasonably incurred by it in disposing of the waste from the occupier of the premises or from the owner of the premises, if the premises are unoccupied.

11.14 CROWN IMMUNITY

Crown immunity from the controls under the Radioactive Substances Act 1960 was largely removed from January 1991. The Crown are therefore now bound by RSA subject to exceptions in relation to premises occupied for military or other defence purposes or by a visiting military force (section 42(1),(2)).

In relation to Crown premises which are now subject to RSA controls, contravention of RSA does not render the Crown criminally liable. However, SEPA may obtain a declarator that a contravention of RSA by the Crown was unlawful (section 42(3)).

In relation to defence and visiting forces premises, administrative arrangements may be made whereby radioactive waste is not disposed of except with the approval of SEPA. Where the waste is to be disposed of at a local authority site, the local authority must receive the waste (see paragraph 11.7.4). The local authority are entitled to be consulted in advance as to any special precautions necessary and can recover the costs of such precautions (ibid).

Department of the Environment Circular 22/92, Local Authority Responsibilities for Public Access to Information under the Radioactive Substances Act 1960 etc, indicates that although the Radioactive Substances Act 1960 (and presumably now RSA) did not apply to defence and visiting forces, similar controls are in fact exercised over them on an administrative basis. Instead of certificates of registration, defence premises and visiting forces premises receive certificates of notification in respect of holding radioactive substances and instead of authorisations approving the disposal of radioactive waste they receive certificates of agreement. Copies of these documents are sent to local authorities except where there are overriding matters of national security. The circular indicates that the defence and visiting forces have indicated a wish to comply with the spirit of public access to information. Although this circular applies in England and Wales, it appears that a similar position pertains in Scotland since, for example, the HMIPI report for 1st April 1988 to 31st March 1992 details inspections etc of Crown premises, including the Clyde submarine base at Faslane.

11.15 PUBLIC INFORMATION
11.15.1 Registers of information

Much information is available to the public under RSA. This is partly achieved by means of public registers operated by SEPA and local authorities. SEPA's register must contain copies of all applications made to it under RSA; all documents issued by it under RSA; all documents sent by it to any local authority in pursuance of directions by the Secretary of State; and details of convictions as are prescribed by the Radioactive Substances (Records of Convictions) Regulations 1992 (SI 1992/1685) — details of the offence; the name of the offender; the date of the conviction; the penalty imposed; and the name of the court. Spent convictions must be removed from the register under the Rehabilitation of Offenders Act 1974 (section 39(1)).

This information must be available to the public except to the extent that it would involve disclosure of information relating to any process applied for the purposes of or in connection with the production or use of radioactive material or a trade secret or would involve disclosure of information which the Secretary of State has directed should be restricted on grounds of national security (ibid).

Local authorities must also keep and make available to the public copies of all documents sent to them by SEPA unless directed by SEPA that all or any part of the document is not to be made available for inspection (section 39(2)). Such a direction can only be made for the purpose of preventing the disclosure of relevant processes or trade secrets (section 39(3)).

It should be noted that copies of documents need not be in documentary form so they could be stored on microfiche, computer disks or CD-ROMS (section 39(4)). The public may inspect documents without charge at all reasonable times and for payment of a reasonable fee they can obtain copies of documents (section 39(5)).

For a general discussion of access to environmental information, see Chapter 4.

11.15.2 Duty to display certificates of registration or authorisation

A person who is registered or authorised in respect of any premises must keep copies of the registration or authorisation posted at all times while the registration or authorisation is in force (section 19). Copies which are displayed must be in such characters and positions as to be conveniently read by persons having duties on those premises.

11.16 NUCLEAR INSTALLATIONS

The following paragraphs are intended to give a brief outline of the nuclear installation controls only.

A nuclear site licence is required under the Nuclear Installations Act 1965 for the use of any site within the UK for the purpose of installing or operating a nuclear reactor or any other prescribed installation for (a) producing or using atomic energy; (b) carrying out any process which is preparatory or ancillary to the production or use of atomic energy and which involves or is capable of causing the emission of ionising radiation; or (c) storing, processing or disposal of nuclear fuel or of bulk quantities of other radioactive matter produced or irradiated in the course of the production or use of nuclear fuel. Such sites include nuclear power stations (eg, Torness) and spent-fuel reprocessing facilities (eg, Sellafield).

Licences are available only to bodies corporate and are not transferable. They must be obtained from NII (part of HSE) not from SEPA. Conditions may be attached to the licence which NII considers necessary or desirable in the interests of safety, whether in normal circumstances or in the event of an accident or emergency. The licence may be revoked at any time. It may also be surrendered at any time but the licensee continues to remain responsible regardless of revocation or surrender until NII gives written notice that the danger from ionising radiation from anything on the site has ceased.

The holder of a site licence is under various express statutory duties, including the duty to secure that no occurrence involving nuclear matter causes injury to any person or damage to any person's property. These duties are not absolute in the sense that the licensee does not need to demonstrate that no such occurrence will ever take place (*Re Friends of the Earth* [1988] JPL 93, CA). The duties impose strict liability. There are certain defences available including an exception where the injury or damage is attributable to hostile action in the course of any armed conflict, including one within the UK. Furthermore, there is a defence available to reduce compensation payable where the claimant was at fault. This would apply, for example, in the case of terrorist action against nuclear installations. However, site licence holders will be liable where the injury or damage is attributable to a natural disaster even where this is of an exceptional character.

Provided a claim is brought timeously and no foreign court has jurisdiction, compensation is due. There is an overall limit of £140 million in respect of any one incident, excluding payments in respect of interest and costs. In general there is a statutory bar on any claims made after thirty years from the date of the occurrence although there are certain exceptions to this. The compensation available extends only to injuries and property damage and does not include pure economic loss as where the value of a house had been adversely affected by the presence of radioactive dust which was not held to constitute actual physical damage (*Merlin v British Nuclear Fuels* [1990] 3 All ER 711). However, it has been held that damages for economic loss, including losses associated with the failure to sell a property, resulting from radioactive contamination which constituted actual physical damage and required to be decontaminated, were recoverable even though the contamination did not pose a risk to human or animal health and was confined to a small part of the property (*Blue Circle Industries plc v Ministry of Defence* [1997] Env LR 341) (see also paragraphs 2.3.5, 2.6.3).

11.17 CARRIAGE OF RADIOACTIVE MATERIAL

There are extensive controls over the carriage of radioactive material including the Radioactive Material (Road Transport) Act 1991, the Radioactive Material (Road Transport) (Great Britain) Regulations 1996 (SI 1996/1350) made thereunder and the Packaging, Labelling and Carriage of Radioactive Material by Rail Regulations 1996 (SI 1996/2090). Shipments of radioactive substances within the EC are governed by Euratom Directive 92/3/EEC and Regulation 1493/93. The directive is implemented in the UK by the Transfrontier Shipment of Radioactive Waste Regulations 1993 (SI 1993/3031), which set up a system of prior notification and requirement for acceptance of shipments of radioactive waste.

APPENDIX 1 FINE LEVELS – STANDARD SCALE

Levels	Amount
Level 1	£ 200
Level 2	£ 500
Level 3	£1,000
Level 4	£2,500
Level 5	£5,000

These levels were last revised with effect from 1st October 1992.

The standard scale prescribes the fines applicable to statutory offences which can only be tried summarily. In circumstances, however, where a statutory offence is triable either summarily or on indictment, then the maximum penalty available on summary conviction is the 'statutory maximum' or such other (and usually larger) sum as may be specifically referred to (in quite a number of cases, £20,000). A reference to the 'statutory maximum', without any figure being specified, is currently a reference to a fine of £5,000.

APPENDIX 2   FRAMEWORK OF CONTAMINATED
LAND LEGISLATION, GUIDANCE AND REGULATIONS
(NOT YET IN FORCE)

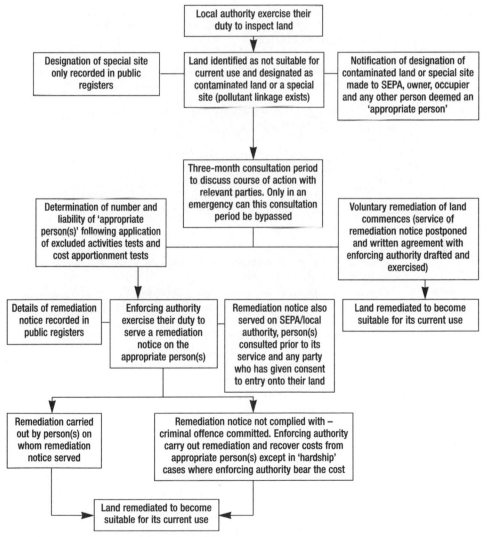

Note: The complex and detailed appeal procedures do not form part of this framework as a result of constrictions of space. See paragraph 6.5.8 for grounds of appeal.

APPENDIX 3 ENVIRONMENTAL PROTECTION ACT 1990, SCHEDULE 2B

CATEGORIES OF WASTE
1. Production or consumption residues not otherwise specified below.
2. Off-specification products.
3. Products whose date for appropriate use has expired.
4. Materials spilled, lost or having undergone other mishap, including any materials, equipment, etc, contaminated as a result of the mishap.
5. Materials contaminated or soiled as a result of planned actions (eg, residues from cleaning operations, packing materials, containers, etc).
6. Unusable parts (eg, reject batteries, exhausted catalysts, etc).
7. Substances which no longer perform satisfactorily (eg, contaminated acids, contaminated solvents, exhausted tempering salts, etc).
8. Residues of industrial processes (eg, slags, still bottoms, etc).
9. Residues from pollution abatement processes (eg, scrubber sludges, baghouse dusts, spent filters, etc).
10. Machining or finishing residues (eg, lathe turnings, mill scales, etc).
11. Residues from raw materials extraction and processing (eg, mining residues, oil field slops, etc).
12. Adulterated materials (eg, oils contaminated with PCBs, etc).
13. Any materials, substances or products whose use has been banned by law.
14. Products for which the holder has no further use (eg, agricultural, household, office, commercial and shop discards, etc).
15. Contaminated materials, substances or products resulting from remedial action with respect to land.
16. Any materials, substances or products which are not contained in the above categories.

APPENDIX 4   WATER POLLUTION

APPENDIX 5   CRIMINAL LIABILITY FOR
ENVIRONMENTAL MATTERS

Relevant provision and paragraph	Subject-matter	Offence	Person liable	Corporate liability	Directors' liability
EA s.110(1) (1.5.4)	Powers of entry and inspection	Intentionally to obstruct an authorised person in the exercise or performance of his powers or duties under EA s.108 and s.109	Any person	Yes	No
EA s.110(2) (a) (1.5.4)	Powers of entry and inspection	Failure to comply with any requirement imposed under EA s.108	Any person	Yes	No
EA s.110(2)(b) (1.5.4)	Powers of entry and inspection	Failure or refusal to provide facilities or assistance or any information or to permit any inspection reasonably required by an authorised person in the execution of his powers or duties under or by virtue of that section	Any person	Yes	No
EA s.110(2)(c) (1.5.4)	Powers of entry and inspection	To prevent any other person from appearing before an authorised person or answering any question to which an authorised person may require an answer, pursuant to EA s.108(4)	Any person	Yes	No
EA s.110(3) (1.5.4)	Powers of entry and inspection	Falsely to pretend to be an authorised person	Any person	Yes	No

Members' liability	Defences	Maximum penalty – summary conviction	Maximum penalty – indictment
No	No	Level 5 (for EA s.108 offences) Statutory maximum (for EA s.109 offences)	Unlimited fine and/or 2 years' imprisonment (EA s.109 offences only)
No	Reasonable excuse	Level 5	–
No	Reasonable excuse	Level 5	–
No	Reasonable excuse	Level 5	–
No	No	Level 5	–

Relevant provision and paragraph	Subject-matter	Offence	Person liable	Corporate liability	Directors' liability
EPA s.71(3) (1.5.3)	Powers to obtain information	Failure without reasonable excuse to provide information in response to a notice requiring information to be provided to the Secretary of State or SEPA	Any person	Yes	Yes (EPA s.157)
EPA s.78M(3) (not yet in force) (6.4.2)	Contaminated land	Failure to comply with any requirement of a remediation notice	Person(s) on whom remediation notice served	Yes	Yes (EPA s.157)
EPA s.78M(4) (not yet in force) (6.4.2)	Contaminated land	Failure to comply with any requirement of a remediation notice and the contaminated land to which the remediation notice relates is industrial, trade or business premises	Person(s) on whom remediation notice served	Yes	Yes (EPA s.157)
EPA s.33(1)(a) (7.8.2) (7.8.3)	Deposit, treatment or disposal of waste	Deposit controlled waste, or knowingly cause or knowingly permit controlled waste to be deposited in or on any land	Any person	Yes	Yes (EPA s.157)

Members' liability	Defences	Maximum penalty – summary conviction	Maximum penalty – indictment
Yes, if managing the affairs of the company (EPA s.157)	Reasonable excuse	Statutory maximum	Unlimited fine and/or 2 years' imprisonment
Yes, if managing the affairs of the company (EPA s.157)	Reasonable excuse	Level 5 with a further fine of one-tenth of level 5 on the standard scale for each day on which the failure continues after conviction and before the enforcing authority have begun to carry out the remediation in terms of s.78N	–
Yes, if managing the affairs of the company (EPA s.157)	Reasonable excuse	£20,000 or such greater sum as the Secretary of State may from time to time substitute with a further fine of an amount equal to one-tenth of that sum for each day on which the failure continues after conviction and before the enforcing authority have begun to carry out the remediation in terms of s.78N	–
	(The following apply to EPA s.33(1)(a), (b) and (c))		
Yes, if managing the affairs of the company (EPA s 157)	(1) Waste management licence authorising the deposit is in force and the deposit is in accordance with the licence (EPA s.33(1)(a) and (b) only)	£20,000 fine and/or 6 months' imprisonment	Unlimited fine and/or 2 years' imprisonment or 5 years' imprisonment if offence relates to special waste

Relevant provision and paragraph	Subject-matter	Offence	Person liable	Corporate liability	Directors' liability
EPA s.33 (1)(b) (7.8.2) (7.8.3)	Deposit, treatment or disposal of waste	Treat, keep or dispose of controlled waste, or knowingly cause or knowingly permit controlled waste to be treated, kept or disposed of in or on any land or by means of any mobile plant	Any person	Yes	Yes (EPA s.157)
EPA s.33(1)(c) (7.8.2) (7.8.3)	Deposit, treatment or disposal of waste	Treat, keep or dispose of controlled waste in a manner likely to cause pollution of the environment or harm to human health	Any person	Yes	Yes (EPA s.157)
EPA s.34(6) (7.8.2)	Duty of care as respects waste	Breach of the duty of care imposed by EPA s.34(1): Section 34(1) imposes a duty of care on any person who has control of such waste to take all such measures applicable to him in that capacity as are reasonable in the circumstances: – to prevent any contravention by any other person of EPA s.33 (the offence of treating, keeping, disposing of or depositing	Any person who imports, produces, carries, keeps, treats or disposes of controlled waste, or who has control of it as a waste broker	Yes	Yes (EPA s.157)

Members' liability	Defences	Maximum penalty – summary conviction	Maximum penalty – indictment
Yes, if managing the affairs of the company (EPA s.157)	(2) All reasonable precautions taken and all due diligence exercised to avoid the commission of the offence	£20,000 fine and/or 6 months' imprisonment	Unlimited fine and/or 2 years' imprisonment or 5 years' imprisonment if offence relates to special waste
Yes, if managing the affairs of the company (EPA s.157)	(3) Acted under instructions from his employer and the person neither knew nor had reason to suppose that the acts done by him constituted an offence under EPA s.33(1) (4) The acts done which constituted the contravention were done in an emergency to avoid danger to the public and that as soon as reasonably practicable after the acts were done particulars of them were furnished to SEPA	£20,000 fine and/or 6 months' imprisonment	Unlimited fine and/or 2 years' imprisonment or 5 years' imprisonment if offence relates to special waste
Yes, if managing the affairs of the company (EPA s.157)	(1) Occupier of domestic property as respects household waste produced on the property (2) All reasonable measures taken to avoid breach of duty	Statutory maximum	Unlimited fine

Relevant provision and paragraph	Subject-matter	Offence	Person liable	Corporate liability	Directors' liability
		waste without a licence); – to prevent the escape of the waste from his control or that of any other person; – on the transfer of the waste to secure: – that the transfer is only to an 'authorised person' or to a person for authorised transport purposes, and – that there is transferred such a written description of the waste as will enable other persons to avoid a contravention of EPA s.33 and to comply with the duty under EPA s.34(1) as respects the escape of waste			
EPA s.44 (7.4)	Waste management licences	(1) Making, in purported compliance with a requirement to furnish any information imposed by or under any provision of Part II of EPA, or (2) Making, in an application for a waste management licence, for a modification of the conditions of a waste management licence or for the transfer or surrender of a waste management licence any statement which he knows to be false in a material particular or	Any person	Yes	Yes (EPA s.157)

Members' liability	Defences	Maximum penalty – summary conviction	Maximum penalty – indictment
Yes, if managing the affairs of the company (EPA s.157)	(1) Statement not knowingly or recklessly made (2) False entry not intentionally made	Statutory maximum	Unlimited fine and/or 2 years' imprisonment

Relevant provision and paragraph	Subject-matter	Offence	Person liable	Corporate liability	Directors' liability
		recklessly makes any statement which is false in a material particular (3) Intentionally making a false entry in any record required to be kept by virtue of a licence			
EPA s.59(5) (7.9)	Removal, elimination or reduction of the consequences of controlled waste deposited on land in contravention of EPA s.33(1)	Failure to comply with a notice served in accordance with s.59(1) to remove, eliminate or reduce the consequences thereof	Occupier	Yes	Yes (EPA s.157)
EPA s.63(2) (7.8.2) (7.8.3)	Unauthorised deposit of waste which is not controlled waste	To deposit, or knowingly to cause or permit the deposit of waste which is not controlled waste but which, if it were, would be special waste	Any person	Yes	Yes (EPA s.157)
COPA s.30F (8.4.6)	Water pollution	To cause or knowingly permit (1) Any poisonous, noxious or polluting matter or any solid matter to enter any controlled waters (2) Any matter other than trade effluent or sewerage effluent to be discharged from a sewer or from a drain in contravention of a prohibition imposed under COPA s.30G (3) Any trade effluent or sewerage to be discharged (a) into any	Any person	Yes	Yes (COPA s.87)

Members' liability	Defences	Maximum penalty – summary conviction	Maximum penalty – indictment
Yes, if managing the affairs of the company (EPA s.157)	(1) Reasonable excuse (2) Person neither deposited nor knowingly caused nor knowingly permitted the deposit (3) Material defect in notice	Level 5 fine with a further fine of an amount equal to one-tenth of level 5 for each day on which the offence continues after conviction and before SEPA exercises its powers itself to do what the notice required	–
Yes, if managing the affairs of the company (EPA s.157)	(1) As EPA s.33 (2) The deposit was permitted by any consent, licence, approval or authority granted under any enactment (excluding any planning permission)	£20,000 and/or 6 months' imprisonment	Unlimited fine and/or 5 years' imprisonment
Yes, if managing the affairs of the company (COPA s.87)	(1) The entry is authorised by an environmental licence or by local act, statutory order or prescribed enactment (COPA s.30I(1)). (2) The entry is caused or permitted in an emergency in order to avoid danger to life or health and all steps are taken as are reasonably practicable in the circumstances for minimising the extent of the entry or discharge and of	£20,000 fine and/or 3 months' imprisonment	Unlimited fine and/or 2 years' imprisonment

Relevant provision and paragraph	Subject-matter	Offence	Person liable	Corporate liability	Directors' liability
		controlled waters; or (b) from land in Scotland, through a pipe, into the sea outside the seaward limits of controlled waters (4) Any trade effluent or sewerage to be discharged, in contravention of any prohibition imposed under COPA s.30G from a building or from a plant (a) on to or into any land; or (b) into any waters of a loch or pond which are not inland waters (5) Any matter whatever to enter any inland waters so as to tend (either directly or in combination with other matter which he or another person causes or permits to enter these waters) to impede the proper flow of the waters in a manner leading or likely to lead to a substantial aggravation of (a) pollution due to other causes; or (b) the consequences of such pollution			

Members' liability	Defences	Maximum penalty – summary conviction	Maximum penalty – indictment
	its polluting effects and the particulars of the entry or discharge are furnished to SEPA as soon as reasonably practicable after the entry occurs (COPA s.30J(1)) (3) The entry is trade or sewerage effluent discharged from a vessel (COPA s.30J(2)) (4) The entry is water permitted to enter controlled waters from an abandoned mine or an abandoned part of a mine (COPA s.30J(3)–(6) available to 31st December 1999 only) (5) In certain circumstances the deposit of the solid refuse of a mine or quarry on any land so that it falls or is carried into inland waters (COPA s.30J(7)) (6) Unless it is a contravention of a prohibition notice a roads authority will not be guilty of any offence in relation to a discharge made from any drain which they are obliged or entitled to keep open (COPA s.30J(8)) (7) Discharge by a sewerage authority (or other person in whom a sewer or works is vested) which they were not bound to receive or the conditions under		

Relevant provision and paragraph	Subject-matter	Offence	Person liable	Corporate liability	Directors' liability
COPA s.46D (not yet in force) (8.4.3)	Water pollution	Failure to comply with a works notice which requires persons to carry out anti-pollution operations	The person on whom the works notice is served by SEPA	Yes	Yes (COPA s.87)
COPA s.49 (8.4.6)	Water pollution	(1) The removal from any part of the bottom, channel or bed of any inland waters of a deposit accumulated by reason of any dam, weir or sluice holding back the waters in such a manner as to cause the deposit to be carried away in suspension in the waters (COPA s.49(1)(a)) (2) The cutting or uprooting of any	Any person	Yes	Yes (COPA s.87)

Members' liability	Defences	Maximum penalty – summary conviction	Maximum penalty – indictment
	sewerage authority were bound to receive the discharge were not observed and the authority could not reasonably have expected to prevent the discharge into the sewer or works (COPA s.30H(2), (3)) (8) A person causes or permits a discharge to be made into a sewer or works vested in a sewerage authority, or other person, and that discharge had to be received by the authority or that person either unconditionally or subject to conditions which were observed (COPA s.30H(2), (3))		
Yes, if managing the affairs of the company (COPA s.87)	The works relate to water permitted to enter controlled waters from an abandoned mine (to 31st December 1999 only)	£20,000 fine and/or 3 months' imprisonment	Unlimited fine and/or 2 years' imprisonment
Yes, if managing the affairs of the company (COPA s.87)	(1) The act causing the water pollution was carried out in the exercise of statutory powers conferred by or under any enactment relating to land drainage, flood prevention or navigation (2) Consent of SEPA	Level 4	–

Relevant provision and paragraph	Subject-matter	Offence	Person liable	Corporate liability	Directors' liability
		substantial amount of vegetation in any inland waters, or so near to any such waters that it falls into them or is allowed to remain in the waters (COPA s.49(1)(b))			
COPA s.49A (8.4.2)	Water pollution	Failure to comply with an enforcement notice as respects discharge consents	The person on whom the enforcement notice is served by SEPA	Yes	Yes (COPA s.87)
EPA s.23(1)(a) (9.2.8)	Integrated pollution control	To carry on a prescribed process without an authorisation or in breach of its condition	Any person	Yes	Yes (EPA s.157)
EPA s.23(1)(c) (9.2.8)	Integrated pollution control	Failure to comply or contravention of any requirement or prohibition imposed by an enforcement notice or prohibition notice	The person on whom the enforcement notice or prohibition notice is served	Yes	Yes (EPA s.157)
EPA s.23(1)(l) (9.2.8)	Integrated pollution control	Failure to comply with an order made by the court under EPA s.26	The person against whom the order is made	Yes	Yes (EPA s.157)
EPA s.23(1)(b) (9.2.8)	Integrated pollution control	Failure by a person to whom an authorisation is transferred to give notice of transfer within the time-limit prescribed by EPA s.9	The person to whom the authorisation is transferred	Yes	Yes (EPA s.157)

Members' liability	Defences	Maximum penalty – summary conviction	Maximum penalty – indictment
Yes, if managing the affairs of the company (COPA s.87)	No	£20,000 fine and/or 3 months' imprisonment	Unlimited fine and/or 2 years' imprisonment
	The following are all the defences for s.32(1)(a), (c) and (l)		
Yes, if managing the affairs of the company (EPA s.157)	A person is not liable under s.23(1)(a) and (c) so far as the offences continue during the time fixed for compliance by an order under EPA s.26	£20,000 and/or 3 months' imprisonment	Unlimited fine and/or 2 years' imprisonment
Yes, if managing the affairs of the company (EPA s.157)		£20,000 and/or 3 months' imprisonment	Unlimited fine and/or 2 years' imprisonment
Yes, if managing the affairs of the company (EPA s.157)		£20,000 and/or 3 months' imprisonment	Unlimited fine and/or 2 years' imprisonment
Yes, if managing the affairs of the company (EPA s.157)	None	Statutory maximum	Unlimited fine and/or 2 years' imprisonment

Relevant provision and paragraph	Subject-matter	Offence	Person liable	Corporate liability	Directors' liability
EPA s.23(1)(g) (9.2.8)	Integrated pollution control	Failure to comply with any requirement imposed by a notice under EPA s.19(2) which requires that person to furnish information within such form and period as specified in the notice	The person on whom the notice is served	Yes	Yes (EPA s.157)
EPA s.23(1)(h) (9.2.8)	Integrated pollution control	Knowingly or recklessly making a statement which is false or misleading in a material particular where the statement is made (1) In purported compliance with a statutory requirement to furnish information or (2) For the purpose of obtaining the grant of an authorisation to himself or any other person or the variation of an authorisation	Any person	Yes	Yes (EPA s.157)
EPA s.23(1)(i) (9.2.8)	Integrated pollution control	To intentionally make a false entry in any record required to be kept by virtue of a condition attached to an authorisation by virtue of EPA s.7	The person to whom the authorisation is granted	Yes	Yes (EPA s.157)
EPA s.23(1)(j) (9.2.8)	Integrated pollution control	With intent to deceive, to forge or use a document issued or authorised to be issued under EPA s.7 or for any purpose thereunder or to make or have in his possession a document so closely resembling any such document as to be likely to deceive	Any person	Yes	Yes (EPA s.157)

236

Members' liability	Defences	Maximum penalty – summary conviction	Maximum penalty – indictment
Yes, if managing the affairs of the company (EPA s.157)	Reasonable excuse	Statutory maximum	Unlimited fine and/or 2 years' imprisonment
Yes, if managing the affairs of the company (EPA s.157)	Statement not knowingly or recklessly made	Statutory maximum	Unlimited fine and/or 2 years' imprisonment
Yes, if managing the affairs of the company (EPA s.157)	No intention to make	Statutory maximum	Unlimited fine and/or 2 years' imprisonment
Yes, if managing the affairs of the company (EPA s.157)	No intention to deceive	Statutory maximum	Unlimited fine and/or 2 years' imprisonment

Relevant provision and paragraph	Subject-matter	Offence	Person liable	Corporate liability	Directors' liability
EPA s.80(4) (10.2.5)	Abatement of a statutory nuisance	Failure to comply with any requirement or prohibition imposed by an abatement notice	The person on whom the abatement notice is served	Yes	Yes (EPA s.157)
EPA s.82(8) (10.2.8)	Abatement of a statutory nuisance (summary proceedings by person aggrieved by statutory nuisances)	To contravene any requirement or prohibition imposed by an order under EPA s.82(2)	The person against whom the EPA s.82(2) order is made	Yes	Yes (EPA s.157)

Members' liability	Defences	Maximum penalty – summary conviction	Maximum penalty – indictment
Yes, if managing the affairs of the company (EPA s.157)	(1) Reasonable excuse (2) Best practical means were used to prevent or to counteract the effects of the statutory nuisance. NB: this defence is only applicable in restricted circumstances as defined by EPA s.80(8) (3) If the statutory nuisance is an EPA s.79(1)(g) or an EPA s.79(1)(ga) offence then it is a defence to prove that (a) the alleged offence was covered by a notice served under COPA s.60 or a consent given under COPA s.61 or s.65; or (b) the level of noise emitted from the premises did not contravene a notice in force in relation to the premises under COPA s.66; or (c) in the absence of a COPA s.66 notice, the level of noise did not exceed a level fixed under COPA s.67.	(1) Level 5 with a further fine of an amount equal to one-tenth of that level for each day on which the offence continues after conviction (2) £20,000 if offence committed on industrial, trade or business premises	– –
Yes, if managing the affairs of the company (EPA s.157)	(1) Reasonable excuse (2) Best practical means were used to prevent or to counteract the effects of the statutory nuisance.	Level 5, with a further fine of an amount equal to one-tenth of that level for each day on which the offence continues after the conviction	–

Relevant provision and paragraph	Subject-matter	Offence	Person liable	Corporate liability	Directors' liability
COPA s.60(8) (10.3.2)	Noise pollution from construction sites	Contravention or failure to comply with a notice served in accordance with COPA s.60	Person on whom the notice is served	Yes	Yes (COPA s.87)
COPA s.61(10) (10.3.2)	Noise pollution from construction sites	(1) Knowingly to carry out work or permit works to be carried out in contravention of any condition attached to a COPA s.61 consent (2) For the applicant for the consent to fail to take all reasonable steps to bring the consent to the notice of any other person who is carrying out the works	The holder of a COPA s.61 consent notice	Yes	Yes (COPA s.87)
COPA s.62(1) (10.3.3)	Noise pollution by loudspeakers	To operate or permit the operation of a loudspeaker in a road between 9 pm and 8 am and at any other time for the purpose of advertising any entertainment, trade or business	Any person	Yes	Yes (COPA s.87)
COPA s.65(5) (10.3.4)	Noise pollution, noise abatement zones and noise level registers	(1) If noise emitted from any premises exceeds the level of noise in a noise level register; or (2) Breaches a condition attached to a consent by the council	(1) Any person (2) The holder of the consent	Yes	Yes (COPA s.87)

Members' liability	Defences	Maximum penalty – summary conviction	Maximum penalty – indictment
	NB: this defence is only applicable in restricted circumstances as defined by EPA s.82(10)		
Yes, if managing the affairs of the company (COPA s.87)	Reasonable excuse	Level 5, with a further fine not exceeding £50 for each day on which the offence continues after conviction	–
Yes, if managing the affairs of the company (COPA s.87)	With regard to offence (2) – all reasonable steps were taken to bring the consent to the notice of any person other than the applicant	Level 5, with a further fine not exceeding £50 for each day on which the offence continues after conviction	–
Yes, if managing the affairs of the company (COPA s.87)	The noise is permitted by virtue of COPA s.62(1A), (2) or (3)	Level 5, with a further fine not exceeding £50 for each day on which the offence continues after conviction	–
Yes, if managing the affairs of the company (COPA s.87)	Written consent is obtained from the council	Level 5, with a further fine not exceeding £50 for each day on which the offence continues after conviction	–

Relevant provision and paragraph	Subject-matter	Offence	Person liable	Corporate liability	Directors' liability
COPA s.65(6) (10.3.4)	Noise pollution, s.65(6) court order	Contravention of an order requiring the execution of any works required by the sheriff to prevent the offence for which the person was convicted under COPA s.65(5) continuing or recurring	Person against whom the order is made	Yes	Yes (COPA s.87)
COPA s.66(8) (10.3.4)	Noise pollution – noise reduction notices	Contravention of a noise reduction notice served in accordance with COPA s.66	The person on whom the noise reduction notice is served	Yes	Yes (COPA s.87)
COPA s.68 (10.3.5)	Noise pollution – plant or machinery	To contravene or cause or permit another person to contravene regulations under COPA s.68	Any person	Yes	Yes (COPA s.87)
N & SNA s.9 (not yet in force) (10.3.7)	Noise pollution – audible intruder alarms	(1) The alarm fails to comply with any prescribed requirement (2) The council are not notified within forty-eight hours of its installation	The person who has the audible intruder alarm installed	Yes	Yes (COPA s.87)
RSA s.32(1)(a) RSA s.6) (11.12)	Radioactive substances	To keep or use or cause or permit to be kept or used, radioactive material of any description if that person knows or has reasonable	Any person	Yes	Yes (RSA s.36)

Members' liability	Defences	Maximum penalty – summary conviction	Maximum penalty – indictment
Yes, if managing the affairs of the company (COPA s.87)	Reasonable excuse	Level 5, with a further fine not exceeding £50 for each day on which the offence continues after conviction	–
Yes, if managing the affairs of the company (COPA s.87)	(1) Reasonable excuse (2) If the noise is caused in the course of a trade or business it is a defence to prove that the best practicable means (as defined in COPA s.72) were used for preventing or counteracting the effect of the noise	Level 5, with a further fine not exceeding £50 for each day on which the offence continues after conviction	–
Yes, if managing the affairs of the company (COPA s.87)	It is a defence to proceedings under s.68(1)(a) only, that means used for the purpose of reducing the noise in question were not less effective for the purpose than the means used by the regulations	Level 5, with a further fine not exceeding £50 for each day on which the offence continues after conviction	–
Yes, if managing the affairs of the company (COPA s.87)	No	Offence (1) – level 5 Offence (2) – level 2	–
Yes, if managing the affairs of the company (RSA s.36)	(1) Registered under RSA s.7 (2) Exempt under RSA s.8 from registration under RSA s.7 (3) The radioactive	£20,000 fine and/or 6 months' imprisonment	Unlimited fine and/or 5 years' imprisonment

Relevant provision and paragraph	Subject-matter	Offence	Person liable	Corporate liability	Directors' liability
		grounds for believing that the material is radioactive			
RSA s.32(1)(a) (RSA s.9) (11.12)	Radioactive substances Mobile radioactive apparatus	(1) To keep, use, lend or let on hire mobile radioactive apparatus of any description, or (2) Cause or permit mobile radioactive apparatus of any description to be kept, used, lent or let on hire	Any person	Yes	Yes (RSA s.36)
RSA s.32(1)(a) (RSA s.13) (11.12)	Radioactive substances	To dispose or cause or permit to be disposed of without an authorisation radioactive waste if a person knows or has reasonable grounds for believing that the material in question is radioactive waste and it: (1) is disposed on or from any premises used by a person for the purpose of carrying on any undertaking (note RSA s.13(5) addition; meaning of premises); (2) arises from any mobile radioactive apparatus; or (3) is received by a person, in the course of carrying on an undertaking, for the purpose of disposal (but no authorisation is required in these circumstances if the waste concerned falls within the provisions of an authorisation granted in relation to (1) or (2) above and the disposal complies with the terms of that authorisation)	Any person	Yes	Yes (RSA s.36)

Members' liability	Defences	Maximum penalty – summary conviction	Maximum penalty – indictment
	material consists of mobile radioactive apparatus in respect of which a person is registered or exempt from registration under RSA s.10		
Yes, if managing the affairs of the company (RSA s.36)	(1) Registered under RSA s.10 or (2) Exempt from registration under RSA s.10	£20,000 fine and/or 6 months' imprisonment	Unlimited fine and/or 5 years' imprisonment
Yes, if managing the affairs of the company (RSA s.36)	Exempted under RSA s.15: (1) Radioactive waste arising from clocks or watches (except where it arises on premises on which clocks or watches are manufactured or repaired by processes involving the use of luminous material) (2) Exemptions granted absolutely or subject to limitation or conditions by order of the Secretary of State	£20,000 fine and/or 6 months' imprisonment	Unlimited fine and/or 5 years' imprisonment

Relevant provision and paragraph	Subject-matter	Offence	Person liable	Corporate liability	Directors' liability
RSA s.32(1)(a) (RSA s.14) (11.12)	Radioactive substances	To accumulate radioactive waste with a view to its subsequent disposal without an authorisation if he knows or has reasonable grounds for believing that it is radioactive waste	Any person	Yes	Yes (RSA s.36)
RSA s.32(1)(b) (RSA ss.7, 10) (11.12)	Radioactive substances	Failure to comply with a limitation or condition subject to which he is registered or exempted from registration as a keeper or user of radioactive waste under RSA ss.7 and 10	The person who is registered under RSA s.7 or exempt from registration under RSA s.10	Yes	Yes (RSA s.36)

Members' liability	Defences	Maximum penalty – summary conviction	Maximum penalty – indictment
Yes, if managing the affairs of the company (RSA s.36)	Exempted under RSA s.15: (1) Radioactive waste arising from clocks or watches (except where it arises on premises on which clocks or watches are manufactured or repaired by processes involving the use of luminous material) (2) Exemptions granted absolutely or subject to limitation or conditions by order of the Secretary of State (3) The disposal of waste has been authorised under RSA s.13 and in accordance with that authorisation the waste is required to be accumulated with a view to its subsequent disposal – no further authorisation required (4) The accumulation of radioactive waste on any premises situated on a nuclear site	£20,000 fine and/or 6 months' imprisonment	Unlimited fine and/or 5 years' imprisonment
Yes, if managing the affairs of the company (RSA s.36)	No	£20,000 fine and/or 6 months' imprisonment	Unlimited fine and/or 5 years' imprisonment

Relevant provision and paragraph	Subject-matter	Offence	Person liable	Corporate liability	Directors' liability
RSA s.32(1)(c) (RSA ss.13, 14) (11.12)	Radioactive substances	Failure to comply with a condition or limitation of an authorisation for disposal (RSA s.13) or accumulation (RSA s.14) of radioactive waste	The person to whom the authorisation is granted	Yes	Yes (RSA s.36)
RSA ss.32(1)(d) (RSA ss.21, 22) (11.12)	Radioactive substances	Failure to comply with any requirement of an enforcement notice or a prohibition notice served in accordance with RSA ss.21 and 22	The person on whom the enforcement notice or prohibition notice has been served	Yes	Yes (RSA s.36)

Members' liability	Defences	Maximum penalty – summary conviction	Maximum penalty – indictment
Yes, if managing the affairs of the company (RSA s.36)	No	£20,000 fine and/or 6 months' imprisonment	Unlimited fine and/or 5 years' imprisonment
Yes, if managing the affairs of the company (RSA s.36)	No	£20,000 fine and/or 6 months' imprisonment	Unlimited fine and/or 5 years' imprisonment

APPENDIX 6   LIABILITY FOR CLEAN-UP COSTS
FOR ENVIRONMENTAL MATTERS

Relevant provision and paragraph	Subject-matter	Enforcement agency and clean-up powers
EPA s.78N (not yet in force) (6.4.2)	Remediation notice served in accordance with EPA s.78E-H	Local authority or SEPA may do what is appropriate by way of remediation to the relevant land or waters
EPA s.59(6) (7.9)	Removal, elimination or reduction of the consequences of controlled waste deposited in contravention of EPA s.33(1)	SEPA may do what the occupier on whom a notice under EPA s.59(1) was served was required to do
EPA s.59(7) (7.9)	Removal, elimination or reduction of the consequences of controlled waste deposited in contravention of EPA s.33(1)	SEPA takes immediate action (without the need to serve a notice) to clean up a site: (1) where the waste must be forthwith removed in order to remove or prevent pollution of land, water or air or harm to human health or (2) if there is no occupier of the land, or (3) if the occupier neither made nor knowingly permitted the deposit of the waste
COPA s.46 (8.4.3)	Water pollution	SEPA may carry out remedial or preventive operations where it appears to it that any poisonous, noxious or polluting matter or any solid waste matter is likely to enter, or is or was present in any controlled waters only if (1) SEPA considers that it is necessary that the operations are carried out forthwith, or (2) after reasonable inquiry it appears to SEPA that no person can be found on whom to serve a works notice under COPA s.46A
COPA s.46D Water pollution (not yet in force) (8.4.3)	Water pollution	SEPA may carry out the remedial action required by virtue of the works notice

Person liable for clean-up costs	Corporate liability	Directors' and members' liability	Defence
The 'appropriate person' (see EPA s.78A(9))	Yes	Yes, members liable if managing the affairs of the company (EPA s.157)	Hardship will be suffered by the person(s) liable for clean-up costs
Occupier	Yes	Yes, members liable if managing the affairs of the company (EPA s.157)	Costs not reasonably incurred
For clean-up powers: (1) Occupier of the land For clean-up powers: (2) and (3) The person who deposited or knowingly caused or permitted the deposit of any waste	Yes	Yes, members liable if managing the affairs of the company (EPA s.157)	For clean-up powers: (1) Costs unnecessarily incurred; occupier neither made nor knowingly permitted the deposit of waste For clean-up powers: (2) and (3) Costs unnecessarily incurred
Any person who caused or knowingly permitted the matter in question to be present at the place from which it was likely, in the opinion of SEPA, to enter the controlled waters or to be present in those waters	Yes	Yes, members liable if managing the affairs of the company (COPA s.87)	(1) The costs were incurred unnecessarily (2) The works related to water permitted to enter controlled waters from an abandoned mine (to 31st December 1999 only)
The person on whom the works notice is served	Yes	Yes, members liable if managing the affairs of the company (COPA s.87)	(1) The costs were not reasonably incurred (2) The works related to water permitted to enter controlled waters from an abandoned mine (to 31st December 1999 only)

Relevant provision and paragraph	Subject-matter	Enforcement agency and clean-up powers
EPA s.27 (9.2.8)	Integrated pollution control	SEPA may arrange for steps to be taken towards remedying the harm caused by the commission of an offence under EPA s.23(1)(a) or (c) but only with the written approval of the Secretary of State
EPA s.81(3), (4) (10.2.7)	Abatement of a statutory notice	The council in whose area the nuisance has occurred may abate the statutory nuisance and do whatever may be necessary in the execution of the notice whether or not proceedings have been taken for the offence of failure to comply
EPA s.82(11) (10.2.8)	Abatement of a statutory notice (summary proceedings by persons aggrieved by statutory nuisances)	The council in whose area the nuisance has occurred may be directed by the sheriff to do anything which a person convicted under EPA s.82(8) was required to do by the order to which the conviction relates
EPA s.82(13) (10.2.8)	Abatement of a statutory notice (summary proceedings by persons aggrieved by statutory nuisances)	If neither the person responsible for the nuisance nor the owner or occupier of the premises nor the person responsible for the vehicle, machinery or equipment can be found, the sheriff may direct the council in whose area the nuisance has occurred to do anything which the court would have ordered that person to do
COPA s.69(1)(c) (10.3.4)	Noise pollution s.65(6) court order	The council in whose area the nuisance has occurred may be required by a sheriff to carry out any works in accordance with a COPA s.65(6) order if the person on whom the order is served fails to execute all or any of the works in accordance with the COPA s.65(6) order

Person liable for clean-up costs	Corporate liability	Directors' and members' liability	Defence
Person convicted of the offence under EPA s.23(1)(a) or (c)	Yes	Yes, members liable if managing the affairs of the company (EPA s.157)	(1) Secretary of State's approval not given (2) If steps are to be taken on or will affect land in the occupation of any person other than the person on whose land the prescribed process is being carried out and permission of that person has not been obtained (3) Steps taken by SEPA towards remedying the harm not reasonable
The person by whose act or default the nuisance was caused and, if that person is the owner of the premises, from any person who is for the time being the owner thereof	Yes	Yes, members liable if managing the affairs of the company (EPA s.157)	Costs not reasonably incurred
If the person convicted under EPA s.82(8) is found then they will be liable for clean-up costs, otherwise the council will be liable	Yes (if person convicted of EPA s.82(8) is found) No (if council liable for clean-up costs)	Yes (if person convicted under EPA s.82(8) is found – members liable if managing the affairs of the company) No (if council liable for clean-up costs)	Council not given an opportunity of being heard
The council	No	No	Council not given an opportunity of being heard
The person convicted under COPA s.65(5)	Yes	Yes, members liable if managing the affairs of the company (COPA s.87)	Costs unnecessarily incurred

Relevant provision and paragraph	Subject–matter	Enforcement agency and clean-up powers
COPA s.69(1)(b) (10.3.4)	Noise pollution Noise reduction notice	The council may carry out the works required by a noise reduction notice if the person on whom the order was served does not carry out all or any of the works in accordance with the notice
RSA s.30 (11.13)	Radioactive substances	If SEPA is satisfied there is radioactive waste on any premises and also satisfied that (1) the waste ought to be disposed of, but (2) by reason that the premises are unoccupied or that the occupier is absent, or is insolvent, or for any other reason it is unlikely that the waste will be lawfully disposed of unless SEPA exercises its powers

Person liable for clean-up costs	Corporate liability	Directors' and members' liability	Defence
The person on whom the noise reduction notice was served	Yes	Yes, members liable if managing the affairs of the company (COPA s.87)	Costs unnecessarily incurred
The occupier of the premises or if unoccupied the owner of the premises	Yes	Yes, members liable if managing the affairs of the company (RSA s.36)	No

APPENDIX 7   CIVIL LIABILITY FOR
ENVIRONMENTAL MATTERS

Relevant provision and paragraph	Subject-matter	Trigger	Person liable	Corporate liability	Directors' liability
Law of nuisance (2.2)	Tolerability	Beyond what is tolerable	Any person	Yes	Yes
Law of negligence (2.3)	Loss or damage	Fault/negligence	Any person	Yes	Yes
Law of property (2.4)	Water pollution	Damage or nuisance	Any person	Yes	Yes
EPA s.78 M(5) (not yet in force) (6.4.2)	Contaminated land	EPA ss.78 M(3), (4)	Person(s) on whom remediation notice served	Yes	Yes (EPA s.157)
EPA s.73(6) (7.7.2)	Waste deposit	EPA ss.33(1), 63(2)	Any person	Yes	Yes (EPA s.157)
COPA s.49A(4) (8.4.2)	Water pollution	COPA s.49A (3)	The person on whom the enforcement notice has been served	Yes	Yes (COPA s.87)

Members' liability	Civil penalties	Defences
Yes	Damages/interdict	(1) Acquiescence (2) In limited and specific circumstances the following defences may be available: (a) nuisance authorised by statute (b) *volenti non fit injuria* (the acceptance of the risk of injury) (c) contributory fault (d) the nuisance has an overwhelming element of social utility (possible defence if interim interdict is sought)
Yes	Damages/interdict	(1) No duty of care owed (2) Damage not foreseeable (3) Damage due wholly to fault of person who suffered it; or (4) *Volenti non fit injuria* (the acceptance of the risk of injury)
Yes	Damages/interdict	Acquiescence
Yes, if managing the affairs of the company (EPA s.157)	Interdict	No
Yes, if managing the affairs of the company (EPA s.157)	Damages	1) As for EPA s.33(1) or s.63(2) (2) Damage was due wholly to the fault of the person who suffered it (3) Damage was suffered by a person who voluntarily accepted the risk of the damage being caused
Yes, if managing the affairs of the company (COPA s.87)	Interdict	No

Relevant provision and paragraph	Subject-matter	Trigger	Person liable	Corporate liability	Directors' liability
COPA s.46D(4) (8.4.3)	Water pollution	COPA s.46D	The person on whom the works notice is served by SEPA	Yes	Yes (COPA s.87)
EPA s.24 (9.2.6)	Integrated pollution control	EPA s.23(1)(c)	The person on whom the enforcement or prohibition notice is served	Yes	Yes (EPA s.157)
EPA s.81(5) (10.2.7)	Abatement of a statutory notice	EPA s.80(4)	The person on whom the abatement notice is served	Yes	Yes (EPA s.157)
RSA s.32(3) (11.8)	Radioactive substances	RSA s.32	The person on whom an enforcement notice has been served	Yes	Yes (RSA s.36)

Members' liability	Civil penalties	Defences
Yes, if managing the affairs of the company (COPA s.87)	Interdict	No
Yes, if managing the affairs of the company (EPA s.157)	Interdict	No
Yes, if managing the affairs of the company (EPA s.157)	Interdict	The alleged offence was covered by a notice under COPA s.60 or a consent given under COPA s.61
Yes, if managing the affairs of the company (RSA s.36)	Interdict	No

INDEX

261